SPIRITUALITY
IN
ARCHITECTURAL EDUCATION

SPIRITUALITY IN ARCHITECTURAL EDUCATION

Twelve Years of the Walton Critic Program at
The Catholic University of America

Julio Bermudez

With Contributions by architects Craig W. Hartman, Juhani Pallasmaa, Alberto Campo Baeza, Claudio Silvestrin, Eliana Bórmida, Michael J. Crosbie, Prem Chandavarkar, Rick Joy, Susan Jones, and Daniel Libeskind.

The Catholic University
of America Press
Washington, D.C.

Cataloging-in-Publication Data available

from the Library of Congress

ISBN 978-0-8132-3481-6

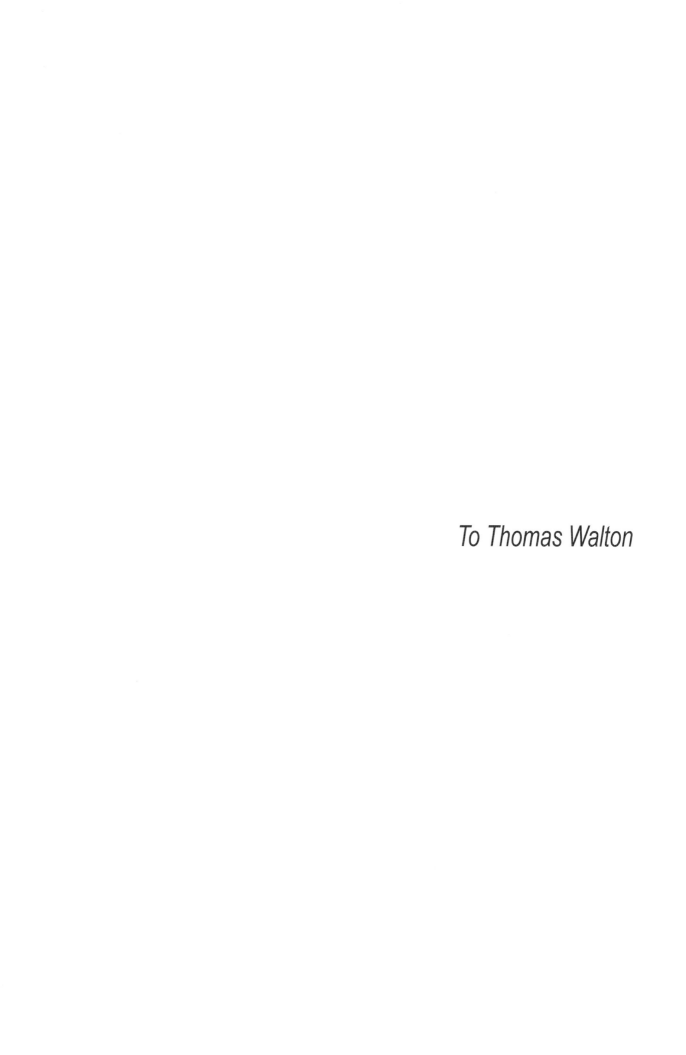

To Thomas Walton

CONTENTS

List of Illustrations   viii

Acknowledgments   xv

Foreword   THOMAS WALTON   xix

Spirituality in the Design Studio: Introducing the Walton Program   JULIO BERMUDEZ   1

Spirituality in Architectural Education. Meditations   JULIO BERMUDEZ   11

The Walton Studio   JULIO BERMUDEZ   34

Being at the Edge of Order   45
    Architecture is Deeply Spiritual, In Conversation with Daniel Libeskind   DANIEL LIBESKIND

Emotional and Material Foundations of Architecture   61
    Tectonically Emotive   SUSAN JONES

Physical, Existential, and Spiritual Home   75
    New Worlds   RICK JOY

Vocation and the Deep Self: Teaching the Voice Within   87
    Teaching the Voice Within   *PREM CHANDAVARKAR*

Changing Notions and Practices of Spirituality and the Sacred   103
    Searching for a New Sacred Space   *MICHAEL J. CROSBIE*

Designing Experiences: Ritual, Narrative, and Embodiment   119
    Architecture as Experience   *ELIANA BÓRMIDA*

Contemplative and Non-Egotistical Improvisation   135
    Spirituality and Designing a Sacred Space   *CLAUDIO SILVESTRIN*

Building Essential Ideas   149
    At Home   *ALBERTO CAMPO BAEZA*
    On Surrender and Universality   *ALBERTO CAMPO BAEZA*

The Sacred Task of Architecture   165
    The Art of Teaching: Objectives in my Walton Studio   *JUHANI PALLASMAA*

Consuming Creation: Rethinking Consumption and Materiality   181
    Finding the Essence: Place and Spirituality   *CRAIG W. HARTMAN*

Intuiting Spirituality Through Making, Space, and Light   195
    ANTOINE PREDOCK

Spirituality in Architectural Education and Practice   199
    BÓRMIDA, CAMPO BAEZA, CHANDAVARKAR, CROSBIE, JONES, PALLASMAA

APPENDIX

    The Voluntary Architecture Simplicity Manifesto   *JULIO BERMUDEZ*   216

    Choosing Being: How to Respond to Today's Unhealthy State of Affairs   *JULIO BERMUDEZ*   219

    On the Architectural Design Parti   *JULIO BERMUDEZ*   222

    Testimonials   226

Contributors   242

Endnotes   250

Bibliography   257

Index   262

ILLUSTRATIONS

Book Cover Figure. Inside the Kursaal Auditorium and Congress Center, San Sebastián, Spain (2004). Photograph by Joshua Hansen.

Figure 1-1. Walton Critic Daniel Libeskind introduces studio exercise. Photograph by Julio Bermudez.   1

Figure 1-2. Six Walton Critics visiting the CUA campus in fall 2018. Photograph by Julio Bermudez.   6

Figure 1-3. Walton Critic Rick Joy discusses work with a student. Photograph by Julio Bermudez.   10

Figure 1-4. Walton Critic Michael J. Crosbie speaks to 10th Anniversary Walton Program Conference participants. Photograph by Julio Bermudez.   10

Figure 2-1. Student working at his desk. Photograph by Bill Sullivan.   11

Figure 2-2. Walton Critic Juhani Pallasmaa communicates with students. Photograph by Julio Bermudez.   18

Figure 2-3. Walton Critic Daniel Libeskind visits the Basilica of the National Shrine of the Immaculate Conception. Photograph by Julio Bermudez.   26

Figure 3-1. Julio Bermudez reviews student's work. Photograph by Julio Bermudez.   34

Figure 3-2. Walton Critic Alberto Campo Baeza expresses his thoughts while speaking to student. Photograph by Julio Bermudez.   37

Figure 3-3. Walton Critic Susan Jones introduces an assignment to the studio. Photograph by Julio Bermudez.   40

Figure 3-4. Walton Critic Prem Chandavarkar with students and guests having dinner. Photograph by Julio Bermudez.												44

Figure 4-1. Studio Libeskind, The Jewish Museum in Berlin - Germany. Photograph by Hufton + Crow.												45

Figure 4-2. Walton Critic Daniel Libeskind and guest lecturer Georgia Saxelby examine design proposals. Photograph by Julio Bermudez.												47

Figure 4-3. Walton Critic Daniel Libeskind responds to students' work. Photograph by Julio Bermudez.												47

Figure 4-4. Students presenting work to Walton Critic Daniel Libeskind. Photograph by Julio Bermudez.												47

Figure 4-5. Walton Critic Daniel Libeskins addressing the studio. Photograph by Julio Bermudez.												47

Figure 4-6. Group photo of the 2019 Walton Studio. Photograph by Julio Bermudez.												47

Featured images and drawings were created by the various students cited.												48-53

Figure 4-7. Studio Libeskind, National Holocaust Museum, Ottawa - Canada. Photograph by Doublespace.												54

Figure 4-8. Studio Libeskind, The Jewish Museum in Berlin - Germany. Photograph by Hufton + Crow.												59

Figure 4-9. Daniel Libeskind. Photograph by Stefan Ruiz.												59

Figure 4-10. Studio Libeskind, Occitanie Tower, Toulouse - France. Rendering by Luxigon.												61

Figure 5-1. atelierjones, Bellevue First Congregational church in Bellevue - Washington. Photograph by Susan Jones.												63

Figure 5-2. Walton Critic Susan Jones first meets with students. Photograph by Julio Bermudez.												63

Figure 5-3. Walton Critic Susan Jones works with student for a desk crit. Photograph by Julio Bermudez.												63

Figure 5-4. Walton Critic Susan Jones gives instructions to students. Photograph by Julio Bermudez.												63

Figure 5-5. Walton Critic Susan Jones talks with students on first day of class. Photograph by Julio Bermudez.												63

Figure 5-6. Group photo of the 2018 Walton Studio. Photograph by Julio Bermudez.												63

Featured images and drawings were created by the various students cited on pages.												64-69

Figure 5-7. atelierjones, Marian Chapel, St. James Cathedral in Seattle - Washington. Photograph by Susan Jones.												70

Figure 5-8. atelierjones, detail of the Bellevue First Congregational Church in Bellevue - Washington. Photograph by Susan Jones.												73

Figure 5-9. atelierjones, skylights and ceiling of the Bellevue First Congregational church In Bellevue - Washington. Photograph by Susan Jones.												74

Figure 6-1. Rick Joy Architects. Desert Nomad House in Tucson - Arizona. Photograph by Jeff Goldberg (Esto).												75

Figure 6-2. Walton Critic Rick Joy in conversation with a student. Photograph by Julio Bermudez.												77

Figure 6-3. Walton Critic Rick Joy in conversation with a student about their design work. Photograph by Julio Bermudez.												77

Figure 6-4. Walton Critic Rick Joy in conversation with a student. Photograph by Julio Bermudez. 77

Figure 6-5. Walton Critic Rick Joy instructing the studio. Photograph by Julio Bermudez. 77

Figure 6-6. Group photo of the 2017 Walton Studio. Photograph by Julio Bermudez. 77

Featured images and drawings were created by the various students cited. 77-83

Figure 6-7. Rick Joy Architects, Sun Valley House - Idaho. Photograph by Joe Fletcher. 85

Figure 6-8. Rick Joy Architects, Princeton University Transit Station with Nakashima benches. Photograph by Jeff Goldberg (Esto). 86

Figure 6-9. Rick Joy Architects, Tubac House, Tubac - Arizona. Photograph by Jeff Goldberg (Esto). 86

Figure 6-10. Rick Joy Architects, La Cabanon - Turks and Caicos. Photograph by Joe Fletcher. 86

Figure 7-1. CnT Architects, Ramaiah House in Bangalore - India. Photograph by Amit Rastogi. 87

Figure 7-2. Photo of final jury for the 2016 Walton Studio. Photograph by Julio Bermudez. 89

Figure 7-3. Student presenting design work to the studio. Photograph by Julio Bermudez. 89

Figure 7-4. Walton Critic Prem Chandavarkar giving summary remarks to the studio. Photograph by Julio Bermudez. 89

Figure 7-5. Walton Critic Prem Chandavarkar reviewing the work of a student. Photograph by Julio Bermudez. 89

Figure 7-6. Group photo of the 2016 Walton Studio. Photograph by Julio Bermudez. 89

Featured images and drawings were created by the various students cited. 90-95

Figure 7-7. CnT Architects, Tata Dhan Academy in Madurai - India. Photograph by Mehul Patel. 96

Figure 7-8. CnT Architects, Brigade Courtyard Apartments in Bangalore - India. Photograph by Koteswara Rao. 102

Figure 7-9. CnT Architects, Ramaiah House in Bangalore - India. Photograph by Amit Rastogi. 102

Figure 8-1. atelierjones, St. Paul's Episcopal Church Renovation in Seattle - Washington. Photograph by Susan Jones. 103

Figure 8-2. Walton Critic Michael J. Crosbie and architect Joan Soranno speak with students. Photograph by Julio Bermudez. 105

Figure 8-3. Student presenting work to Walton Critic Michael J. Crosbie. Photograph by Julio Bermudez. 105

Figure 8-4. Future Walton Critic Susan Jones gives a design crit to a student. Photograph by Julio Bermudez. 105

Figure 8-5. Walton Critic Michael J. Crosbie listens to students' design proposals. Photograph by Julio Bermudez. 105

Figure 8-6. Student presenting work during jury with Walton Critic Michael J. Crosbie. Photograph by Julio Bermudez. 105

Figure 8-7. Students presenting work during jury with Walton Critic Michael J. Crosbie. Photograph by Julio Bermudez. 105

Figure 8-8. Group photo of the 2015 Walton Studio. Photograph by Julio Bermudez.   105

Featured images and drawings were created by the various students cited.   106-111

Figure 8-9. Larkin Architect Limited. St. Gabriel's Passionist Parish Church in Toronto - Canada. Photograph by Roberto Chiotti.   112

Figure 8-10. Anonymous. God as Architect/Builder/Geometer/Craftsman, The Frontispiece of Bible Moralisee. Illumination on parchment (circa 1220-1230). Work in the public domain.   115

Figure 8-11. Joan Soranno, HGA, Bigelow Chapel at the United Theological Seminary of the Twin Cities, New Brighton - Minnesota. Photograph by Joan Soranno.   117

Figure 8-12. Joan Soranno, HGA, Lakewood Cemetery Garden Mausoleum in Minneapolis - Minnesota. Photograph by Joan Soranno.   117

Figure 9-1. Bórmida & Yanzón Arquitectos, central courtyard of the visiting center, Salentein Winery in Tunuyán - Mendoza, Argentina. Photograph by Bórmida & Yanzón Arquitectos.   119

Figure 9-2. Students discuss their work with Walton Critic Eliana Bórmida. Photograph by Julio Bermudez.   121

Figure 9-3. Walton Critic Eliana Bórmida responds to students' presentation. Photograph by Julio Bermudez.   121

Figure 9-4. Walton Critic Eliana Bórmida reviews a student's work. Photograph by Julio Bermudez.   121

Figure 9-5. Walton Critic Eliana Bórmida works with a student at their desk. Photograph by Julio Bermudez.   121

Figure 9-6. Walton Critic Eliana Bórmida listens to a student at her desk. Photograph by Julio Bermudez.   121

Figure 9-7. Walton Critic Eliana Bórmida speaks at the Embassy of Argentina. Photograph by Julio Bermudez.   121

Figure 9-8. Group photo of the 2014 Walton Studio.   121

Featured images and drawings were created by the various students cited.   121-127

Figure 9-9. Bórmida & Yanzón Arquitectos, Interior of the Diamonds Winery in Tunuyán - Mendoza, Argentina. Photograph by Bórmida & Yanzón Arquitectos.   128

Figure 9-10. Bórmida & Yanzón Arquitectos, courtyard of the visitor center, Salentein Winery in Tunuyán - Mendoza, Argentina. Photograph by Bórmida & Yanzón Arquitectos.   132

Figure 9-11. Bórmida & Yanzón Arquitectos, central courtyard of the visitor center, Salentein Winery in Tunuyán - Mendoza, Argentina. Photograph by Bórmida & Yanzón Arquitectos.   132

Figure 9-12. Bórmida & Yanzón Arquitectos, entry way to the visitor center (the Killka), Salentein Winery in Tunuyán - Mendoza, Argentina. Photograph by Bórmida & Yanzón Arquitectos.   133

Figure 9-13. Bórmida & Yanzón Arquitectos, main public entry to Septima Winery in Lujan de Cuyo - Mendoza, Argentina. Photograph by Bórmida & Yanzón Arquitectos.   133

Figure 10-1. Claudio Silvestrin Architects, Neuendorf Villa in Majorca - Spain. Photograph by Claudia Silvestrin Architects.   135

Figure 10-2. Walton Critic Claudio Silvestrin examining the design proposal of Emily O'Loughlin. Photograph by Julio Bermudez   137

Figure 10-3. Walton Critic Claudio Silvestrin in a desk crit with Lillian Heryak and Lisa Nucera. Photograph by Julio Bermudez.   137

Figure 10-4. Walton Critic Claudio Silvestrin checking the work of Marisa Aschettino and Erica Donnelly. Photograph by Julio Bermudez. 137

Figure 10-5. Walton Critic Claudio Silvestrin teaching while Toni Lem works in the foreground. Photograph by Julio Bermudez. 137

Figure 10-6. Interim review of students' work by Walton Critic Claudio Silvestrin and faculty. Photograph by Julio Bermudez. 137

Figure 10-7. Group photo of the 2013 Walton Studio. Photograph by Julio Bermudez. 137

Featured images and drawings were created by the various students cited on pages. 138-143

Figure 10-8. Claudio Silvestrin Architects, Neuendorf Villa in Majorca - Spain. Photograph by Claudio Silvestrin Architects. 144

Figure 10-9. Claudio Silvestrin Architects, Neuendorf Villa in Majorca - Spain. Photograph by Claudia Silvestrin Architects. 146

Figure 10-10. Claudio Silvestrin Architects, Neuendorf Villa De Wec, in front of the Lemanus Lake in Geneva - Switzerland. Rendering by Claudio Silvestrin Architects. 147

Figure 11-1. Initial sketch for the House of the Infinite in Cadiz -Spain. Drawing by Alberto Campo Baeza. 149

Figure 11-2. Walton Critic Alberto Campo Baeza gives a desk crit. Photograph by Julio Bermudez. 151

Figure 11-3. Walton Critic Alberto Campo Baeza commenting on the work of students. Photograph by Julio Bermudez. 151

Figure 11-4. Students present design work to Walton Critic Alberto Campo Baeza. Photograph by Julio Bermudez. 151

Figure 11-5. Walton Critic Alberto Campo Baeza giving instruction to students. Photograph by Julio Bermudez. 151

Figure 11-6. Group photo of the 2012 Walton Studio. Photograph by Julio Bermudez. 151

Feature images and drawings were created by the various students cited. 152-157

Figure 11-7. Alberto Campo Baeza, Casa Moliner in Zaragoza - Spain. Photograph by Javier Callejas. 158

Figure 11-8. Alberto Campo Baeza, Between Cathedrals in Cadiz - Spain. Photography by Javier Callejas. 160

Figure 11-9. Alberto Campo Baeza, Andalucia's Museum of Memory in Granada - Spain. Photograph by Javier Callejas. 164

Figure 12-1. Juhani Pallasmaa. Finnish Institute in Paris - France. Photograph by Gérard Dufresne. 165

Figure 12-2. Walton Critic Juhani Pallasmaa participates in the final thesis review of a student. Photograph by Julio Bermudez. 167

Figure 12-3. Walton Critic Juhani Pallasmaa teaches while students listen. Photograph by Julio Bermudez. 167

Figure 12-4. Walton Critic Juhani Pallasmaa works with students on a design proposal. Photograph by Julio Bermudez. 167

Figure 12-5. Walton Critic Juhani Pallasmaa responds to the design proposal of two students. Photograph by Julio Bermudez. 167

Figure 12-6. Group photo of the 2011 Walton Studio. Photograph by Julio Bermudez.   167

Featured images and drawings were created by the various students cited.   168-173

Figure 12-7. Juhani Pallasmaa (in collaboration with Kristian Gullichsen). Moduli 225. Prefabricated Vacation   174
Home System, Prototype in Finland. Photograph by Kaj Lindholm.

Figure 12-8. Juhani Pallasmaa, entrance foyer, Rovaniemi Art Museum and Music Hall in Rovaniemi - Finland.   178
Photograph by Arto Liiti.

Figure 12-9. Juhani Pallasmaa, Sami Lapp Museum in Inari, Lapland - Finland. Photograph by Rauno Traskelin.   179

Figure 13-1.Craig W. Hartman, SOM, praying chapel inside the Cathedral of Christ the Light in Oakland -   181
California.

Figure 13-2. Walton Critic Craig W. Hartman discusses work with a student. Photograph by Julio Bermudez.   183

Figure 13-3. Walton Critic Craig W. Hartman and other reviewers make final comments during a studio jury.   183
Photograph by Julio Bermudez.

Figure 13-4. Student presenting work to Walton Critic Craig W. Hartman. Photograph by Julio Bermudez.   183

Figure 13-5. Student presenting work to Walton Critic Craig W. Hartman. Photograph by Julio Bermudez.   183

Figure 13-6. Group photo of the 2010 Walton Studio. Photograph by Julio Bermudez.   183

Featured images and drawings were created by the various students cited on pages.   183-189

Figure 13-7. Craig W. Hartman, SOM, The Cathedral of Christ the Light in Oakland - California.   190
Photograph by SOM.

Figure 13-8. Craig W. Hartman, SOM, praying chapel inside the Cathedral of Christ the Light in Oakland -   194
California. Photograph by SOM.

Figure 13-9. Craig W. Hartman, SOM, praying chapel inside the Cathedral of Christ the Light in Oakland -   194
California. Photograph by SOM.

Figure 13-10. Craig W. Hartman, SOM, main worship space of the Cathedral of Christ the Light in Oakland -   194
California. Photograph by SOM.

Figure 14-1. Nelson Fine Arts Center at Arizona State University, Tempe - Arizona. Photograph by   195
Julio Bermudez.

Figure 14-2. Walton Critic Antoine Predock considering a student's work. Photograph by Julio Bermudez.   197

Figure 14-3. Walton Critic Antoine Predock talking to Thomas Walton. Photograph by Julio Bermudez.   197

Figure 14-4. Group photo of the 2009 Walton Studio. Photograph by Ann Cederna and Andreea Mihalache.   197

Figure 14-5. Students' presenting his work. Photography by Ann Cederna and Andreea Mihalache.   198

Figure 14-6. Photo of the 2009 Walton Studio final review. Photograph by Ann Cederna and Andreea Mihalache.   198

Figure 14-7. Student pinning up their work for design review. Photograph by Ann Cederna and Andreea   198
Mihalache.

Figure 14-8. Photo of Walton Critic Antoine Predock with various staff and students. Photograph by Ann Cederna and Andreea Mihalache.   198

Figure 15-1. Panel of previous Walton Critics during the 2018 Walton Symposium. Photograph by Julio Bermudez   199

Figure 15-2. Bórmida & Yanzón Arquitectos, Alfa Crux Wines, San Carlos, Mendoza — Argentina. Photograph by Bórmida & Yanzón Arquitectos.   201

Figure 15-3. Photo of Walton Studio roundtable speakers. Photograph by Julio Bermudez.   206

Figure 15-4. Claudio Silvestrin, Victoria Miro Private Collection Space, London — England. Photograph by Marina Bolla.   210

Figure 16-1. Detail of Richard Serra's "Sylvester" (2001) sculpture at the Glenstone Museum in Potomac - Maryland. Photograph by Alexandra Garner.   215

Figure 20-1. Photo of Walton Program alumni reunion in 2018. Photograph by Julio Bermudez.   231

Figure 20-2. Photo of Walton students with Walton Critic Alberto Campo Baeza. Photograph by Julio Bermudez.   236

Figure 20-3. Photo of Walton Program alumni reunion in 2016. Photograph by Julio Bermudez.   240

ACKNOWLEDGMENTS

This book could have never been done without a large number of individuals generously devoting their resources, time, skills, knowledge, and effort. Because there are so many, I am afraid that I will inevitably forget someone, to whom I apologize in advance.

My first and biggest thanks go to the very person who made it all possible, Thomas Walton, and, through him, to his family, especially his wife, Kathleen Walton. Thomas unexpectedly passed away about a year ago, which profoundly shocked and saddened us at the CUA School of Architecture and Planning. I had talked to him just a few days before about this book's cover and begun discussing the program for the 2020 Walton Studio in the context of COVID-19. From the moment I joined the CUA architecture faculty in Fall 2010 and started to direct the Walton Critic Program, Thomas was always supportive, positive, open-minded, engaged, and extraordinarily generous. He never once intervened or tried to sway me toward this or that choice of an architect for the program and embraced everyone I brought in with warmth and intelligence. During any particular year, we would find ourselves sharing lunches or walks in which we would talk about many things,

including the Walton Program. I looked forward to these times of friendship, reflection, and peace. I cannot express my gratitude to Thomas in words. I only hope that this book documents and recognizes the incredible legacy of his vision, love, and commitment to education, spiritual growth, architecture, and, of course, our school and students.

I also want to thank my faculty colleagues who invited me to join their school family 11 years ago and trusted me with directing the remarkable Walton Critic Program. I won't name all the twenty-some faculty who made that choice, for they are too many, but I still need to express my gratitude to them. I hope you are satisfied with the result of my efforts.

Turning to the Walton Critic Program itself, I must start by recognizing the eleven renowned architects that left everything behind to come to our campus to teach architecture: Antoine Predock (2009), Craig W. Hartman (2010), Juhani Pallasmaa (2011), Alberto Campo Baeza (2012), Claudio Silvestrin (2013), Eliana Bórmida (2014), Michael J. Crosbie (2015), Prem Chandavarkar (2016), Rick Joy (2017), Susan Jones (2018), and Daniel Libeskind (2019). In their coming to

Washington DC (some from across the globe), these remarkably accomplished individuals demonstrated their profound commitment to teaching and architecture. I want to thank each one of them for trusting the school and me for this educational adventure. The results have been well beyond my highest expectations. One of these outcomes has been the friendships that have grown over the years through direct and indirect contacts and visits. The essays that these professionals wrote for this book were voluntarily done, demonstrating their closeness and commitment to the values behind the Walton Program. It has been my honor and privilege to meet and work with such talented people.

What can I say to the 186 (115 graduate and 71 senior undergraduate) students that decided to enroll in the eleven Walton Studios? Since these courses are elective, they would have never happened unless students decided to join them. Registering for such a class usually required a leap of faith given their unconventional nature: they addressed the relationship between architecture and spirituality. But, of course, the students did a lot more than enrolling. They did the heavy lifting, the actual work. Their time and effort are a testament to their dedication to learning architecture and, at the same time, exploring the big questions in life. I have been impressed by these young people's eagerness and openness to consider what matters vis-à-vis architecture. For all this and so much more, thank you!

A program like this demands a large and continuous administrative support to succeed. Many people at my school deserve mention. I want to thank past Walton Critic Program coordinators Ann Cederna, Andreea Mihalache, and Kathleen Lane (2008-2010); Associate Deans for Administration Michelle Rinehart, August Runge, and Cate Sullivan; Academic Associate Deans Ann Cederna, Luis Boza, Hollee Becker, Judy Meany, and Patricia Andrasik; Assistants to the Dean Kathy L. Fayne and Patricia Dudley; Staff members Nora Petersen,

Kaitlyn R. McLoughlin, Bob Willis, Jerry Mosby, Hussam Elkhrraz, and Davide Prete. I also owe gratitude to our present Sr. Director of Advancement, Andrew Browne, and Staff member Justin McPherson. A special thanks goes to past Dean Randall Ott for his trust and support in running the Walton Program from the very beginning. Acknowledgment should also go to CUA International Student and Scholar Services (especially Gudrun Kendon) for their critical assistance with the visa and other administrative work necessary to bring five foreign visitors to campus. I would like to register my appreciation for the six faculty that agreed to teach the Walton Studio with the renowned guests and me: Gregory Upwall (2010 and 2011), Luis Boza (2012), Randall Ott (2013), Matthew Geiss (2014), and Ana Maria Roman Andrino and Lavinia Fici Pasquina (2016). I don't want to forget to recognize my colleague and friend Travis Price, leader of 24 outstanding Spirit of Place projects at CUA (1993-2017), for his endless commitment and work for the Sacred Space and Cultural Studies concentration as well as the Walton Program over all these years.

The Catholic University of America deserves much credit for creating the academic and spiritual conditions that enabled the Walton Studio's pedagogy and vision to flourish. It's hard to imagine this type of initiative happening in public institutions, especially for a sustained period of time - something I discuss in Chapter 2.

The Walton Program brought some of its activities outside campus into the professional and cultural community of the Washington, DC metro area. In this regard, I want to acknowledge the PR, logistic, and financial support of the embassies of Argentina, Finland, India, Italy, and Spain. In addition, the American Institute of Architects, Washington DC Chapter (through Kathleen Spencer), and the Dadian Gallery at the Wesley Theological Seminary (through Deborah Sokolove) deserve credit for collaborating with the Walton Program in hosting exhibitions of our studio work (both) and lectures (the AIA-DC).

Design reviews are essential to help students during the design process and eventually assess the quality of their final work. Therefore, it is imperative that such juries, as we call reviews in architecture, be composed of professionals outside one's institution to avoid group thinking and conflicts of interest. Over the 12 years, the Walton Program involved 40 to 50 architectural practitioners and academics — about 1/3 from out of town and 2/3 from the large Washington, DC, metro area. Our school, students, and I are very grateful to all of them, whom I cannot name here because of their number. Regarding the book itself, let me recognize the 33 Walton Studio alumni that sent their testimonials for inclusion in this book's Appendix. My appreciation also goes to the 14 participants in a book cover competition we conducted in May 2020, and particularly the three finalists (John Allen, Alex Garner, and Matthew Schmalzel) for their extra effort in working with me afterward. Although we decided to go with a different cover, their efforts helped us arrive at the right choice. In this regard, I want to thank Trevor C. Lipscombe, Abigail Brady, Odette Leal, and Kristen Weller for serving in the book cover competition jury.

I would like to thank several scholars for their advice in writing various parts of this book: Thomas Barrie, Michael Benedikt, Karla Britton, Prem Chandavarkar, Michael J. Crosbie, Norman Crowe, Thomas Fowler, Tammy Gaber, Anat Geva, Francie Hankins, Matthew Niermann, and Phillip Tabb. Additionally, I want to acknowledge the following individuals who reviewed and provided helpful feedback on the full manuscript: Michael J. Crosbie, Nesrine Mansour, Lorena Checa, Tami Wolfgang, Amirali Ebadi, Cesar Chirinos, and Patty Rayman. Lastly, I need to recognize the Architecture, Culture, and Spirituality Forum (ACSF) and its community of 650 members

from 56 countries for providing me with a nourishing academic, social, and professional context that encouraged the vision and activities upon which the Walton program operated all these years.

The book design and production were in the able hands of graduate assistants Odette Leal (2018-19) and Abigail Brady (2019-20) under my supervision. We based the layout on the one used in my book "Transcending Architecture" (CUA Press, 2015) that book designer Anne Kachergis developed. I owe much gratitude to Odette and Abigail for their selfless effort, commitment, and dedication. Abigail deserves special mention, as she continued working with me long after her graduation and ad honorem. I am delighted with the result, which speaks highly of their design capability. Regarding research assistance for this book, I want to thank Cesar Chirinos (2019-21) and, again, Abigail Brady. In terms of the selection and formatting of the design work included in this book, it was done by myself with the help of Amanda Ocello (2018), and graduate assistants Alexandra Garner (2018), Odette Leal, and Abigail Brady. I want to thank all four of them very much.

This book is in your hand courtesy of CUA Press, which means that many people worked on its production and marketing. Here I must point at the leadership and continuous support of director Trevor C. Lipscombe. He saw the value and potential of this project from the moment it was brought to his attention. Additionally, I need to thank Theresa Walker (Managing Editor) and Brian Roach (Sales and Marketing Director). I truly enjoyed working with designer Anne Kachergis on the book's final cover, which, I hope the reader will agree, is both alluring and beautiful. Lastly, I want to record my indebtedness to James Michael Reilly for his outstanding copy-edit of the final drafts of this book.

Much happened in my life in the past 11 years. Good and bad, sad and joyful, with gains and losses. Through it all, there were friends, family, close relationships, and pets that provided me with life-sustaining emotional, caring, and emotional support, caring, and encouragement. And yet, dedicating so much time and effort to a project like this inevitably took me away from them. Still, they were kind, understanding, and patient with me and, more than once, brought me back from moments of doubt, tiredness, sorrow, and frustration. I owed so much to them and would like to express my deepest gratitude for their continuous love over these many, many years. They are Andrea Kalvesmaki, Carlos and Maricarmen Reimers, Tami Wolfgang, Greg Upwall, Thomas Barrie, Gerardo Aleu, Patty Rayman, Rachel Christenson, Lucia Irazabal, Ellie Cook, and my late father Adan Bermudez, whom I miss very much. I can't fail to mention Reina and (late) Pepe, my two best furry friends. They unconditionally accompanied me and were always happy to see me, lay down next to me while I worked on the computer, and greet students, colleagues, and renowned visitors.

In the end, the most significant acknowledgment has to go, as I said in the beginning, to Thomas Walton, who made all this possible and to whom I dedicate this book.

Julio Bermudez
June 21, 2021

FOREWORD
THOMAS WALTON

Imagine an environment and an architecture so compelling that you couldn't not approach it. I am sure that has happened to you. And then imagine that, as you explored it, the path, the landscape, the forms, the light, the materials, the sounds surrounded you with experiences that touched your soul, that moved you emotionally, that left you speechless as you took it all in. I am sure that has happened to you as well. These are intense and treasured moments. And while in some ways overwhelming, they leave you thirsting for more.

Well, you are in luck, because this volume is all about these kinds of experiences. It is about vision and visions. It is about shaping those liminal boundaries that are the gateways to spirituality. It is a reminder that we can craft space to catch a glimpse of, or even step into, the world that transcends our day-to-day existence. What a journey! It is one that, in these pages, captures the shared wisdom of teachers and students, as they together seek to discover how architecture can embody spirituality.

In a very special way, this challenging and collaborative adventure happens in the School of Architecture and Planning at The Catholic University of America in Washington, DC. It is a quest underwritten by the Clarence Walton Fund for Catholic Architecture, an endowed program in the School established in 2008 in honor and memory of the late Clarence C. Walton. Dr. Walton was the first lay president of this national Catholic University and committed to promulgating the Catholic identity and distinguished leadership of the University across its many disciplines.

The architecture program was a clear, but untapped, arena for this quest. The Church has, for centuries, been at the forefront of Western culture's expression of architecture and spirituality. The luminous mosaics that dematerialize the walls of the basilicas at Ravenna, the tranquil cloisters and glowing light under the vaulting of Romanesque monasteries, the jewel-like fire of Gothic stained glass, the harmonious human proportions of Renaissance chapels, the grandeur of Baroque cathedrals, and stunningly spare modern edifices such as those by Le Corbusier and Alvaro Siza are all pathways to transcendence.

In this context, it is a natural fit to celebrate and extend this legacy at CUA. The premise of the Walton Distinguished Critic Program is to have funds to invite the finest minds in the profession to explore architecture and spirituality as a studio partnership with graduate and undergraduate students. And so it has transpired. The contributors to this book have acclaimed reputations for their design and writing in this field. Moreover, they bring perspectives and insights from around the globe. They share their ideas in a studio experience, in lectures, and in panel discussions in a process that guides students to advance their personal approaches to architecture and spirituality.

In these pages, you hear from renowned critics and see the work they have inspired. The panorama is wide, covering a range of project types, some explicitly religious, others that seek to imbue secular environments with spiritual meaning. In words and images, this book hopes to nurture your own reflections and strategies.

Thomas Walton suddenly died before finishing. But I would like to offer some final words in his place.

First, Thomas wished to thank Ann Cederna and Julio Bermudez for their efforts, energy, and leadership of this program. Ann got the program off on its feet and began the legacy. Julio has stewarded it for the last ten years with great enthusiasm and a belief that this unique educational opportunity can encourage students to think of "sacred spaces" as non-traditional and yet inspiring. The Walton Program would not exist without the work of both Ann and Julio.

Secondly, Thomas strongly believed that spirituality could be found outside of a traditional church building. Faith and prayer, or other food for the soul, can and should be found in various places that make you think and feel and be. That belief was central to the development of the Walton Program. Thomas taught architectural history, and so he appreciated and admired traditional church architecture. But as life evolves, so do tastes

and norms and traditional ways of life. Thomas believed that sacred spaces should not just be defined by what was in the past, but what is in the present and future. The work and thinking of the renowned architects in this book are prime examples of that.

Finally, this endowment was dedicated to Dr. Clarence Walton but is a work of love for the entire Walton family. Dr. Walton and his wife Betty were firm believers in sharing one's gifts with others, be it in time, talent, money, prayer, or any combination. The Clarence Walton Fund for Catholic Architecture was one of their ways of sharing their gifts with others, and Thomas's family will continue this legacy in both Dr. Waltons' names. Thomas wanted this to be the first of many volumes, and so we are looking to the future.

Kathleen E. Walton

SPIRITUALITY
IN
ARCHITECTURAL EDUCATION

SPIRITUALITY IN THE DESIGN STUDIO

SPIRITUALITY IN THE DESIGN STUDIO:
introducing the walton program
JULIO BERMUDEZ

Our first and foremost task in life is to take hold of our spiritual destiny. 'Spiritual destiny' or 'vocation' are not words that are encountered often in educational circles. Nevertheless, we are beginning to see a concern in education that opens up the possibility of considering education as a spiritual venture.

Edmund O'Sullivan[1]

How does spirituality enter the education of an architect? Should it? What do we mean by 'spirituality' in the first place? Isn't architectural education a training ground for professional practice and, therefore, technically and secularly oriented? Is there even room to add something as esoteric if not controversial as spirituality to an already packed university curriculum? The humanistic and artistic roots of architecture certainly invite us to consider dimensions well beyond the instrumental, including spirituality. But how would we teach such a thing? And why, if spirituality is indeed relevant to learning architecture, have we heard so little about it?

Since 2008, the ***Walton Distinguished Critic in Design and Catholic Stewardship*** program, or "Walton Program," has been addressing these and many other philosophical, disciplinary, pedagogic, and practical questions related to the

spiritual dimension of professing architecture. It proposes that architecture can and should assist the spiritual growth of humanity in the service of tackling both our urgent and enduring challenges. Its vehicle has been an advanced design studio strategically located between the physical and the metaphysical, culture and nature, life and intention, the worldly and the transcendental. This studio, called the "Walton Studio," also anchors the Sacred Space and Cultural Studies graduate concentration — a unique curriculum inviting architecture students, faculty, and professionals to reflect, learn, research, and profess the deepest spiritual and cultural roots of the built environment. Offered every fall, the Walton Studio is intended for graduate students in the concentration and usually available to senior undergraduates as an elective studio. The voluntary nature of taking this class is important because engaging spirituality demands willingness, maturity, and interest.

The other distinctive characteristic of the Walton Program is recruiting world-class architects to help envision and teach it. The Walton Critics, as the renowned guests are called, have come from the four corners of the earth — three from Europe: *Alberto Campo Baeza, Juhani Pallasmaa, and Claudio Silvestrin*; one from Asia: *Prem Chandavarkar*; one from South America: *Eliana Bórmida*; and six from North America:

Michael J. Crosbie, Craig W. Hartman, Susan Jones, Rick Joy, Daniel Libeskind, and Antoine Predock. Over the past dozen years, their lectures, teaching, and interactions with students and faculty as well as the architectural community of the Washington, DC metro area have sparked renewed design, pedagogic, and scholarly interest in the unmeasurable dimension of architecture. The cumulative effect of these activities has enormously enriched not only our school but also the architectural discipline.

I am not saying this lightly. The high caliber and continuous commitment to spirituality of the Walton Program loom large in architecture, a field that has largely ignored it. The avoidance of spirituality is well documented by several architectural scholars and practitioners.[2] Although architectural education is slowly changing in academic scholarship and professional practice, architectural education remains resistant. How else do we explain the very few courses, publications, and discussions on the topic? I am here not speaking of teaching about religious buildings or designing sacred spaces. Rather, I am talking of curricula that address, facilitate, and/or develop spiritual sensibilities, worldviews, skills, and experiences through architecture. This is not something easy to do and may partially account for the lack of educational engagement. There are many challenges, starting with the belief that architectural education is a training ground for professional practice and therefore technically and secularly oriented. Yet, the humanistic and artistic roots of architecture extend well beyond the instrumental and therefore invite us to consider more significant dimensions of architecture, including spirituality.

A generation ago the influential "Boyer Report" recommended architectural schools to steer their mission, curriculum, and service towards what could be fairly described as spiritual concerns. Similarly, another important document intended to guide future architectural education, this one by the International Union of Architects, was explicitly advising schools to incorporate spirituality into their professional programs.[3] And these pointers have not been the only ones. Spirituality has been an area of increasing attention and study in higher education since the early 2000s. Nevertheless, as we will review in the next chapter, the interest of architectural educators in spirituality remains inconsequential, at least officially. Perhaps this has to do with secular colleges and universities considering anything spiritual as defying the mandated separation between church and state. While these institutions allow some experimentations in the name of academic freedom, it is something else to institutionalize a spirituality inclusive curriculum. However, examples of sustained attention to spirituality are also missing in faith-based schools of architecture, a fact that suggests a system-wide avoidance of the topic as earlier noted. But let us not dwell on negative criticism towards our existing educational model. Instead, let us observe what it is missing as an opportunity to make things better.

Let us include and appreciate traditional methods as the very source and energy from which we can spring forward. There is definitely much to learn, think, and argue about the relationship between architectural education and spirituality. Unfortunately, as far as I know, no such focused study has been done before. There certainly are references to spirituality in pedagogy-centered papers or recorded teachings (most notably of Louis Kahn). But these examples (already few and far between) address spirituality indirectly, generally, or specifically to the topic at hand and stay clear of any consideration of its potential contribution (as a worldview, sensibility, skill, or experience) to architectural education. The absence of such larger educational, professional, and philosophical thinking explains by itself where we are today and demands addressing. For this reason, I will devote the entire next chapter to this task. Those readers that want to continue with this conversation are invited to leap forward.

Returning to the Walton Program, some

questions may be raised about the role of famous architects in a studio advancing spirituality. Isn't putting other human beings on a pedestal, particularly those enthroned by market capitalism and media societies, subversive to the very Walton enterprise? Critiques of the "star architect" system abound. A few responses may be advanced and, in the process, further illuminate the nature of this program. One answer has to do with the uncontestable quality of the architectural work and thinking these Walton Critics have gifted the world with and bring to the studio. Excellent role models do matter when we are trying to educate the next generation of professionals. Second, and while several of these eleven architects could be thought of as "star architects," it is also true that they have provided ample evidence in their actions, writings, and buildings of a commitment to spirituality. In fact, they were selected precisely because of this. But louder than any words is the fact that, however expensive it was for our school to bring them to campus, today's financial reality made these architects lose substantial income by spending time with us and not at their offices. They were on campus teaching our students because they wanted to give back, to share, to educate. Anyone witnessing their dialogues with students during an ordinary desk crit or responding to their works during a public pin-up knows of their genuine devotion to teaching. Indeed, having closely worked with ten of the eleven Walton Critics myself, I can attest to each person's authentic commitment to spiritual values in architecture and education. A fourth response refers to inspiration and validation. Having a highly recognized architect sitting, listening, and discussing their ideas side-by-side at their desk gives students an unmistakable message: they have something valuable to share with the world. American poet and playwrite E.E. Cummings makes this point beautifully:

> We do not believe in ourselves until someone reveals that deep inside us something is

valuable, worth listening to, worthy of our trust, sacred to our touch. Once we believe in ourselves we can risk curiosity, wonder, spontaneous delight or any experience that reveals the human spirit.

Who in youth hasn't suffered the debilitating insecurity of realizing how little we know? Even if we feel that we have something to say, great doubt and anxiety remain. In many ways, we don't believe in ourselves and are looking for external validation. This is an important job for the regular teacher to fulfill, no doubt. But if this confirmation comes from a world-class professional that the student admires, its impact is likely to be much greater. Besides, witnessing that such individual is very much like them, a human being that breathes, has doubts, and makes jokes offers students invaluable, humanizing lessons. The power of these experiences are profound and, for some students, life-changing. The last but no less important reason for bringing a recognized professional to campus has to do with the already mentioned lack of attention to spirituality in architectural education. Not only does the presence of respected figures confer upon immediate credibility to the effort but also each unique iteration builds a body of educational precedents in an area with hardly any. If we now add the longevity of the Walton Program and the quality of the work produced, we have enough evidence to claim (and for others to judge) the value of bringing spirituality into the teaching of architecture.

MAPPING THE BOOK
As previously stated, the next chapter examines the role and relevancy of spirituality in architectural education. This section provides definitions, context, examples, and an overview of the main issues and questions surrounding the inclusion of spirituality in architectural education. Its substantial length is due to the complexity of the topic and the need to present appropriate arguments along with references and data when

possible. Writing this chapter stretched my capacities as a teacher and scholar to the limit as I confess in the text. My hope is that, despite any shortcomings, the essay establishes a place to begin discussing and advancing the spiritual dimensions of teaching and learning, practicing, and experiencing architecture.

Chapter Three shares the fundamental organizational strategy, principles, curriculum, and pedagogy shaping all the Walton Studios. An overview of the warm-up and main assignments, the "big questions" posed, building programs utilized, "factoids," and general outcomes is also included. Following this introduction, there are eleven sections that document the particular iterations of the studio. They go from the most recent effort in 2019 to the first one in 2009. The experiences are titled after their most defining characteristic, whether topical or pedagogical.

— 2019 Walton Studio with *Daniel Libeskind.* Being at the edge of order.
— 2018 Walton Studio with *Susan Jones*. Emotional and material foundations of architecture.
— 2017 Walton Studio with *Rick Joy.* Physical, existential, and spiritual home.
— 2016 Walton Studio with *Prem Chandavarkar.* Vocation and the deep self.
— 2015 Walton Studio with *Michael J. Crosbie*. Changing notions and practices of spirituality and the sacred.
— 2014 Walton Studio with *Eliana Bórmida.* Designing experiences: ritual, narrative, and embodiment.
— 2013 Walton Studio with *Claudio Silvestrin.* Contemplative and non-egotistical improvisation.
— 2012 Walton Studio with *Alberto Campo Baeza.* Building essential ideas.
— 2011 Walton Studio with *Juhani Pallasmaa.* The sacred task of architecture.
— 2010 Walton Studio with *Craig W. Hartman.* Consuming creation: rethinking

consumption and materiality.
— 2009 Walton Studio with *Antoine Predock.* Intuiting spirituality through making, space, and light.

Each section starts with a summary of the studio intentions and characteristics, continues with three examples of students' work, and finishes with an essay by (or interview with) its Walton Critic. In their writings, the architects reflect on the relation between architecture and spirituality, sometimes relating it to the teaching experience. Given the rarity of such meditations in the disciplinary record, these essays are likely to become an important source of reference and guidance. The exception to this presentation format is the 2009 Walton Studio, as I could neither retrieve most of the students' work nor secure an essay from architect Antoine Predock, things that I apologize for. Next, I will briefly introduce the 10 essays in the order they appear in the book

Daniel Libeskind is well known for his commitment to transcendent values and meaning. In this interview, he considers the relationship between architecture and spirituality from multiple, often provocative vantage points that expand our views and understanding. Libeskind acknowledges that *"architecture is deeply spiritual"* and that his work seeks to *"go beyond what is given in the apparent reality of architecture."* His technique consists of designing buildings that invite our ordinary habits to drop off so that what lies beyond is revealed in all its sacred wonder. He advises us to make ample use of the arts and interdisciplinarity to get in the right mindset for true cultural and architectural questioning. For at its very core, the 2019 Walton Critic convincingly tells us, *"Architecture is a quest. This is what makes it spiritual."* He concludes by exhorting students to be (radically) themselves, take the path less traveled, and not believe what they hear or are told but ask for themselves.

Susan Jones reflects on how three underestimated sources of architectural ideation in the academy and profession – feelings, embodiment, and subjectivity—may be utilized to open up, explore, and respond to the spiritually charged topic of death and grief. She deployed these ideas in her 2018 Walton Studio utilizing a pedagogy of experiential emotivity, tectonic improvisation, and empathic design. Students accustomed to remain at a safe distance from anything emotionally or spiritually compromising were drawn into a design-making process where body, feelings, and spirit were brought together in a dramatic process. This unleashed the transformative power of architecture to create spaces that connect us to the deepest plane of being.

Rick Joy writes like he does architecture: simply and meaningfully. The result is a short and to the point message: life is all about the spirit, whether we seek or find it within (soul, mind), without (nature), or with others (fellow human beings); and that each person may be naturally inclined to one or another of these paths. He makes no effort to hide which approach speaks to him, a sensibility that defines his buildings so well and which he eloquently spoke and taught about during his residency at CUA in Fall 2017.

Prem Chandavarkar questions today's

architectural education grounded on modernity's values of individualism, objectivity, and instrumentalism. Not only does such a system disable the student's authentic engagement of others and the world, but it avoids or denies the sacred dimension of life. He proposes that teaching architecture ought to awaken each student's vocation which is not self-bound but rather, as the root of the word "vocation" indicates, a call from a sacred source beyond ego that includes *"the inner voice of others and the higher voices of the world."* The 2016 Walton Critic argues that since the student's inner voice can be most easily recognized with the instructor's assistance, a teacher-student centered pedagogy should form the core of architectural education. Such a model of learning depends on the full interaction between both parties through an exercise of passion (to spark the inner voice and encourage its flourishing) and compassion (to balance the inevitable difficulties of doing so). In other words, bringing spiritual depth to architectural education *will require recasting the act of teaching, where it still valorizes knowledge, but is primarily an act of love."*

Figure 1-2. Six Walton Critics visiting campus in Fall 2018. From left to right: Susan Jones, Prem Chandavarkar, Eliana Bórmida, Julio Bermudez (host), Randall Ott (School Dean), Alberto Campo Baeza, MIchael J. Crosbie, and Juhani Pallasmaa. Photograph by Julio Bermudez.

Michael J. Crosbie reflects on the intentions and pedagogy behind his 2015 Walton Studio: an open inquiry into the nature of sacred space today, a time when a majority people (and youth in particular) describe themselves as "spiritual but not religious" or "nones." What kinds of activities and building programs support our search for the transcendent today? Can there be sacred space without religious consecration or beliefs of some type? Is there sacred architecture beyond monasteries, temples, cemeteries, or memorials? Crosbie's essay dives into the challenging, sometimes uncomfortable, but insightful questions surrounding the new, faith-unbound forms of spirituality in contemporary American culture. He invites us to consider that the *"sense of the sacred is not static and unchanging, and that every age needs to ask and try to answer what it is."*

Eliana Bórmida shares how her experiential approach to architecture was organically developed over two decades of designing buildings for the wine industry in Mendoza, Argentina. She points out that when we approach building programs phenomenologically, the fundamental relationships between nature, culture, and spirituality become synergized and opened to realization and enjoyment by all. The result is an architecture that invites beauty, identity, intimacy, meaning, embodiment, memory, emotions and transcendence, as those who have visited her buildings can attest. Bórmida finishes by sharing the design methodology her office uses to approach architectural commissions and that she taught in her 2014 Walton Studio with excellent results.

Claudio Silvestrin states that designing sacred space is the highest calling of architecture, one that demands architects to be *"humble and put aside our school teaching, our degrees, our professional habits, and our self-referential ego to start afresh with a new mind."* This translates to thinking with our hearts and exercising careful spiritual discernment. Only then will we *"design and build a bridge between Earth and Heaven, divinities and mortals and at the same time, make*

ourselves feel like we can be both citizens of the material world and the spiritual world." The fact that Silvestrin used improvisation to ground the design of buildings normally considered not sacred in his Walton Studio has two far reaching implications: (1) intuition, if properly applied, leads to the best architectural outcomes and (2) the *"sacred"* domain may extend into the secular realm if a building's activities have spirituality at heart. These two inferences align with much of the 2013 Walton Critic's writings and work.

The first and short text of **Alberto Campo Baeza** may seem a bit informal. However, it is when this writing is paired with his second piece *"On Surrender and Universality"* that this architect's mind and approach come to light. Let me explain. Campo Baeza approaches the world empathically, assuming the goodness of his fellow human beings and acting likewise. He puts himself in the other individual's shoes and tries to connect at a personal level. If we read his second essay with this attitude at heart, we will understand that his passionate argument for a universality grounded on selfless style and simplicity is not advocating for a cold, detached, stoic, or puritan architecture. Rather, he is telling us that beauty, the radiance of being, shines forth when we stop embellishing or adding to things and remove ego from the equation. Campo Baeza invites us to join him and his five inspiring *"friends"* (T.S. Eliot, Orgega y Gasset, and Alejandro de la Sota along with Grombrich and Melnikov) in letting go of provincialism, individualism, and noise to find our true, spiritual home.

In *"The Art of Teaching"*, **Juhani Pallasmaa** offers ways to move beyond today's limited and limiting model of architectural education. His diagnosis is compelling. Architectural education focuses too much on "externals" and little if at all on the inner reality of the students. Yet, *"the very essence of learning in any creative field is embedded more in the student's sense of self and his/her unconsciously internalized image of the world than in detached and external facts."* Addressing the situation, the 2011 Walton Critic tells us, demands that we recognize and restore the central but often ignored role that emotions, embodiment, poetics, experience, existential meaning, authenticity, the unconscious, and empathy play in the dialogic act of teaching and learning architecture. These insights agree with ongoing discussions in higher education about how to integrate the spiritual dimension of humanity in the cognicentric, instrumental, and impersonal pedagogy and curricula of most universities. In this context, Pallasmaa explains the importance of teachers in the learning process (reminding us of Chandavarkar's essay), what characteristics they should personify, and how to measure their success. He concludes by sharing examples of such "art of teaching" in the design studio. It would be hard to find another writing that so succinctly offers so many insights and directions on how to improve today's architectural education.

Craig W. Hartman considers the great challenges of our age and proposes an architecture that honors nature and assists human flourishing *"through principles both ancient and contemporary."* This means acting sustainably, responding to local place and history, and seeking beauty without giving up the positives gains of 21st Century. He invites architects to use *"space, form and the poetics of light to create a modern humanism that serves the culturally diverse"* communities of today. Hartman then conducts a comparative analysis of five outstanding modern churches (Le Corbusier's Chapel of Ronchamp in France, Eladio Dieste's Church of Christ the Worker in Uruguay, E. Fay Jones' Thorn-crown Chapel in Arkansas, Peter Zumthor's Bruder Klaus Field Chapel in Germany, and his own Christ the Light Cathedral in Oakland, California). This study reveals a variety of ways in which our immanent and transcendent natures may be mediated through sacred architecture. The 2010 Walton Critic concludes his essay by inviting both the academy and the profession to use architecture to bring spirituality to our global urban civilization.

The book closes with the **round-table discussion** that launched a four-day long event that celebrated the 10th anniversary of the Walton program in October 2018. Moderated by Michael J. Crosbie, he and another five Walton Critics — Juhani Pallasmaa, Alberto Campo Baeza, Eliana Bórmida, Prem Chandavarkar, and Susan Jones — shared their meditations on *"Spirituality and Architectural Education and Practice."* I will never forget that night. The level of attention in the audience was only matched by their silence. As each Walton Critic added their heartfelt reflections to the one before, the atmosphere in the room became increasingly charged with more clarity, depth, gratitude and spirit. In my thirty-five years in academia, I had never witnessed a more compassionate, direct, and authentic teaching. I was not the only one with tears in my eyes as many colleagues and students confessed to me later. This transcript cannot fully account for what happened that memorable evening but it does capture the words elicited. In them, the reader will find many insights, ideas, references, and recommendations to take home and put to good use.

An **Appendix** with testimonials from Walton Program alumni and three short essays I wrote completes this volume. Since I regularly employed my texts in the Walton Studios, it is appropriate to include them in this volume. They also provide another vantage point from which to view the discussion about spirituality in architecture. The first one is the *"Voluntary Architectural Simplicity (VAS) Manifesto."* Originally written in 2003 and improved throughout the years, it proposes an ethical-aesthetic way to respond architecturally (and spiritually) to the challenge of our time. The second paper is *"Choosing Being,"* a critical reflection on today's cultural hallucination with having and doing. The argument calls for refocusing our personal and social efforts in developing being to bring spirituality and balance back to our lives and world. Last is *"On the Architectural Design Parti,"* my most popular writing based on web views (nearly 25,000 in early - February 2021, counting its English and Spanish versions posted in Academia.edu). This short piece is a meditation on the nature and function of the design *"parti"* that seeks to illuminate the subject without undermining its truly magical if not mystical quality.

PARTING WORDS

Spirituality is behind the best examples of architecture across space and time. In fact, it may well be what originated it — if we understand architecture to be more than physical shelter. The archeological evidence of Göbekli Tepe in Southeastern Turkey, a temple built for the worship needs of large numbers of prehistoric people, strongly supports this possibility. Built 6,000 years before Stonehenge and the Giza Pyramids, more time had passed between when those ancient structures were built and Göbekli Tepe than between them and us![4] And ever since, the most accomplished works of architecture, regardless of place or culture (at least until the late 19th Century), have been overwhelmingly associated with spiritual drives. This is a fact that architecture educators and practitioners readily accept. Yet their consent doesn't translate into an openness to spiritual engagement. The reason may have to do with the way they approach those masterpieces: dispassionately, analytically, like someone who has never swam a lap commenting on the swimming performance of an Olympic champion on TV. Such third-person perspective is unable to grasp that those great works of architecture are amazing because the people that conceived and built them were living the spirituality they were expressing. Simply put, historical, scientific, typological, or any such removed analysis will not get us to attain (or understand) the extraordinary results of old as much as experiencing a similar spiritual mindset. Swimming and competing (not necessarily winning) will enable us to understand and say something meaningful about the Olympic swimmer.

But who wants or needs to engage architecture or spirituality in such a personal way in our secular age? Perhaps we do. If we looked at many of today's best buildings with an open mind, we would discover that at least some of them have been shaped by visions or sensibilities that are certainly spiritual —whether the architect of record realized (or acknowledged) it or not. Design, knowledge, technology, skills, labor, materials, finance, management, and the rest are all fundamental. Still, it is what brings them together with love, commitment, and vision that makes greatness possible. Without spirit, the type of efforts required to attain such excellence succumbs. It takes something extraordinary within to accomplish something extraordinary without. We know this to be true in our bones but, somehow, we need to keep reminding ourselves, don't we? And, if we sense this to be true, if we think, feel, or know that spirituality is at work in our best architecture (even today's), shouldn't we reexamine our discipline's attitude towards it?

For twelve years the Walton Program has been working with the conviction that spirituality is an important part of learning how to profess architecture. Because of its novel and untested nature, this effort started as and continues to be an ongoing experiment in architectural education. For this reason, traditional metrics may not be the best way to evaluate its success — not to mention that experiments may fail. Perhaps, the authenticity of the effort and what it teaches us should be used instead. By documenting eleven experimental trials and as many reflections, this book seeks to raise awareness, spark discussion, and offer a precedent for the role that spirituality can play in training future architects and, transitively, practice. May this work be a contribution, however small, to a world in dire need of spiritual sensibility.

Figure 1-3. 2017 Walton Critic Rick Joy discusses graduate student Madeline Amhurst's reflections on "home." In the background, Caroline Winn, Alex Garner, Emily Oldham (from left to right) as Anh-Tu Nguyen and Ian Walker consider the site. Photograph by Julio Bermudez.

Figure 1-4. Michael J. Crosbie reflects on the intentions and results of his 2015 Walton Studio during the exhibition celebrating the 10th anniversary of the Walton Program at CUA School of Architecture and Planning in October 2018. Photograph by Julio Bermudez.

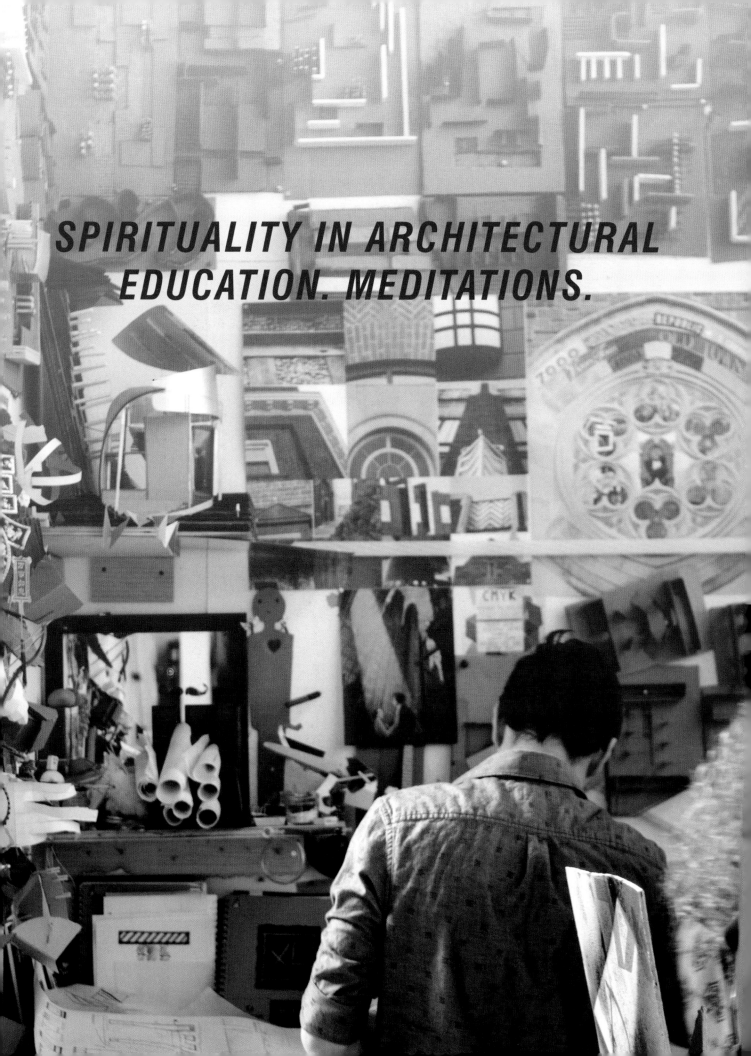

SPIRITUALITY IN ARCHITECTURAL EDUCATION. MEDITATIONS.

SPIRITUALITY IN ARCHITECTURAL EDUCATION. MEDITATIONS.
JULIO BERMUDEZ

Higher education looses upon the world too many people who are masters of external, objective reality, with the knowledge and skill to manipulate it, but who understand little or nothing about inner drivers of their own behavior. Giving students knowledge as power over the world while failing to help them gain the kind of self-knowledge that gives them power over themselves is a recipe for danger —and we are living today with the proof of that claim in every realm of life from economics to religion. We need to stop releasing our students into the wild without systematically challenging them to take an inner as well as outer journey.
Parker J. Palmer[1]

Writing an essay about spirituality in architectural education seems like a daunting if not impossible task. Every time I sat down to work on it, doubts, concerns, and questions would invade my mind and paralyze me. Who was I to attempt a project like this? How could I be so naïve to approach such an academic minefield where losing if not a limb, certainly scholarly, professional, and pedagogic credibility seemed all but certain? But my heart, intuition, and faith would raise their voices loud and clear asking me to engage the topic. Over and over again, they would rescue me from the grip of fear and misgiving and

point to the urgent, unavoidable need to address spirituality today. How could anyone pretend to offer professional education without dealing with the deepest, most meaningful dimensions upon which architectural design, thought, and practice find their ethos?

I realized that to move forward, I had to acknowledge my clumsiness at the effort. It was not that I was unprepared or knew nothing about spirituality in architecture. This would be far from the truth as my academic and personal paths indicate. It was because I knew something, perhaps just enough to attempt this risky endeavor, that I could see how little I knew. Some term this condition "learned ignorance" and contend that it only grows with time: the more we learn and "know," the more we realize our real ignorance.[2] With this humble attitude at heart, I recorded the following meditations on spirituality in architectural education. I call my considerations "meditations" to indicate their tentative, in-progress, and naturally arising quality. This label also frees me from having to unpack every topic or argument, an impossible proposition as many of them would demand a book onto themselves. I will certainly not claim that spirituality is the most important subject in the architectural curriculum. This would be inappropriate and wrong. Instead, I will posit that traditional teaching should be complemented with experiences that invite the full range and depth of our humanity, particularly those associated with the spirit. Doing so would go a long way to address the type of concerns (along with many others) cited in the initial quote. These meditations are therefore intended to advance and not criticize architectural education. At the very least, they seek to start the conversation.

It is intimidating to reflect and write on spirituality in architectural education for many reasons. One is undoubtedly the very few precedents or discussions available even in organizations with professed interest on the subject like the Association of Collegiate Schools of Architecture (ACSA) in the United States. Searches for articles covering "spirituality" and related topics (e.g., "faith," "religion," "authenticity") concerning education in its Journal of Architectural Education (the oldest and most prestigious publication covering research and commentary on architectural education) find nothing! Nor are many articles on the topic found in other well-known journals such as Places, Design Issues, Space and Culture, and the International Journal of Islamic Architecture.[3] Queries on 25 years of proceedings from Regional, National, and International ACSA conferences retrieve a minimal number of articles.[4] Inquires on the published record of other academic groups with a stake in architectural teaching and scholarship such as the Architecture Research Centers Consortium (both its conference proceedings and ENQ journal) and the Society of Architectural Historians don't fare much better. On the other hand, a search of 30 National Conference on the Beginning Design Student (NCBDS) proceedings more readily finds pedagogic work with spirituality in mind. Still, this positive result — a total of 25-35 papers (about one article per conference) — underscores the low coverage of the topic: they represent about 2% of the total number of published works.[5] The Architecture, Culture, and Spirituality Forum (ACSF) and ARCHNET deserve a special note. ACSF was founded in 2007 with the expressed mission to address the lack of

attention to spirituality in architecture. Although architectural education figures significantly in its agenda, only 3% of all the papers presented at its ten annual symposia cover pedagogic issues.[6] Something similar occurs with ARCHNET. Despite offering an impressive diversity and quantity of work related to Muslim spirituality in architecture and related fields, attention to architectural education is reduced to providing resources (e.g., syllabi, PowerPoint presentations) rather than reflective discussions or case studies.[7] The fact that there is a lack of conversation on spirituality in architectural education, even in these two groups that hold spiritual issues central to their mission, further demonstrates the low attention the topic receives. Not surprising, open web queries about spirituality in architectural education only affirm the analyses: the very few results obtained usually point back to the examples found in the cited sources.[8] In fact, there is not one conference paper, web posting, journal article, or book chapter solely devoted to articulating or reflecting on the relationship between architectural education and spirituality. Do I need to say that there are no books about it either?

This overall silence indicates that at least officially (i.e., in the published record), neither schools of architecture nor their faculty are too eager to offer students experiences related to spirituality. It is a muteness that extends to the architectural discipline at large — an avoidance that has been recognized and lamented by several architectural scholars and practitioners over the past decade.[9] Yet, paradoxically, the dialogues of Louis Kahn and his students, as well as his thinking, continue to be a source of spiritual wonder if not a central part of our discipline's lore.[10] And there are other few other examples such as the living legacy of John Hejduk's teachings at Cooper Union or the influential workshops that Juhani Pallasmaa continues to give around the world.[11] Who hasn't heard professionals or academics refer to the ineffable and immeasurable during design studio reviews —allusions that indisputably refer to some type of transcendent realm or dimension? And what about architecture classes and studios that do engage the highest quality of architecture — even though their teachers may refrain from calling that quality "spiritual"? Indeed, the best architectural teachers (and practitioners) that I know never fail to acknowledge the spiritual dimension of architecture even though they may refer to "it" with other names. Does this uneasiness or fear of using or addressing the topic with the word "spirituality" explain the official silence?[12] Any reasonable observer would expect no such attitude from people who generally define themselves as religious or spiritual as Americans repeatedly do in national polls.[13] In fact and consistent with such statistics, most of the students entering American colleges and universities consider themselves spiritual (72%) and/or religious (54%) with faculty following a similar pattern (81% spiritual and 64% religious).[14] Professing a faith is quite common around the globe too. A majority of the world population believes in God or a deity and/or practices some form of spirituality.[15] The reality that these data paint leaves us with the same basic question: why does architectural education ignore or avoid something important to most people? In order to understand this puzzle, we need to consider the nature and implications of spirituality as well as the concerns it raises.

ON SPIRITUALITY

Defining "spirituality" in depth could occupy the rest of this chapter, if not the entire volume.[16] Since we don't have such luxury, we will have to accept a much shorter interpretation. Three excellent definitions by recognized education scholars and observers provide us with the right framework. For writer, speaker, and activist Parker J. Palmer, spirituality is *the diverse ways we answer the heart's longing to be connected with the largeness of life —a longing that animates love and work.*[17] For UCLA education researcher extraordinaire Alexander W. Astin, spirituality is a multi-layered quality involving *"… an active quest for answers to life's 'big questions'; a global worldview that transcends ethnocentrism and egocentrism; a sense of caring and compassion for others coupled with a lifestyle that includes service to others; and a capacity to maintain one's sense of calm and centeredness, especially in times of stress."*[18] For author and social activist bell hooks, *"spiritual life is first and foremost about commitment to a way of thinking and behaving that honors principles of inter-being and interconnectedness. When I speak of the spiritual, I refer to the recognition within everyone that there is a place of mystery in our lives where forces that are beyond human desire or will alter circumstances and/or guide and direct us. I call these forces 'divine spirit'."*[19] These and so many other definitions denote that *"spirituality"* is a deeply seated awareness, worldview, attitude, and/or way to perceive/act in the world that emerges from, responds to, and/or expresses

(1) a realm, order, or being beyond the limits, understanding, and control of individual and socio-cultural consciousness; sharing, which often lead to the adoption/creation of a belief system, rituals (whether institutionalized or personally articulated), and a community where it feels at home and grows. Let us remember that "religion" is usually defined as a social institution supporting or organizing a group of individuals' ways to practice, express, explain, believe, and transmit spiritual information/experiences/meaning. But we would be mistaken to equate the two. It is possible to be spiritual and non-religious, as in the case of environmental atheists committed to preserving nature, agnostic humanists fighting for social and economic justice, or the growing number of individuals describing themselves as "nones" (i.e., religiously unaffiliated people) in national surveys on faith.[21] Spirituality is a broader concept, sensibility, or experience than religion.

We may think of spirituality as the common ground on which all faiths build their foundations. The interest that many of us have in spirituality is not due to a prejudice against creeds. Rather, it is a recognition that in today's diverse societies, spirituality provides a more reliable platform than religion for connecting people at the deepest level. Because spirituality doesn't demand or expect agreement in doctrines and practices — only a *"belief that there is an unseen order and that our supreme good lies in harmoniously adjusting ourselves thereto,"* as American psychologist-philosopher William James puts it[22] — it facilitates the engagement and communication of this essential dimension of being among individuals from all backgrounds. For all its virtues (and like all things in life), spirituality does have a dangerous side. It is a tendency to devolve into an "existentialization" of religion, cultish devotion, misplaced desire and projections, or other expressions that cheapen or betray its transcendent and all-encompassing nature.

SPIRITUALITY IN HIGHER EDUCATION

If we were to integrate the essential characteristics of spirituality into higher education, two general and related actions would be necessary: (1) to bring transcendent and relational perspectives into what is being taught, and (2) to involve the whole being of the learner.

The first recommended action would require us to present the world as a non-fragmented, interconnected whole. This would mean to recognize the essential relationship between self and others that is implicit in the web of life, culture, and spirit where we dwell. Here lies the source of all compassionate and interpersonal understanding. Explicitly, every dealing with the world should be taught as involving not just a distant "I-it" (i.e., objective, third-person) but, most likely, an "I-Thou" (i.e., intersubjective,

second-person) interaction. [23] Education ought to assist students in realizing that beliefs, customs, language, knowledge, and more are frameworks through which "others" are directly influencing or participating in their consciousness and behavior —mostly beyond their awareness. These actions are facilitated by asking the "big questions" in life because responses will inevitably reveal intentions and values that, in turn, will make clear otherwise invisible cultural, religious, social, and-or philosophical frameworks ruling the learners' lives. Additionally, big questions have the benefit of bringing personal and social perspectives together. Issues of trustworthiness, ethics, beauty, purpose, belonging, and integrity—all expressions closely tied to spirituality—inevitably come up. Once students can see their worldview, they start to perceive those of others. This enables the consideration of multiple paradigms of self, society, relationships, and reality (including education, architecture, the curriculum). The importance of flexibility in taking perspectives and shifting those perspectives cannot be overstated, particularly when we are able to bring any gained realization to empathic and personal levels. This is why service-learning courses, study abroad, and interdisciplinary classes work so well in terms of holistic learning and spiritual growth. [24] They provide direct ways for students to cognitively and emotionally access and understand alternative views of the

(2) fundamental connectedness with others, nature, and/or divinity; and/or

(3) serving or helping other living beings.

By providing a transcendent, holistic, and compassionate context, spirituality offers a "Big Picture."[20] This all-encompassing perspective puts ordinary life, society, and the world in their right place. Meaning, purpose, truth, goodness, and beauty are naturally brought forth and have the larger whole in mind and heart. Egocentrism and ethnocentrism are kept out. This reverent, humble, and inclusive understanding is not abstract or detached. On the contrary, the literature shows that spirituality involves our whole being (physical, emotional, intellectual, and social), hence its power and significance. For these reasons, spirituality is associated with the highest aspirations and values of humanity (e.g., empathy, authenticity, equanimity), a sense of unity, awe and the sacred, and particularly religion. Its connection to faith is strengthened by the fact that spirituality usually seeks understanding and world and act or help accordingly. In short, integrating spirituality into higher education means teaching how to perceive and operate from an interpersonal, dialogic viewpoint.

The second necessary action for bringing spirituality into higher education has little pedagogic novelty. We have long known that the best learning occurs when a person is fully participating. Over the past two decades, science has confirmed that all knowledge is fundamentally shaped by our feelings, body, intentionality, and culture. Hence the ongoing discussion on 4E cognition (embodied, embedded, enactive, and extended). If students don't establish a personal relationship with what is being taught, the gained knowledge will be superficial and forgotten. Finding significance depends on a person's interest, social context, trust in the source, and-or emotional-behavioral interaction. In short, personal engagement is vital. If we were speakers of a Romance language, we would be using *"sapere/saber/à savoir"* (i.e., "savoring") and not *"cognoscere/conocer/conhecer"* (i.e., knowing) to describe the aim of true education. Sapere demands we are directly connected with what we come to know. It is a knowledge gained by acquaintance. On the other hand, "cognoscere" is to know from a distance, by reading, hearing, or watching. It is an awareness that is intellectual and detached. Whereas sapere is first-person knowing, cognoscere is third-person knowing. For this reason, integrating spirituality in education implies that *"the ontological standing of experience [be] elevated from mere secondary appearance to a central position ..."*[25]

These two recommendations challenge the cognicentric, fragmented, and utilitarian paradigm shaping most higher education today, including architectural schooling. Its third-person approach limits curricula and pedagogy to intellectual (i.e., logical, detached, analytical), instrumental (i.e., technical, pragmatic, productive), disciplinary (i.e., focused, divided, incomplete), and-or objectivist (i.e., empirical, measurable, materialist) frameworks. This model also accentuates individualism and personal success over the common good, competitiveness over collaboration, productivity over reflection. Although third-person perspectives and related values are useful, powerful, and necessary, they leave out fundamental aspects of our humanity and the world, namely the interior life of the student, empathy and compassion, the socio-cultural "multiverse" contextualizing all experiences and beliefs, and the fundamental interconnectedness of it all.

Starting in the 2000s, many educators, philosophers, and scholars began to point at these significant shortcomings of higher education, criticism that go beyond the traditional liberal arts arguments.[26] A balanced or integral learning experience, they argue, is necessary to present educational content in ways that complement outer (third-person), inner (first-person), and relational (second-person) dimensions of knowledge, behavior, and being. And, since the former approach has been dominant, increased attention to the latter two is necessary. Simply put,

A truly integrative education engages students in the systematic exploration of the relationship between their studies of the 'objective' world and the purpose, meaning, limits, and aspirations of their lives. The greatest divide of all is often between the inner and outer [worlds], which no curricular innovation alone can bridge. The healing of this divide is at the heart of education during the college years, rightly understood.[27]

It is a healing that naturally brings spirituality into the picture. For the moment we include students' inner lives into any educational endeavor, spirituality becomes unavoidable. As Astin et al. say:

Spirituality is fundamental to students' lives. The "big questions" that preoccupy students are essentially spiritual questions: Who am I? What are my most deeply felt values? Do I have a mission or purpose in my life? Why am I in college? What kind of person do I want to become? What sort of world do I want to help create? [28]

College students are supposed to ask these big questions. From a developmental psychology perspective, this is where young adults are in their lives.[29] Avoiding such inquiries invalidates their concerns and is counter-productive to their education.

Unfortunately, colleges and universities have been moving in the opposite direction. The growing market, social, and political pressures to account for educational outcomes (job placement, graduation rates, starting salary, etc.), costs (student debt, tuition increases, etc.) and accessibility, have pushed higher education to become ever more "superficial," secular, and utilitarian.[30] Universities and colleges have continued to apply their familiar cognicentric-instrumental paradigm because of its more efficient capacity to market, package, and measure educational programs, curricula, and outcomes respectively — what some call the "business model" of education.[31] But this is poor practice because delivering fragmented and decontextualized knowledge out of artificially siloed academic departments through outdated discipline-narrow teaching methods is not how to prepare students for our complex 21st Century. And if this were not bad enough, there are indications that in this turmoil, university and college leadership and faculty are losing track of the ultimate mission of higher education: to assist students to *grow up, learn who they are, to search for a larger purpose for*

their lives, and to leave college as better human beings." [32]

Education analysts and critics alike recommend that turning things around requires us to adopt integral models of education in which spirituality plays a significant role. We are talking of a shift from traditional cognitive and instrumental goals toward meaning-making and personal transformation objectives, including self-discovery, emotional interests, motivations, values, etc. This "ontological turn" has as much to do with practical imperatives as with spirituality. In today's changing world, the best education is not occupied with knowledge and skills that may become obsolete or are superficial. Instead, it focuses on the structural and qualitative dimensions of the learner (e.g., deep self, character, emotional intelligence, social skills) whose development confer better adaptability to heterogeneous and rapidly changing cultural and natural environments.[33] The value of this approach is evident in the "post-truth," "fake-news" reality where we live. In this world, what matters is not so much third-party knowledge but life experience, that is, how the self deals with ambiguous, ever-shifting, and new information. Trustworthiness is built rhetorically (i.e., we listen to who we trust) and functionally (i.e., a skill matters if it is useful). In other words, learning new knowledge cannot and should not be separated from personal intelligent behavior and being.[34] The brings us again to the point that the new education arcs toward "sapere" over "cognoscere."

An essential piece in this discussion is the well-known UCLA study of spirituality and religion in higher education. Directed by renowned educator Alexander W. Astin, this multi-year and large-scale investigation documented (1) how students grow spiritually and religiously during college, (2) how institutions may support such development, and (3) its effects on traditional educational outcomes. The project surveyed over 112,000 freshman students from 236 U.S. colleges and universities at the start of their studies, and 15,000 of these were polled again in their junior year. Additionally, the study included individual interviews and focus groups with students attending eleven different campuses. Finally, the work surveyed faculty at the same institutions during a full academic year. The results of this remarkable study are summarized in the influential 2011 book *Cultivating the Spirit. How College Can Enhance Students' Inner Lives.*[35] If there were doubts about the relevancy of spirituality in higher education, this investigation puts the matter to rest. I will not get into the particulars of this fascinating study — the reader is encouraged to go to the source — but I offer the following citation as a good summary of their conclusion:

> … *providing students with more opportunities to touch base with their 'inner selves' will facilitate growth in their academic and leadership skills, contribute to their intellectual self-esteem and psychological well-being, and enhance their satisfaction with the college experience … In short, we believe that the findings of this study constitute a powerful argument in support of the proposition that higher education should attend more to students' spiritual development.*[36]

Integrating spirituality into higher education strengthens and expands learning opportunities and outcomes. It doesn't erase or replace traditional types of knowledge and teaching methods but instead includes and transcends them by adding usually ignored first- and second-person perspectives. Furthermore, by providing an all-encompassing—even if fuzzy or too general— perspective (i.e., a "big picture"), spirituality encourages education to take on six endemic fragmentations afflicting contemporary life:[37] (1) fragmentation of worldviews (separate frameworks of meaning); (2) fragmentation of knowledge (different disciplines, methods, technologies); (3) fragmentation of society (individualism, racism, xenophobia, wealth); (4) fragmentation between economic life and nature

(environmental destruction); (5) fragmentation of our inner and outer lives (see earlier quote); and (6) fragmentation within our selves (heart and mind, body and mind). Notice that fragmentations (3) through (6) correspond to "ontological" fragmentations (being in its social, ecological, and self expressions). In contrast, the first two are about the mental constructs used to put the world together. The transcendent and relational framing that spirituality affords empowers education to seek connections, patterns, commonalities, and unity among the parts.

Figure 2-2. Architect and educator Juhani Pallasmaa communicates with students using the full range of human expressions (cognition, emotion, embodiment, spirit) during his teaching at CUA School of Architecture and Planning.

RESISTANCE TOWARD SPIRITUALITY

Despite these arguments, positive research results, and reasonable requests for change, there remains resistance to intergrating spirituality into higher education. Three main obstacles are preventing change. The first comes from fears that engaging spirituality risks brainwashing students into irrational thinking and behavior. The second sees spirituality as steering away from proven, good educational practices, and causing poor learning outcomes. The last obstacle has to do with seeing spirituality as challenging the mandated separation of church and state in public institutions in the U.S. Let us review these concerns.

The first, most severe, and understandable worry has to do with religious indoctrination. History is littered with the awful consequences of blindly following spiritual faiths: from the tragedy of Jim Jones' Peoples Temple in Jonestown, Guyana (1978) to the unspeakable abuses of the Holy Inquisition in medieval Europe and the horrors of contemporary ISIS (Islamic State of Irak and Syria). And there are also plenty of less dramatic or known but still repulsive cases of psychological, social, political, or military control exercised in the name of "holy" wisdom. However, we must also recognize that religion usually plays a positive role in contemporary free societies. Examples of its beneficial impacts abound: charity for the poor, care for the elderly, social and racial justice, volunteer work, community building, psychological support, etc. The fact that a majority of citizens (at least in the U.S.) define themselves as religious indicates that people see faith as good and necessary for daily life. Regarding abuse, it is fair to say that the public associates it with religious institutions and not with the faith. But let us remember here that our focus is spirituality and not religion, and that some of the major differences between the two originate precisely in spirituality's lack of institutional control and indoctrination. Spirituality is a deep-seated awareness, worldview, attitude, and/or way to experience/act where doctrine or belief plays a much lesser role. For this reason, some of the apprehensions people have about religion should be soothed with spirituality. Still, even a skeptic should accept that including (not suppressing) spirituality in education, especially at the university/college level, makes sense not only to improve an already heavily utilized mode of reasoning but also, more cynically perhaps, to keep an eye on it. Transparency and not denial or censorship is the best path to address difficult topics in democratic, free societies.[38] Unfortunately, this is not what we are doing in higher education. Something has gone wrong with how we, as a society, perceive both religion and spirituality vis-à-vis education. Blaming it all on rationalists, atheists, or scientists would be gravely mistaken. As Waldorf Education professor Jost Schieren argues, fear and cynicism towards spirituality are historically and culturally built and widespread across society, including among religious people. They evolved as a societal safeguard against naïve spiritual pursuits going wrong and causing enormous personal and collective harm: fanatism, sectarianism, and anarchism.[39] This cultural attitude was taken up by the secular forces of the 20th Century and rationalized into common-sense beliefs that justified keeping spiritual concerns out the classrooms. Despite its good and understandable original intentions, the effects have been far from perfect.

In his book "*Religion and American Education,*" Warren A. Nord convincingly shows that conventional wisdom against integrating religion into education makes three wrong assumptions: (1) "*the secular and the sacred can be separated, and the greater part of our world can be understood in purely secular terms;*" (2) "*secular ways of understanding the world are neutral and therefore secular education is neutral;*" and (3) "*critical reason is the ally of modern secular thought, whereas religion lives and dies by irrational faith. As education must be objective and rational, education must be secular.*"[40] The shortcomings of these postulations are not hard to identify. The world is certainly not a vast profane territory peppered with a few sacred areas. Who can deny that the lack of reverence towards nature implied by secularism is at least partially to blame for the massive environmental destruction around the earth? Regarding the neutrality of secularism, we know that there is no unbiased perspective. Every perception or action (whether secularly or spiritually framed) is taken from a particular ideological position or intention (even if unconsciously). Furthermore, any implementation of a secular-only education in the name of neutrality proves itself utterly partial. As Nord says, *just as racially segregated schools are inherently unequal, so an exclusively secular education is inherently not neutral.*[41] Besides, assuming a position's neutrality is very dangerous because it leads to denial and abuse. Lastly and related, unchecked faith in reason and objectivity has proven as problematic as blind faith in religion. The Frankfurt School of philosophy has shown that rationality is a tool that always depends on a value-system external to itself to operate. Moreover, the myth of objectivity has been put to rest by modern physics, post-structuralism, and cognitive science. In other words, there is no neutral point of view, no value-free rationality, and no objectivity. This doesn't mean thawt we must fall into chaos, radical relativism, or solipsism but rather that other more nuanced ways to address the world are needed. Here Nord appropriately argues that inviting religion (or spirituality) back into education does require its critical examination but that such interrogation ought to be extended to science and reason as well. After all, and despite their incredible contributions to our civilization, these secular operations are dangerously narrow-minded, particularly in their modernistic or positivistic expressions.

The second concern about integrating spirituality into higher education has to do with concrete learning outcomes. Won't attention and time devoted to spiritual matters (e.g., self-searching, "big questions," various worldviews) result in diminished or inferior university education? Even more poignantly:

The critique of cognicentrism and the emphasis on the nondiscursive and spiritual elements of human inquiry can easily raise the specter of anti-intellectualism. The basic concern is that the incorporation of somatic, vital, and emotional experience into the educational container may jeopardize intellectual rigor. In other words, if we make too much room for somatic, emotional, and intuitive knowing, don't we run the risk of debilitating intellectual standards of analytical rigor and rational criticism? Can we really escape the degeneration of educational practice into a fluffy, warm, but ultimately uncritical process that bypasses the meticulous elaboration and appraisal of knowledge?[42]

The answer coming from the cited, large-scale UCLA study of spirituality and religion in higher education is a resounding "no." As briefly discussed, this investigation found that engaging spirituality augments, not lessens, the academic experience and performance of students. In fact,

Spiritual development turns to be highly compatible with many of the more 'traditional' outcomes of higher education such as academic performance, leadership development, self-esteem, satisfaction with college, and motivation for further education. Further, most of the programs and practices that contribute to spiritual development also promote these traditional outcomes.[43]

As articulated in this study, but also by other educators, integrating spirituality into higher education does not mean introducing controversial, strange, or difficult curricula and pedagogies. Many existing programs, courses, and teaching methods can do the job or need just some minor modification. For example, interdisciplinarity, travel abroad, interracial interaction, service learning, interfaith dialogue, and leadership training are common ways to advance spirituality in colleges and universities.[44] And there are others, like the adoption of contemplative practices in a variety of educational venues.[45] The fact that bringing spirituality onto campus improves learning outcomes should ease the concerns of those focused on educational accountability.

The third major obstacle against including spirituality in higher education has to do with the mandated separation between church and state in public institutions. In a nation with great religious and cultural diversity, we all agree that the state should not be in the business of promoting any faith. Of course, this is also what the United States Constitution establishes.[46] But there is a great difference between affirming this policy and banning spirituality from campus. First, spirituality is not religion, as we have articulated earlier on.[47] Incorporating spirituality in the classroom is not about discussing a doctrine, creating a community of believers, or practicing particular rituals. Instead, it seeks to unleash students' capacity to perceive and question things from more comprehensive, non-egocentric, and non-ethnocentric perspectives without losing connectedness and empathy with the world. This is "the" spiritual outlook if there is one, and what develops equanimity and compassion as well as promotes considerations of meaning, purpose, and authenticity. Second, banning spirituality from the classroom creates an artificial barrier that discourages naturally arising curiosity, sharing, conversation, and, therefore, deep learning. Since spirituality is present in all aspects of our existence, trying to keep it out is like trying to stop water from flooding a boat with a thousand holes. Third, censoring spirituality has serious negative consequences. Without developing spiritual sensibility in future citizens, society becomes unprepared to deal with problems that demand value appraisal, multiple perspectives, integrative thought, empathy, and balanced judgment —the type of challenges that increasingly characterize our present and future worlds. Holistc educator John P. Miller summarizes the response to this third type of resistance towards spirituality rather well:

Because the spiritual is not connected to a particular set of religious beliefs, it does not fit within some of the legal rulings on the separation between church and state that have been applied to schools in the United States. Because the spiritual can permeate every aspect of life, it is impossible to keep it out of the classroom.[48]

Lastly, there is the legal precedent of Zorach v. Clauson (1952), where the U.S. Supreme Court accepted that religion could be accommodated in public education under certain conditions. Since we are talking of spirituality and not religion, the case could be made much more strongly for integrating spiritual sensibility into secular schools, indicating a possible legal path forward.[49]

Whether the concern against spirituality in education is about manipulating students into cultish irrationality, wasting time in learning useless or controversial material, or breaking the law mandating church-state separation, the fact is that young people will inevitably discover and-or explore spirituality in college. As cited, most college students already arrive to campus with interest in religion or spirituality. Being away from their family and socio-cultural cocoon at a time when they are meeting people with other viewpoints, behaviors, cultures, and religions invites students to make spiritual inquiries and reflections. This is also the time when young adults wonder about choices that will impact much of their lives (e.g., a career path, relationships, etc.). So instead of resisting, it would be much wiser to utilize their natural curiosity and openness to advance their education. Addressing these fundamental matters with appropriate guidance is particularly important these days as students have immediate access to anything right on their smartphone.

After reflecting on the biases keeping spirituality off of campuses, it is hard to avoid concluding, along with Nord and other scholars and educators, that spirituality needs to be invited back into secular higher education.

This applies to both undergraduate (because it is when individuals are developing their psychological self and worldviews) and graduate (because future professionals need to have self-understanding and the most encompassing and compassionate perspective possible) education. Without incorporating a spiritual mode of thinking, feeling, and understanding, real education is artificially and fundamentally inhibited and decontextualized from life. We could even interpret such avoidance (if not censorship) as infringing on the rights and needs of students and teachers.

> *To ignore the spiritual side of students' and faculty's lives is to encourage a kind of fragmentation and a lack of authenticity, where students and faculty act either as if they are not spiritual beings, or as if their spiritual side is irrelevant to their vocation or work. Within such an environment, academic endeavors can become separated from student's most deeply felt values, and students may hesitate to discuss issues of meaning, purpose, authenticity, and wholeness with each other and especially with faculty.*[50]

Quite simply, logical reasoning, empiricism, and -or cultural-historical analyses, while useful, do not fully quench students' natural desire for existential depth, connection, belonging, integrity, goodness, beauty, transcendence, and so on.

It goes without saying that in an era hyper-aware of all types of discrimination, the same courtesy is usually not extended to religious and spiritual practitioners. This is not a conservative talking point. I have seen it played out several times at academic conferences and classrooms. It is something that is just beginning to be discussed in the academy, and that will grow in the years to come, I am sure. The acceptance of spirituality as a legitimate area of human learning that this book and many others are arguing for will hopefully assist in this process.

SPIRITUALITY IN FAITH-BASED INSTITUTIONS

Let's now turn our attention toward religious colleges and universities. If the ignorance or censorship of spirituality in public institutions undermines the full education of students, couldn't its promotion in faith-based campuses cause as much harm, albeit in other ways? Alternatively, can a spiritual inquiry encounter resistance in religious institutions if it involves criticism of content deemed theologically unquestionable?

In the foreword to a book examining higher education at faith-based universities and colleges, recognized educator Jon F. Wergin acknowledges his preexisting bias that religious institutions were places where in-depth examinations were avoided for fear of conflict with creed.[51] However, based on the collected data and arguments presented in the volume he is introducing, Wergin confesses that he had been wrong all along. Indeed, in *"Putting Students First. How Colleges Develop Students Purposefully,"* education researchers Braskamp, Trautvetter, and Ward present faith-based universities and colleges delivering a more integral education when compared to public secular colleges where spiritual and religious issues are off-limits. Instead of safeguarding faith or avoiding doubts and critique, religious institutions of higher learning are found to encourage students to look into their vocation, ethics, morals, existence, and relation to something larger than themselves but without indoctrination. Their research shows faith-based higher education as supporting spirituality while still instilling the skills and knowledge that their public, secular counterparts do.

This is congruent with my experience at The Catholic University of America, where I teach. In my ten years here, I have never been told to promote religion nor curb potential criticism towards it. Neither have I ever been questioned by colleagues, administrators, or students about my spirituality-integrated courses. Of course, fundamental Catholic values that the university holds are to be respected (not necessarily agreed with), but they are so humanistic that my students and I have never found them to be a source of friction or trouble. I have been able to utilize the long Catholic tradition of intellectual questioning to advance spiritual inquiry in my teaching. Doing so has invariably involved challenging not only cultural and social practices but also religious convictions. But such examination is healthy and at the heart of all higher education, not to mention being in sync with where young adults developmentally are, as we saw. Raising doubts and issues about a particular faith is not counter religious and spiritual thinking. Most religions are sympathetic to such inquiries because, in the end, they often return the seeker to her/his faith with more clarity and commitment than before. For example, Christianity recognizes that *"faith necessarily seeks understanding"* and that this is fundamentally good because *"… all intellectual inquiry leads eventually to questions of ultimacy that invite faith responses."*[52] Zen Buddhism considers that only a small or weak faith is apprehensive of doubt because it knows that it may not survive it. Great or strong faith welcomes such challenges because it knows that they will only strengthen it. But let us be clear here: even if the spiritual quest takes the student away from their original faith, a religious university would be doing its job.

I am aware that utilizing my own experience at a religious university to generalize what is happening at other such institutions is not ideal. However, my multiple interactions with faculty and scholars from such organizations in the context of the cited research study give me some confidence to risk making these statements. Besides, my quick overview of faith-based higher education concerning spirituality doesn't pretend that everything is okay at these institutions, for they are far from perfect. Nor am I saying that spirituality neatly enters all its classes and teaching methods. The fragmentation of higher education into academic disciplines, departments, and colleges affecting secular universities is also present at religious colleges. So

is the prevalence of the cognicentric, utilitarian, and business model of education. All this means that there are plenty of courses and whole careers in faith-based campuses where spirituality is not part of the students' experience at all, except through some general class requirements, usually placed in the first two years of education. As a result, many cases, students graduating from religious universities have as little exposure to spirituality as in their secular counterparts, especially in STEM and graduate programs, including architecture. Still, spiritual thinking, practice, and discussion are not off the record or discouraged as is often the case in public higher education. And this makes a big difference.

SPIRITUALITY IN SCHOOLS OF ARCHITECTURE

The scarce publication record covering spirituality in architectural education suggests that it is not something usually addressed in schools of architecture. However, the situation is more nuanced. For there are a few courses here and there that include curricula associated with the spiritual.[53] This is at least what my thirty-five years in the architectural academy, visits to dozens of programs, schools' webpages, countless conference attendances, thirteen years of ACSF (Architecture, Culture, and Spirituality Forum) leadership, and continuous discussions with colleagues on the topic strongly indicate. This experience also shows that when spirituality surfaces in a course, it is due to faculty interest or particular circumstances (e.g., hot topics of the day) and not to cover curriculum requirements. In other words, spirituality is not content officially sanctioned or systemically included in architectural education. Except for a couple of exceptions, this is true across North American schools of architecture as far as I have been able to find out.[54]

The case could be made that a more significant number of classes than what I recognize above may be already inviting or implying spiritual considerations. After all, students working under the still influential (even if contested) modern aspiration to think everything anew and seek progress or, alternatively, postmodern relativism and cultural criticism are confronted with challenges that call for the interrogation of existing traditions, habits, and ways of thinking. Although this argument is compelling, I would say that, in the vast majority of such cases, the actual coursework never reaches a sustained consideration of spirituality. Still, the good news is that architectural education does offer conditions ripe for spiritual engagement. This is partially why scholar James Thompson asserts that architectural training is ahead of other disciplines (e.g., engineering, empirical sciences, etc.) in addressing the 'ontological' dimension of education even though, he also acknowledges, the opportunity goes mostly unexploited: *the ontological turn is therefore meant less of a critique of architectural education and more as an opportunity to better understand topics of identity, development, and socialization that remain tacit in everyday practice. I would argue that the implications of directing our attention towards architectural education as an ontologically transformative process remain underexplored.*[55]

While ontological issues may or may not lead to spirituality, spirituality always involves ontological questions (i.e., reflections about being). Perhaps, the reasons for the "under exploration" that Thompson mentions have to do with the concerns about spirituality reviewed earlier (or the ones to be introduced momentarily). But it could also (and most likely) be that faculty prefer to direct their students away from spirituality into more traditional disciplinary, social, or cultural concerns. Still, it is good to realize that without much effort, architecture schools could invite spiritual meditations into its curriculum and pedagogy. Obvious examples of courses potentially addressing spirituality are a design studio on sacred space, an environment-behavior class on wellbeing, a service-learning class supporting social justice, a history offering on religious architecture, and

seminars on the sociology of urban development, aesthetic phenomenology, or the ethics of sustainability. I say "potentially" because, again, it is possible to teach any of these courses without ever approaching spirituality directly, only considering its observable manifestations to deliver technically or scholarly competent responses.[56] However, even when such courses raise spiritual awareness of/in architecture, they may end up having a limited educational impact because of their inconsistent or infrequent presence in the curriculum. Without reinforcement, what was learned fades away under the weight of ever new information. Such minor exposure to spirituality would not change the fact that schools of architecture graduate people ill-prepared to recognize, discuss, respond, and-or advance anything spiritual in their and other people's lives or the world at large.

So what?

Many practitioners and academics will probably ask this very question and argue that spiritual concerns are not germane to training people in a technical, professional field such as architecture. After all, spirituality is not part of the criteria for accrediting architectural programs. Another line of resistance or criticism about integrating spirituality into architectural education will point at the huge and urgent challenges facing our societies: global warming and climate change, vast economic inequality, racism, pandemics, xenophobia, terrorism, massive waves of refugees, political and financial corruption, environmental destruction and death of countless creatures, and the list goes on. In this context, the critics will likely add, spiritual pursuits appear as selfish or elitist distractions from what matters. They will tell us that the way forward is to intensify or expand what the architecture discipline is already doing: working on sustainability, social justice, health and wellbeing, alternative business practices, participatory community development, evidence-based design, etc. Architectural education ought to deal with such concrete visions and solutions and not aloof spirituality. These heartfelt and insightful observations are missing something essential, however: the reason for doing anything at all. Focused on solving problems through design and construction, we architects often lose sight of what makes us take such progressive actions in the first place. When we do, we acknowledge our ethical or empathic drive to "do the right thing." If probed further, many may admit a deeper motivation, such as faith. The point here is that our best architectural intentions and efforts come from a source deep within (call it conscience, "soul") or without (call it love for humanity, nature, God). Thus, whether we realize it or not, there is a spiritual drive behind such actions. Now, if some form of spirituality is already at work in what we do, why is there a need to call it out? The answer is obvious: without awareness, it is easier to fall into technocratic, ideological, aesthetic, scientific, financial, politically-correct, or other delusions. Who can deny that approaches such as "zero-carbon architecture," "social responsibility," "action research," and so many other well-intentioned initiatives often do as much harm as good? It is because we tend to get mentally and emotionally absorbed by a task we love (the design and making of buildings) that we need to bring spirituality to inform and monitor our work consciously.

Calling for spirituality to play a fundamental role in architecture is congruent with what it means to "profess." An architect is not someone who just possesses the technical and artistic competency to solve design and building problems. While such knowledge is necessary, it is limiting, if not dangerous, when the spiritual dimension of professing is missing. For professing architecture also demands us to hold a deep-seated commitment to people, life, and the world. Spirituality is (or ought to be) where the why and what of architectural professing come from, and the guiding light for the how. Professing is where meaning and knowledge, caring and discipline, transcendence and immanence come

together in the here and now of practice. Only a spirituality-guided professing gives architects the capacity to approach today's urgent needs without missing the sacred dimension of humanity, life, and nature. But this spiritual sensibility and skill, like all others, don't come overnight but must be sparked, practiced, and developed. This is why spirituality should be part of architectural education.

Teaching architecture is, therefore, educating students in the spirit, art, and technique of professing —a pursuit far from easy. If excellence and rigor are expected under ordinary circumstances, having spirituality as part of learning to be an architect requires all the more clarity, discipline, quality, care, and scrutiny. In addition, many "moving parts" must be in place, coordinated, and working for this educational vision to succeed, namely curriculum, pedagogy, faculty, and students. Following, I will briefly share meditations on each one of these components. These considerations are not intended to be comprehensive nor 100% correct. As said at the start of this chapter, I aim to start the conversation.

COURSE CURRICULUM, CONTENT

Professional programs are packed with required courses and little space for anything else. The good news is that incorporating spirituality does not necessarily mean to create new classes. In its most straightforward application, spiritual issues only need inclusion in the content of some (certainly not all) of the courses already offered. Common sense would suggest dedicating one studio, given its central role in architectural schooling, and maybe 1 or 2 other classes to engage the topic. If appropriately placed in the curriculum, they would provide enough continuity and reinforcement. Let me add that covering spirituality may not need to extend to the whole class or studio. One or two learning units or assignments out of the several a course includes may be sufficient.

How do you bring up spirituality in a

course? I would recommend, based on arguments I made elsewhere,[58] to focus on one of the three fundamental ways in which architecture and spirituality meet and inform each other:

- the architectural object : the programmatic, typological, and physical ways that buildings manifest and invite spirituality;
- the semiotic or communicative dimension of architecture : social, cultural, and symbolic purposes vis-à-vis spirituality; and
- the design/making process and the experience of architecture: spiritual dimensions of the production and-or reception of the built environment.[59]

These three manners in which architecture and spirituality intersect bring us back to third-person (i.e., external, "objective"), second-person (i.e., dialogical, or "intersubjective"), and first-person (i.e., internal, or "subjective") ways ways we relate with the world.[60] As discussed earlier, architectural training, like most higher education, has traditionally emphasized third-person knowledge, skills, and methods. This is particularly true and reasonable in the design studio and technical classes (e.g., construction, CAD, structures, etc.). Still, if a course uses the architectural object as an entry point to spirituality, the teacher should make sure that the semiotic and phenomenological dimensions of architecture are also taken into account. Second-person perspectives have been most often deployed in history-theory-criticism courses, but more can and should be done. Perhaps the most forgotten or avoided dimension in architectural education has been first-person experiences. Many accuse design education as being overly "subjective," while in truth, it is mostly built upon third-person and the commonly unrecognized but hugely influential second-person (i.e., cultural and professional) perspectives. Pedagogic improvements in this area do not mean to emphasize the capricious or egocentric drives of the students but rather to ask learners to engage the educational process with their full being. Learn-

ing metacognitive abilities would be of particular importance here, but so would be developing the emotional, embodied, interpersonal, and intuitive aspects of the self. We will return to this discussion in a later section and again in the next chapter.

Although the selection of spiritual or religious content does jump-start the study of any spirituality minded curriculum, there are other less obvious and perhaps better ways to do it. An example is an investigation of tectonics that raises spiritual considerations within a

Figure 2-3. The CUA community has the Basilica of the National Shrine of the Immaculate Conception next to campus. Religious practice is thus always available to students and faculty. In this photo, Daniel Libeskind visits the church during his residence as Walton Critic. Photograph by Julio Bermudez.

construction course or design studio (as Susan Jones and Antoine Predock did in their Walton Studios).[61] The point is that the curriculum should include opportunities for architectural students to engage in spiritual questioning. Readings, the arts (film, theater, painting, etc.), precedents, lectures, oral and written argumentation, brainstorming, field trips, research, and of course, design are ways to approach such content. Interdisciplinarity also plays a vital role in an architectural education informed by spirituality. In a very literal way, addressing spirituality through architecture is opening the discipline to non-architectural issues. The holistic perspective and connectedness established by a spiritual worldview naturally generate meditations on culture, the arts, science, the humanities, and beyond. This is something that both Juhani Pallasmaa and Daniel Libeskind remind us in their contributions to this book (as they did when teaching on campus). The best architects are those that don't separate architecture and everything else but those that see buildings as part of the whole milieu. Incorporating spirituality into architectural education prepares students for doing precisely that.

When should the spiritual dimension of professing architecture enter the architectural curriculum? The answer seems obvious: from the beginning. Spirituality should not wait until students have acquired the right technical skills or reach enough "maturity" to consider such matters. We have seen that students are ready and want to look into spirituality as they enter college. It's us teachers and the "system" that are not responding. This is not what the Walton Program does (it happens at the graduate or senior undergraduate level) and, therefore, something that my school (like most) should address.

Finally, college is a time when young adults are being pulled in many directions, including the hard expectations of architectural schooling and society in general. Asking them to try other ways of seeing the world, people, themselves, and life may be too much and not the right thing to do for many students. The teacher should always be aware of and accept this possibility. By the same token and when appropriate, teachers should be ready to raise questions *"concerning the meaning of life or 'what life is for.'"*[62]

PEDAGOGY

Although the obvious way for spirituality to enter architectural education is through a course's content, what makes it happen is enacting it. In order to work, this engagement cannot be detached but must be involved, participatory, personal. In other words, the curriculum is an invitation that works if it compels the student to study, search, and question. As Daniel Libeskind said in his interview later in the book, spirituality is found in the quest. For this reason, how we go about the process (i.e., what method is utilized) is critical. This highlights the central role of pedagogy in a spirituality informed architectural education. How we teach determines the breadth, depth, directionality, involvement, relationships, and much more of what is learned. Let us examine this for a moment. There is the course "it-content" that is affected by the way it is delivered (i.e., taught). This implies that there is also an "it-delivery" that provides a significant, if not the most crucial part of the teaching. By this, I mean the possibility of learning not only procedural knowledge and problem-solving skills (i.e., research, design methods) but also (and often ignored or unnoticed but crucial for a pedagogy seeking spiritual outcomes) that the learning process itself becomes an object of study. In other words, learning can become a gate to self-discovery if the student turns it into a contemplative journey —a skill that the learner might need to get instruction for. Here is when the true emancipatory nature of education begins fulfillment, something that great educators and activists such as John Dewey and Paulo Freire spoke so much about.[63] This is an operationalization of the ancient injunction "know thyself" that goes much further than "metacognition" because it thoroughly involves spirituality. From this perspective, even if an architectural topic does not lend itself easily to spiritual questions, it may be fruitful if the right pedagogy is applied.

A spirituality informed teaching deploys a 1-2-3-person perspectives wheel to guarantee balanced learning, never to dwell too long in one point of view and yet to make sure to attend to fundamental issues in every pass. Teaching thus empowers the deep/big self (soul, conscience, the "true self" as the great spiritual teacher Thomas Merton refers to it) but not the superficial/small self (ego). Particular attention should go to the inner world of the student, a fundamental focus in a spirituality minded education as we have seen.

This is something well articulated by Juhani Pallasmaa in his essay. Such first-person work should be complemented with a second-person perspective to assist learners in recognizing their biases as closing their minds.

The alternative worldviews beyond binary oppositions and their consequences should be explored. Empathic attempts at interpreting class content should be regularly exercised. The "objective" or external world should always remain in clear sight, and third-person responses demanded. All of this while tolerating ambiguity, uncertainty, insecurity, paradox, contradiction, and multiplicity.[64] The goal is to keep an equanimous attitude through it all, even if this is not always possible. Finally, the teaching should create opportunities for learners to find, explore, or assess their vocation. This is why the teacher needs to allow each student to find their own way to the task at hand.

Another related approach to the learning process in a spirituality-seeking architectural education could use what physicist and educator Arthur Zajonc calls "epistemology of love." This is a knowledge-seeking inquiry that is respectful, caring, dialogical, and embedded. It implies enacting the scientific method using a second- instead of a third-person frame of reference. An epistemology of love makes more sense in an ar-

chitectural inquiry than in empirical science. The labels of the stages necessary to deepen its application are clear enough to give a glimpse of what they would entail: (1) respect, (2) gentleness, (3) intimacy, (4) vulnerability, (5) participation, (6) transformation, and (7) imaginative insight.[65] The epistemology of love finds some coincidences with Chandavarkar's interpretation of teaching as an "act of love." It also echoes some of the arguments made by Alberto Perez-Gomez in his inspiring book *Built Upon Love*.[66]

Social interaction (i.e., collaboration, sharing, debate, community) is also an essential component in a spirituality-raising pedagogy. By asking students to partake and discuss their thinking, feeling, and doing, social interaction naturally lends itself to the 1-2-3-person perspective cycling. Not only do social relationships affirm the second-person nature of all learning and of architecture (a profession depending on teamwork) but also train students to do both. The communal dimension of studying architecture is enormously influential in architectural education. If well directed, its intense and all-involving nature may play a definitive role in fostering spiritual growth. It is impossible to go through architecture school without existential and socio-cultural interrogation. Long hours, pressure, burnout, success or lack thereof, and demands of critical thinking make every student question commitments, vocation, and themselves. The transition from academia to practice doesn't make things any easier, bringing up more questions, challenges, uncertainty, etc. In all these trying times, it is the community and relationships (with peers, trustworthy teachers, friends, family) that enable students to succeed. Stated differently, big questions, meditations, and social bonding are built-in spiritual opportunities in the professional training of architecture.

Creativity opens yet another powerful pedagogical opportunity to relate spirituality and architectural education. The design process is entirely dependent on creativity and, along with it, exhibits intuitive and contemplative traits that invite spiritual sensibility and states. During its best creative moments, design "thinking" enables brief contacts with what seems to be a realm well beyond ordinary reality. This is made possible through intuition. Pope John Paul II puts it beautifully:

> *Every genuine artistic intuition goes beyond what the senses perceive and, reaching beneath reality's surface, strives to interpret its hidden mystery. The intuition itself springs from the depths of the human soul, where the desire to give meaning to one's own life is joined by the fleeting vision of beauty and of the mysterious*
> *unity of things. All artists experience the unbridgeable gap which lies between the work of their hands, however successful it may be, and the dazzling perfection of the beauty glimpsed in the ardour of the creative moment: what they manage to express in their painting, their sculpting, their creating is no more than a glimmer of the splendour which flared for a moment before the eyes of their spirit.*
>
> *Believers find nothing strange in this: they know that they have had a momentary glimpse of the abyss of light which has its original wellspring in God.*[67]

Creativity offers one other connection between spirituality and architecture: the act of building itself. A new building does create a reality that will affect many people and things for years, if not decades, to come. For some, this architectural addition (or gift) to the world could be interpreted as an echo of the natural or metaphysical act of "creation." The creative act of constructing human reality invites not only intriguing philosophical reflections but also, if taken seriously, a real and compassionate commitment toward its natural, cultural, and spiritual contexts. Embracing such tasks and its implications are well beyond our comprehension, no matter how great our tools and knowledge

may be. This demands our utmost care, humbleness, and reverence.

Saying that spirituality enters architecture during its creative processes (design and building) has profound implications. Unfortunately, not everybody sees it this way. Creativity for many architects and teachers has been demystified, instrumentalized, and monetized. They consider the creative experience as "just" a bunch of psychological, organic, social, or physical processes. Yet, somehow, there remains a bit of candor and wonder about it, let us recognize it. This is because it is hard for anyone who has experienced the creative process in depth to deny that something extraordinary takes place —something that, in some cases, extends to erecting buildings, which is what Pope John Paul II is referring to. For this reason, there is hope that a rekindling of the mystery of architectural imagination remains possible. Such a spark would inevitably come along a spiritual awakening, not unlike what Morris Berman so beautifully describes in his book *"The Reenchantment of the World."*[68]

Diverse courses will find different types of pedagogies better suited to their subject matter, particular goals, place in the school curriculum, teacher's expertise, and students. Teaching methods such as curriculum-focused, instructor-led, student-centered, independent study, Socratic, group dynamics, research-driven, and exploratory are available and appropriate depending on the said circumstances. The design studio deserves a special note because of its unique characteristics and role in architectural education. Since the learning process in the design studio is intrinsically tied to the design process, how you engage it defines how students will open to spirituality. This means that the teaching method/process (the pedagogy) and the selected design method/process go hand in hand. The choice of what design methodology the studio pursues is, therefore, not trivial. Different architectural ways to access and explore spirituality will be facilitated or hindered by whether a studio undertakes this or that design methodology (e.g., conceptual vs. contextual vs. functional vs. phenomenological). Still, the teacher should be able to operate within any given design process and nest other types of pedagogy within that order as needed.

THE PEOPLE: TEACHER AND STUDENTS

If the role of the teacher is always significant, its relevancy increases when spirituality enters the classroom or studio. Their job is to encourage spiritual questioning through architecture. We are talking of presenting "big questions" or asking students to consider meaning, purpose, empathy, worldviews, and themselves vis-à-vis what is being studied. This, in no way, means that the architecture faculty becomes a spiritual guide or guru. The teacher is not trained to do such a thing. Yet, it is also apparent that he/she must have a spiritual path, practice, and-or understanding in order to lead a spirituality-integrated architectural curriculum.[69] Perhaps the biggest challenge of a spirituality-sensitive architectural education is to find faculty versed in architecture, teaching, and spirituality. This is likely to be one reason explaining the few courses or discussions on spirituality in the architectural academy. A whole chapter could be written about teaching in a spirituality-minded curriculum. Risking to miss important issues, I will begin by acknowledging that spirituality cannot be directly taught. It is more like instructing someone how to see the dimmest stars in the sky by using peripheral vision. Only by surrendering our direct gaze can the stars appear. But once we succeed a couple of times, we will always know how to do it. The stars have always been and will remain there, waiting. This analogy is helpful, but applying it to practice is more laborious. After the necessary instructions have been given, the students must go into the course content (the sky) and get to sense the spiritual dimension of what is being read, written, discussed, designed, or built (the dimmed stars). This is where the quest, the process, the actual

learning begins. Although there are different teaching methods as explained earlier, a Socratic pedagogy should be applied as much as possible (even if nested within other pedagogies), especially at the start of the journey when the difficult and involved questions come up and students are both most open (because they don't know much yet) and closed (because of possible preconceptions). The teacher must wait for the right time to ask the right question or provide the right advice, using the right leverage. Following is a list of skills, attitudes, practices, conditions, and knowledge that, although familiar to excellent teaching in higher education, acquire particular significance in our case because of the delicate nature of spirituality. The teacher of a spirituality-raising architecture class or studio should:

• Be open-minded, interested, respectful, and tolerant of diverse views and approaches to the spiritual and architectural inquiry. The instructor encourages a "beginner's mind" attitude in the students no matter how advanced in their architectural career they might be. Everybody is a beginner when it comes to spirituality. I will cover "beginner's mind" in the next chapter.

• Have the personal courage to do it. Bravery is needed because, as we have seen, taking on spirituality is (1) largely avoided, suppressed, and-or not well regarded in academia; (2) difficult to teach; and (3) intimate to the teacher and the students.[70]

• Open up, maintain, and never close the quest. The instructor's main job is to ask questions, to be a catalyst for learning. The teacher must learn to let students learn, as Pallasmaa points out in his essay. This means to allow students to (1) do their work without intervening unless necessary, and (2) make mistakes — there is success in failures because they steer the learning process and teach students how to deal with adversity, among other things. The instructor confirms (doesn't tell), points (doesn't give), and encourages and demonstrates (doesn't do).

• Never make themselves the center of attention. Rather, the teacher is silent, listens more than talks, and eventually disappears altogether because their presence is no longer necessary. Making themself obsolete is proof of an outstanding teacher.

• Display both passion and compassion. The faculty shows and demands high commitment, effort, and risk-taking, and delivers robust criticism when deserving ("father's" love). At the same time, the teacher must balance such intensity, expectation, and attitude with caring, acceptance, and encouragement ("mother's" love). Chandavarkar explains these practices very well in his essay, to which I defer.

• Recognize various types of students (i.e., personality, learning styles), tune in to each one individually, and aim at drawing their true self out. The teacher encourages a "know thyself" attitude in the students.

• Teach by example, demonstrating in themselves the qualities that students ought to display. The instructor makes themself vulnerable, shows emotions, and hides neither doubts and questions nor excitement and care for what is happening in the classroom. Only by exposing their own strengths and weaknesses does the teacher gain the students' trust. Authenticity and honesty are a must.

Juhani Pallasmaa and Prem Chandavarkar present an excellent list of pedagogical issues, practices, and arguments in their essays that I consider part of this list.

As hard as it is to teach an architectural course that raises spiritual issues, it is not easy to be a student either. Learners are asked to open their minds and hearts to concerns and questions of significant personal, socio-cultural, and religious sensibility. Therefore a good deal of courage is necessary on their part. This implies trust in the teacher and faith in the value and reality of the educational journey ahead. The students must believe that the faculty will use their dominant role compassionately and wisely, showing much patience, understanding, respect, and assistance because exploring spiritual issues could prove confusing, challenging, disturbing, etc. In other words, the emotional dimension of teaching is as important as, if not more important than, its cognitive counterpart. For this reason, offering a secure learning environment is required for the students to become open enough to explore spirituality. An adverse incident could be very upsetting and produce permanent scars, making it difficult to try new things. Hence, great care, knowledge, and restrain on the part of the teacher are necessary. For all these reasons, the spiritual quest cannot be required or enforced. It has to be voluntarily undertaken by the students, which in turn requires teachers to inform students beforehand properly.

These meditations underscore the interdependence and close relationship between teacher and student. It also clarifies the defining natures of teaching and learning, namely, that teaching is performative and learning transformative. On the one hand, the teacher has to spark and maintain the learning flame burning. Although the student does the actual work (which, of course, is also performative), it is the teacher's burden to keep the learning going. This is why, generally speaking, when a class has poor results, it is the instructor who usually deserves the blame. On the other hand, learning is happening if and only if students are cognitively, emotionally, behaviorally, and-or socially transformed. No transformation means no education. This points out the challenges facing the student as they are the ones that must undergo the mutation. Naturally, the teacher also undergoes change (i.e., learns) through this process, which, given the spiritual dimension of the educational effort, may have profound implications — something I cannot delve into at this time. The dance between the performative and transformative dimensions of education becomes all more entangled, interesting, and also risky when we include spirituality in the mix. We are entering a new pedagogic territory of great opportunity and challenges that, given its complexity, we would be wise to study and discuss. Something seems clear, though: the traditional (i.e., standard) teacher-student relationship must be rethought when spirituality enters a course. Here the old apprenticeship model that hinges in a close relationship between teacher and student appears as a good option to take into account.

LAST MEDITATIONS

I was initially overwhelmed with the prospect of addressing the role of spirituality in architectural education. The task seemed impossible to tackle. While my anxiety was real, I also knew deep down that the job could not be that hard. For who doesn't understand that learning architecture is figuring out that buildings are more than physical shelters, performance instruments, symbolic monuments, zero-carbon machines, affirmative action tools, pretty forms, real estate investments, or conceptual provocations? Who doesn't agree that true architectural professing transcends egocentric, ethnocentric, technocentric, money-centric, building-centric, or any other narrowminded interest? Shouldn't architecture assist us in migrating from our current cultural focus on *consumption* and *busyness* to one on *being*? If there is an urgent task today, it should perhaps be to awaken our being to all its interdependent richness: personal, social, ecological, and transcendent.

In architectural terms, this translates into creating soulful buildings and places that support our spiritual growth and wellbeing. It is a vision that, as we look into the future and consider how much we will have to build, acquires relevance and urgency.[71] Regrettably, there is little discussion and understanding about what this means and how we can go about doing it. This must change. Given the conditions of architectural practice, schools of architecture appear better able to take on the study of a mutually

reinforcing relationship between architecture and spirituality. The architectural academy would thus recruit another reason to take on spirituality beyond (1) improving the limited and limiting teaching model presently utilized and (2) preparing future citizen-architects for dealing with an ever-more challenging world. Why not use a spirituality-informed professional training as the platform to investigate and develop ideas, methods, and knowledge that advance such architectural vision? Attending to these three goals in no way would diminish the quality of architectural education, only enhance and make it more meaningful, thus taking care of the responsibility that schools of architecture have with the profession, the public, earth, and, for those with faith, God.

I will close with a reflection inspired by this 100-150 years-old adage:

Education is what remains after one has forgotten what one has learned in school.[72]

There is something mystical in this statement that resonates with a spirituality-minded architectural education. It is telling us that the instrumental reasons for going to college are not the point. But, if education is not what can be remembered (i.e., information, knowledge), then what is it about? A pointer is found in a distinction earlier made between knowing as "sapere" and knowing as "cognoscere." Whatever has been learned indirectly is the first to go for the simple reason that it remains attached through weak links. "Sapere-knowing," on the other hand, involving us directly, establishes deep roots and an extensive network of connections that makes the gained knowledge inalienably ours. "Sapere" is so much part of our being, so "us," that it cannot be forgotten. Yet, "sapere" becomes hard, if not impossible, to describe consciously or verbally. And it is this tacit nature of "personal knowledge," as polymath Michael Polanyi calls it,[73] that reveals what remains when all that was taught is forgotten. If we meditate on this, we soon realize that "sapere" makes any distinction between knowledge and being untenable. We are transformed by what we come to know, and the knowledge gets shaped by who we are. In other words, there is an intimate dance between being and knowledge taking place (in which others, the context, and more have an influence). Learning is the result of such dance, and, when performed enough times in the right way, it turns into development. To put it differently, education is an epistemologically and ontologically transformative process.[74]

Today's cognicentric, utilitarian, and fragmented education leads us away from what the adage points at. While we may need some of that teaching, we cannot accept that it is all that education has to offer. Hence our call for a spirituality-minded education, one that expands and transcends the existing learning paradigm. We want an education that skillfully and compassionately arranges the conditions for knowledge and being to meet and transform one another.

We aspire for an education that seeks to occasion transformations that are so structural, profound, intimate, and thorough that learners cannot tell what they have learned because it has become one with them. In other words, we envision an education in pursuit of the "ineffable" that frees learners and encourages them to become ever more themselves by gaining "sapere-knowledge" that cannot be forgotten. We want an education that is emancipatory for all and with spirituality at its heart.

THE WALTON STUDIO

THE WALTON STUDIO
JULIO BERMUDEZ

The academy is not paradise. But learning is a place where paradise can be created. The classroom, with all its limitations, remains a location of possibility. In that field of possibility we have the opportunity to labor for freedom, to demand of ourselves and our comrades, an openness of mind and heart that allows us to face reality even as we collectively image ways to move beyond boundaries, to transgress. This is education as the practice of freedom.
bell hooks[1]

Education is the kindling of a flame, not the filling of a vessel.
Various[2]

GENERAL ORGANIZATION AND PRINCIPLES

Do I dare to say that the Walton Studio floats in the educational space between these two inspiring quotes?

By providing a compelling vision, a safety net, and audacious but straightforward instructions, the Walton Studio sends students off to the little-explored territory where architecture and spirituality meet. Transgressing the ordinary boundaries of architectural education is difficult, but the rewards are worth it: freedom in thinking, feeling, and making reality anew. The flame burns bright!

Immersing students in such an architectural-spiritual journey is not an esoteric academic endeavor. On the contrary, as we learned in the previous chapters, it covers curricular and pedagogic needs largely ignored by higher education and schools of architecture alike. Because of the lack of precedents and its uniqueness, the Walton Studio began as and continues to be an in-progress experiment on how to integrate spirituality into architectural education. Eleven experimental trials have been attempted thus far. Each one was developed in response to three questions:

(1) How is architecture/spirituality going to be spiritually/architecturally explored? Will it be through architecture's artifactual, communicational, or experiential dimension?
(2) What spiritual concern(s), "big questions," building type/program, and design-teaching methodology are to be addressed/utilized?
(3) What type of architectural *transcendence* will be emphasized?

The first two questions and the issues/implications behind them were covered in the last chapter, so that I won't repeat them. The third one needs discussion. All spiritual traditions establish some sort of "transcendence" (of self, culture, world, etc.) as a prerequisite to access the *"unseen order of things"* as William James called "it." In our case, this means the removal of whatever architectural condition is used to arrive at the sought-after spiritual state, realization, or action. This architectural transcendence is not far off the mark. The best buildings and professional practices have the paradoxical quality to "transcend" themselves. For, as I have argued elsewhere, [3] architecture is barely realized when a structure guarantees the (legally required) health, safety, and welfare of its users. Instead, the promise of architecture is fulfilled when such expectations have been met and vastly surpassed. This can be accomplished by (1) **inducing transcendent experiences** (e.g., beauty, unity, joy, the numinous), (2) **serving activities that advance a transcendent cause** (e.g., human dignity, social justice, environmental preservation), or (3) **enabling architects** (through design or making) **to go well beyond cultural, social, professional, or other hardwired conventions**. In the first two cases, the building is "used up," as it were, in the very act of facilitating the experience or providing assistance. When architecture completely fulfills its mission, it leaves no traces. It "disappears." In the third possibility, it is the individual architect that enacts the transcendence by transgressing existing boundaries and expectations. These three ways to transcend architecture have spirituality writ large. The Walton Studio challenges students to design buildings that transcend.

Holding the three previous considerations in mind, a fundamental fourth question shaping the design of a Walton Studio is then asked:

> (4) Who is the guest, and how do her/his philosophy, work, and expertise play out with the general intentions of the Walton Program?

It has been my honor and privilege to select the Walton Critic on nine of eleven occasions. The choice of the outstanding individual has always been based, as said in Chapter 1, in how the architect's track record played out with the spiritual intentions of the Walton Program. Built works, writings, interviews, lectures, and (when possible) direct or indirect acquaintance with the potential candidate were taken into account. I also wanted to have a variety of voices and approaches represented over the years. The idea was to build (and eventually share) a valuable precedent of how to teach a spirituality-informed design studio. Looking back, I must honestly say that I am delighted with the people the Walton Program has been able to bring to campus. Each in their way came open-heartedly, interested in dialogue and sharing, committed to teaching, and eager to engage our students and community. The relationships that grew out of these experiences have remained alive ever since, something proven by the Walton Critics' writing contributions to this book years after they visited Washington, DC.

Developing the Walton Studio, therefore, means a collaborative enterprise between the future visitor and myself throughout the summer before their Fall residency. These interactions are usually time-consuming but very rewarding. They have expanded my ideas, knowledge-base, and critical ability as well as teaching and design methodologies. The result has been eleven very different studios. A studio with, for example, Alberto Campo Baeza will never (and cannot) be the same to one with Eliana Bórmida or Rick Joy. Yet, common ground and patterns among them are clear. They arise from my continuous coordination and co-teaching of the Walton Studio (in 10 of the 11 iterations) and (in addition to the vision and considerations laid out in the past two chapters) the following six principles:

1. Spiritual Focus

The Walton Studio proposes that today's massive problems will never be sincerely addressed (and thus solved) unless we acknowledge the ultimate meaning, wholeness, or trans-personal nature of reality and all beings. While this position does not require a divinity, it doesn't shy away from the metaphysical either. Spiritual sensibility is raised and developed by employing topics, experiences, worldviews, and-or issues related to the three "transcendences" of architecture. This usually involves "big questions" directly or indirectly related to the good, the true, and the beautiful. Discussions on faith and religious practices are allowed, sometimes encouraged. It would be absurd to address spiritual issues without permitting an open conversation on faith for those that so desire. Two rules apply to such dialogues, though: (1) there is no denial or criticism of someone else's faith or lack thereof, and (2) the focus is placed on spirituality and not dogma. Commonalities among different spiritualities are sought without being naïve in believing that fundamental agreement or synthesis is possible.

2. Cultural Questioning
Once spiritual issues are raised, whether by "big questions" or a specific subject, students are asked to analyze the responses offered by society.

Figure 3-2. The authenticity, honestty, and passion of the teacher are fundamental to lead spirituality-minded courses. Here is Alberto Campo Baeza clearly expressing how he feels/thinks about what he is telling students.Photograph by Julio Bermudez

Unexamined beliefs and attitudes towards "the good life," purpose, home, relationships, wealth, the sacred, nature, death, and more are brought forward, discussed, and their points of view (i.e., biases) noted. Thus, spiritual questioning turns into cultural criticism and existential interrogation. Awakening to social prejudice and one's "deep" self is not easy but results in an expansion of the students' worldview and knowledge of themselves. My short text "Choosing Being" in the Appendix offers one way in which the Walton Studio invites cultural and spiritual inquiries at once.

3. Contemporary Architectural Discourse
The Walton Studio enlists contemporary languages, theories, technologies, materials, and methods to approach the production (i.e., design, construction) and reception (i.e., use, experience) of architecture. The ways these instruments are chosen and utilized by the designer are examined in relation to cultural and spiritual worldviews and intentions.

4. Voluntary Architectural Simplicity (VAS)
The Walton Studio often recruits VAS as a concrete way to respond to today's zeitgeist. Its renewed aesthetics and ethics of "less is more" encourages a turn towards the minimal, the fundamentally uncomplicated, the direct, and conscious as a potent antidote to our culture of excess, schizophrenia, simulacra, and unconsciousness. VAS advances an architecture of clarity, sustainability, embodiment, and essentialism. The VAS manifesto in the Appendix articulates this philosophy.

5. Phenomenology
Sooner or later, everything comes down to experience and this is as true for architecture as for spirituality. It is in the lived moment when building and spirit converse through embodied, emotional, social, and intellectual experiences.

Since architecture presents itself "narratively" (i.e., in a story-type format unfolding in time) and poetically at its best, design methodologies ought to follow suit. The Walton Studio, therefore, resorts to phenomenology to develop and assess the artifactual and communicative dimensions of architecture. The studio emphasizes knowing by acquaintance (i.e., in first-person, "sapere") over knowing at a distance (i.e., in third-person, "cognoscere"). Empathy and hermeneutics are the bridges connecting first- and third-person perspectives of reality.

6. Integral Pedagogy

The studio topic and building program are skillful means to get students to start and continue the *architectural inquiry*. The aim is to use design to investigate, reveal, and develop spiritual realities, sensibilities, ideas, and experiences. For this reason, the way the studio is programmed to unfold is fundamental.

Consistent with earlier arguments, the Walton Studio employs a 1-2-3-person perspective cycling pedagogy. This means that the three points of views are being taken, rotated, and coordinated throughout the entire learning/design process.[4] The studio pays special attention to first- and second-person sensibilities for two motives: (1) to balance the object-oriented, third-person approaches dominating the discipline and higher education (something reviewed in chapter two); and (2) phenomenology and worldviews are where spirituality and culture find their natural homes and leverage points.

Concretely, the first-person driven pedagogy follows two thrusts. The most obvious one is using phenomenology to guide the design of buildings as described above. The other refers to instilling the ancient "know-thyself" injunction in the students by turning the design process into a mirror to see themselves (i.e., as decision-maker, rational, emotional, embodied, social being). Teaching advances in both directions and supports (a) subjectivity/self, not caprice/ego; (b)

working with the intellect, not intellectually; (c) emotional involvement, not drama; (d) listening to the body, not blind desire; and (e) trusting intuition but verifying it critically. In terms of advancing a second-person perspective, the Walton Studio asks students to respect yet interrogate culture and faith (existing worldviews), connect to the greater (interdisciplinary, social, ecological, and spiritual) world around them, and exercise compassion and charity. The Walton Studio usually requires work in teams in most assignments. This plays a vital role by facilitating the 1-2-3 cycling pedagogy, developing collaborative skills, and relationally illuminating individuals' strengths and weaknesses. The second-person pedagogy is also activated when asking students to empathically consider the effect of design actions on people (clients, users, the public, living beings). Although phenomenology and empathy may often lead the way in architectural design, the third-person perspective still plays a crucial role in the Walton Studio. This indicates that traditional architectural pedagogies are necessary and very much at work in the formal, functional, tectonic, contextual, etc. design of the "objective" dimensions of the building.

By utilizing a 1-2-3 cycling pedagogy, the Walton Studio seeks a more holistic or integral learning experience than traditional studios. This intention finds a strong parallel in Catholic Ignatian spirituality with its emphasis on balancing head, heart, and hand. Pope Francis explains it very well in a talk he delivered at the Catholic University of Chile. True education, he tells us,

> ... integrates and harmonizes intellect (the head), affections (the heart) and activity (the hands) ... [It] offer[s] students a growth that is harmonious not only at the personal level but also at the level of society. We urgently need to create spaces where fragmentation is not the guiding principle, even for thinking. To do this, it is necessary to teach how to reflect on what we are feeling and doing; to feel what we are thinking

and doing; to do what we are thinking and feeling. An interplay of capacities at the service of the person and society.[5]

As to how to foster spiritual awareness and questioning, the Walton Studio usually asks students to work through intuitive actions facilitated by physical and emotional participation within a collaborative and supportive social climate. These intuitive actions are loosely framed by ideas, directions, or questions, that is, intellectual constructs. Intuition is the force or voice of creativity, which, in turn, leads to spiritual states and realities —as we saw in Chapter 2. There is undoubtedly an art to this process. It consists of teaching students how to manage their thinking to avoid disrupting access to intuition. Practically, it means to use the intellect for (1) setting up the appropriate conditions for creativity, (2) excusing itself so other actors (body, emotions, intuition) may enter the scene undisturbed, and (3) returning to observe, evaluate, and articulate what has ensued. This use of the mind is not only skillful but also very relevant, humble, and respectful. It lets go of our controlling ego in order to invite intuition, creativity, and, ultimately, the spirit to step in. This is a well-known contemplative technique in many spiritual traditions. It is called "beginner's mind" in Zen Buddhism and refers to an intensely curious, reverent, attentive, open, relaxed, wondrous, innocent, and contemplative awareness.[6] Approaching spirituality with a beginner's mind makes total sense, even in the absence of any reference to Zen Buddhism. Who is not but a beginner when facing the mystery of spirituality? This is true whether our pursuit is done through architecture or anything else. Thus and in the conditions we are discussing, surrendering intellectual control and knowledge facilitates rather than hinders good design, learning, creativity, and spirituality. This is contrary to common sense (and existing cultural, educational, and professional paradigms). It should be noted that establishing a beginner's mind doesn't guaran-

tee results, only that the chances are improved. Three Walton Critics employed this approach, namely Antoine Predock, Claudio Silvestrin, and Susan Jones. I also used it in the warm-up assignments (i.e., the analog-digital media workshops) I led in the 2010 and 2019 Walton Studios. An essay-long discussion on the application of a beginner's mind attitude in architectural education is available elsewhere.[7]

There is only one last point to make regarding the Walton Studio pedagogy, and it refers to the "other" pedagogy at play: the one exercised by buildings. For there is powerful teaching implicit in the ethical, social, and cultural function of architecture. Here the Walton Studio asks students to study how architecture may instill spiritual sensibility, support, experiences, or values in those who inhabit, visit, or just pass by it. The pedagogic function of buildings is always taking place. Still, when the goal is to occasion the spiritual wellbeing and flourishing of humanity, the stakes are higher and must be included in the teaching of architectural professing.

STUDIO RECORD
NOTE: various documentation materials of the Walton Studios are available online.[8]

WARM-UP EXERCISES
All the Walton Studios employed warm-up assignments to launch the architectural/spiritual quest. The goals of these short exercises (1 or 2 weeks long) varied depending on the studio. They have ranged from the focused study of a topic to teaching concrete technical and methodological skills, to open-ended design improvisations. A few start-up assignments have been experimental (2013, 2014, 2019) while others traditional (2012, 2017). Here is the list:

• Light/tectonic exploration (2009, 2018)
• VAS Manifesto writing (2010)
• Analog-digital media design workshop (2010, 2019)

- Design charrette of an object, installation, or space (2010, 2011, 2014, 2015, 2016, 2019)
- Art inquiry (2011, 2019)
- Precedents Analysis (2012, 2014, 2017, 2018)
- Design Improvisation (2013)
- Phenomenological reflections (2014, 2016)

Every Walton Studio required readings about the topic under investigation. A variety of religious texts covering spiritual issues have been used over the years, including those from the Catholic/ Christian, Buddhist, Hindu, and Sufi traditions.

MAIN ASSIGNMENTS

Different building types and programs have been used as primary teaching vehicles. However, as said, the method and process by which the design was conducted (the inquiry) is what mattered the most. The choice of parameters and design method was defined in response to the four main organization questions described at the start of the chapter. Although spiritual issues or programs were often recruited, only three of the eleven studios worked on a sacred space with another two studios doing mixed secular-religious buildings. Regarding scale, buildings were generally around 20,000-30,000 sq.ft. with a couple of exceptions (a 5,000 sq.ft. home in 2017 and a 500,000 sq.ft. National Immigration Museum in 2013). Following is a list of the different architectural programs used in the eleven Walton Studios.

Sacred Space Programs
- 21st Century Catholic Monastery on the east bank of the Potomac River in Maryland in Washington, D.C. (2012)
- Non-denominational Burial Chapel in down town Washington, D.C. (2011)
- Ecumenical Chapel on CUA Campus in Washington, D.C. (2009)

Mixed Space Programs (Sacred/Secular)
- Funerary Complex in a memorial park in Seattle, WA (2018)

- A Place for Spirit and Wellbeing in a neighborhood of Washington, D.C. (2015)

Secular Space Programs
- Center for Just Being in a neighborhood of Washington, D.C. (2019)
- A Single-family home in a Maryland suburb outside Washington, D.C. (2017)
- Vocation Center in a neighborhood of Washington, D.C. (2016)
- National Immigration Museum on the National Mall, Homeless Shelter in Chinatown, and a Nursery/Kindergarten in downtown, all in Washington, D.C. (2013)
- Spiritual Retreat in Nature in the Shenandoah Mountains, VA (2014)
- Nature's Observatory on the east bank of the Potomac River in Washington, D.C. (2012)
- Treatment-Rehabilitation Center for Consumption Addiction in the Redrock desert of southern Utah (2010)

Figure 3-3. 2018 Walton Critic Susan Jones introduces an assignment to the studio as Antonio Ugarte, Federico Witzke, and Fai Almahmoud listen. Photograph by Julio Bermudez.

BIG QUESTIONS

"Big Questions" were embedded in all the projects. These inquiries demanded meditations of existential, social, cultural, and philosophical importance where spirituality played a substantial role. For example,

- What is and how do we practice spirituality? (2009, 2014, 2015, 2016)
- What is and how do we develop "b/Being"? (2010, 2019)
- What is the "good life"? (2010, 2012, 2014, 2016, 2017)
- What is our relationship with Nature? (2010, 2012, 2014)
- What is authenticity? (2011, 2014, 2016)
- How do we deal with death? (2011, 2018)
- What is contemplative life? (2012)
- What are social justice and human dignity? (2013, 2015)
- What is Home? (2013, 2017)
- What is the role of every day in life? (2014, 2017)
- What is sacred? (2015)
- Do we have a vocation? (2016)

PATTERNS AND FACTOIDS

Of the eleven visits by renowned architects, three were concentrated in short and intense (charette-type) design workshops (2009, 2010, 2019). The other eight lasted at least three weeks. Three studios intentionally avoided architectural precedents to free the design inquiry (2010, 2013, 2019). Three iterations placed great importance on theoretical investigations (2010, 2015, 2016), whereas intuition and improvisation were central to another four (2009, 2013, 2018, 2019). Five studios gave students a great latitude to develop the building program (2013, 2014, 2015, 2017, 2019), whereas two provided a list of spaces with square footage (2012, 2018). Four studios emphasized the role of a "concept" or "idea" to direct the architectural inquiry (2012, 2013, 2017, 2019). Phenomenology was the driving force in most iterations (2009, 2010, 2011, 2014, 2016, 2018) with par-ticular focus on embodiment (2009, 2011, 2014, 2018), light (2009, 2018), making/tectonics (2009, 2018), and emotion (2009, 2011, 2016, 2018). All but four studios required teamwork in the main course assignment (2010, 2011, 2012, 2013, 2014, 2015, 2016). The most experimental studios (through the whole semester, not a particular assignment) were 2010, 2013, 2015, 2016, and 2019. The majority of studios stressed simplicity/VAS (2010, 2012, 2013, 2016, 2017, 2018), but a few didn't at all (2009, 2011, 2019). Finally, several iterations used design methodologies combining strong phenomenological and conceptual processes (2010, 2012, 2017, 2018, 2019).

ABOUT THE STUDENTS AND FACULTY

Since the Walton Studio is required for graduate students enrolled in the Sacred Space and Cultural Studies graduate concentration and elective for senior undergraduates, the students are aware of and interested in the exploration of spirituality through architecture. This is imperative because learners should not be required to pursue a spiritual inquiry. In terms of religious affiliation, the majority of the students have been Catholic. Still, a good number of non-religiously affiliated and Muslim (most of them coming from the Middle East) students have always joined the studio. Of the 11 Walton Studios, only two were composed of just graduate students (2010, 2015). The other nine included both graduate and undergraduate students. When the number of students was too high for one studio section, another instructor joined the Walton Critic and me. This was the case in the 2010 and 2011 (Gregory Upwall), 2012 (Luis Boza), 2013 (Randall Ott), 2014 (Matthew Geiss), and 2016 (Ana Roman Andrino and Lavinia Fici Pasquina) offerings.

OUTCOMES AND IMPACT

The Walton Program has been productive and influential. Its 11 iterations have

- served 186 students (115 graduate and 71 undergraduate),
- involved seven different faculty,
- invited about two dozens out-of-town architects and twice as many local professionals to studio reviews,
- delivered 29 lectures (22 at CUA, four at Embassies, and three at the American Institute of Architects, Washington, D.C. chapter),
- collaborated with five extramural partners (the AIA-DC and five embassies —Argentina, Finland, India, Italy, and Spain), and
- had its works exhibited in 5 venues (2 at AIA-DC, one at the Dadian Gallery at the Wesley Theological Seminary, and two at CUA) and published in 2 journals.

In addition, the Walton Program supported the organization of two symposia. The first one was in the Fall of 2011 and coincided with the 100th-anniversary celebration of the beginning of architectural education at CUA. This meeting brought world-class speakers and a large number of attendees. It resulted in the book *"Transcending Architecture. Contemporary Views on Sacred Space"* that I edited and was published by CUA Press in 2015. The second event was in Fall 2018 and organized to commemorate the 10th-anniversary of the Walton Program. On this occasion, 6 of the 10 Walton Critics were brought back to campus to lecture, engage faculty, give crits to students, and more. The idea of this book was born during this second symposium.

Regarding the students' performance, it varied from student to student and studio to studio. Some learners made the most of the opportunity, and some stayed lukewarm. Still, it is fair to say that the overall quality of the work has been higher than comparable studios at CUA and other schools. I believe the reason for this success has to do with the unique focus and pedagogy of the Walton Studio, along with the inspiring presence of a renowned architect. The fact that the students freely chose the studio played a role as well. In the following pages, the reader will be able to review over 30 student projects (three per studio) selected out of at least 105 works.

The influence of the Walton Program may also be assessed by the type of Master's thesis that students pursued after taking the studio. The chosen topics or building programs generally related to the spiritual dimension of architecture and-or involved cultural criticism. Concerning our graduate student population, Walton Studio students have won a larger proportion of thesis design awards. However, the most crucial impact of the Walton Program remains invisible because the work output of a class cannot fully capture what has been learned by the students. This is only known much later. In this respect, the Appendix includes a section with testimonials from Walton Studio graduates reflecting on their experience.

The Walton Program has spawned a group of 75 alumni that meets every year during the time a new illustrious architect teaches at CUA. This has become a festive reunion to socialize and celebrate the Walton Studio alumni's growth as professionals and people. Most of them are now practicing (and many registered) architects at a variety of firms. Although a majority live in the Northeast or mid-Atlantic region of the U.S., alumni are distributed around the country, with many having their home abroad. A few have opened their own offices. Some regularly participate in studio reviews at CUA. In other words, the Walton Studio graduates have fared well professionally. When I talk to them about architecture and the world, they tend to have a "big picture" perspective along with an empathic response to what is happening, attitudes I would define as spiritual. As their past teacher, I am very proud of what they have already accomplishedand, and I look forward to witnessing their contributions to the world in ways that, I hope, are spiritually sound.

CONCLUSION

It is hard not to feel demoralized, disempowered, or skeptical about the world today. Who doesn't want things to be better or work towards improving them? But the path to a new and better reality cannot be one of avoidance, appeasement, subversion, or adoption of some sexy new idea. Nor can we fall back to easy reactionary models. Instead, the path forward should come, at least initially, from inside ourselves as individuals and society. And, what better place to start than in a classroom or studio devoted to drawing those ideas, visions, and more out of students? Isn't this what "education" is all about anyway?

Originating in the Latin word "educare," education means "to draw out." In order to teach/learn, something inside the student must be brought forward, probably from the deep — otherwise, it would have surfaced already! The attention to the inner world of students that a spirituality grounded architectural education depends on and enables naturally aligns with this goal. But, how do we most successfully occasion such "drawing"? Should the teacher invite or provoke such coming out? Should it be a "calling"? Is this the vocation we usually talk about? These are all questions that a spirituality-minded education must deal with. One thing is clear. An education that genuinely draws out is not a one-time, individualistic, and secluded event but a process involving others that takes time, patience, openness, care, and all we have been discussing thus far.

But as much as there is more to architecture schooling than learning to put a building together, there is a lot more to a spirituality-growing architectural education than bringing out a student's inner world. There is also, and significantly, the questioning of today's reality and the envisioning of better ones that can only be done in conjunction with others, as bell hooks tells us in the citation starting this chapter. None of this can be done unless "big questions" and a "big picture" are invited in. Compassion, patience, social bonding, authenticity, and

the rest cannot be demanded or intellectually learned but must be organically, lovingly, patiently grown. Such developments would best happen if integrated and not separated from the intense educational experience students of architecture undergo. Keeping spiritual and ordinary lives apart is not only artificial but has negative consequences. Social philosopher and architectural critic Lewis Mumford warned us about it 80 years ago:

> *the segregation of the spiritual life from the practical is a curse that falls impartially upon both sides of our existence.*[9]

Don't we want to graduate students versed in the spiritual dimension of professing architecture? For twelve years, the Walton Studio has been working towards this goal. A summary of the results is presented in the following pages. May this experience assist all of us in the never-ending task of learning (and teaching) architecture.

Figure 3-4. The camaraderie between instructor and students is a genuine feature of the Walton Studios. This is the dinner after the final review of the 2016 Walton Studio (only half of those attending are shown). From Left to right: guest, Tatianna Woodard Freeman, Nina Chandavarkar, (Walton Critic) Prem Chandavarkar, Amanda Ocello, Ian Walker, Ana Maria Roman Andrino (teacher), Billy Wantz, Tatiana Admundsen, Madeline Wentzell, and Anh-Tu Nguyen. Photograph by Julio Bermudez.

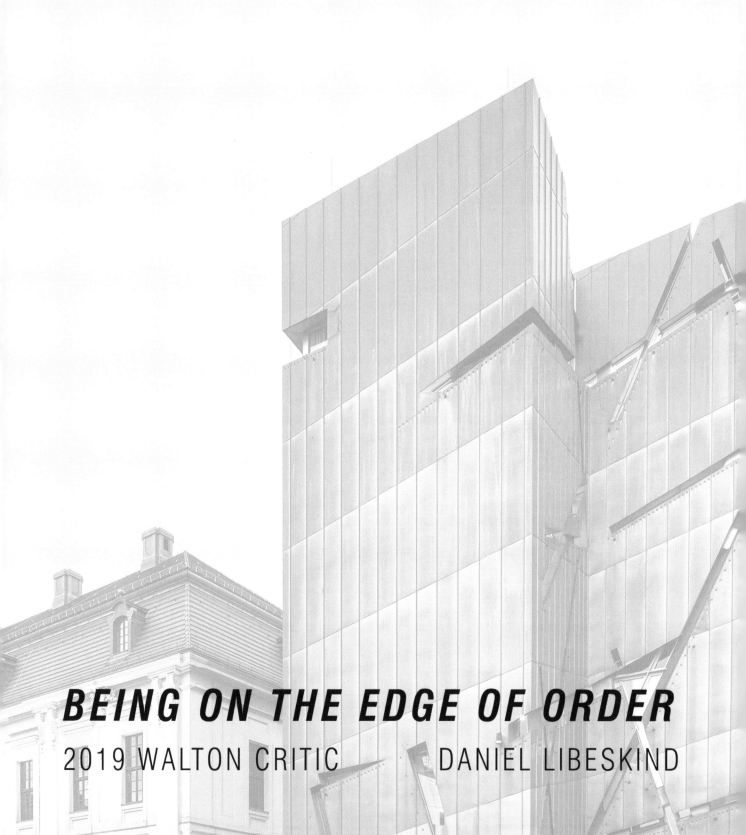

BEING ON THE EDGE OF ORDER

2019 WALTON CRITIC   DANIEL LIBESKIND

BEING AT THE EDGE OF ORDER
2019 Walton Studio
Walton Critic: Daniel Libeskind

STUDIO TOPIC

New architectural responses are necessary to address a host of new situations confronting our civilization. This was the task of the 2019 Walton Studio. We started by studying contemporary architects whose work offer deep meaning, reverential contextualism, cultural criticism, and experiential transcendentalism. Of central importance was detecting the process and methods by which they are able to produce their remarkable work. As 2019 Walton Critic Daniel Libeskind puts it, we were after the *"Art of Architecture."* This meant to conduct a design studio devoted to experimentation, willing to question, and able to take risks. It translated into three pursuits. One consisted in using design maneuvers based in intuitive action as sole provocateurs of architectural ideas, issues, and arguments. Students were given certain rules and tools and asked to surrender to a doing-driven process wherein meaning/understanding came only after the act. In other words, the *Art of Architecture* was sought and found by means of *playing* — a creative condition that arises at the edge between order and chaos. The productivity of this pedagogy was hinged in the concept of *"reading,"* that is, in the association of value, ideas, or meaning to the perceivable qualities of the produced artifacts.

The second effort was directed by Libeskind. He invited students to first meditate on the dialogue between three artworks (a music piece, two engravings, and a poem) and then apply the gained insights to designing a minimal inhabitable space: a monk's or a prisoner's cell. His intense design charrette taught students the power of the arts to illuminate the interdisciplinary, cultural, and spiritual nature of architecture.

These experiments laid the groundwork to launch the third and last pursuit: the programing and design of the *FOJUBE (FOr JUst BEing) Place*, an institution without precedent in the post-enlightenment West: a secular space where to experience *"being"* rather than *"doing"* or *"having."* By silencing the constant socio-cultural pressures to be busy, *FOJUBE* was to encourage visitors to notice their own functioning self. This 20,000 sq.ft. urban retreat was to be located in Southwest Washington DC, and foster not-doing, not-having, and letting be. As a haven from the real world, it had to promote organic emotional, mental, and spiritual healing through activities directed to the subjective (individual self), intersubjective (collective self), objective (environmental/no-self), and transcendent (spirituality) dimensions of being. This was to translate into practices aimed at observing, studying, exercising, and expressing being in itself (e.g., mind, heart, body, spirit) and in relation to others, nature, and God.

Figure 4-2. Libeskind and Saxelby examining the design proposal by Ahmed Almohanna and Madison Moore.

Figure 4-3. Daniel Libeskind responding to the scheme of Emilio Bustamante and Simon Talago.

Figure 4-4. Sekely and Nabbie presenting their work.

Figure 4-5. Libeskind addressing the whole studio (right).

Figure 4-6. *Faculty:* Daniel Libeskind, Julio Bermudez, and Georgia Saxelby
Graduate Students: Morgan Allen, Paula Balmori, Abigail Brady, Ted Chillingworth, Cesar Chirinos, Ana Garcia, Joshua Murray, and Antonio Ugartte
Undergraduate Students: Ahmed Almohanna, Andrew Beiner, Emilio Bustamante, Isabella Laccetti, Madison Moore, Jake Nabbie, Abigail Sekely,and Simon Talago. Photograph by Julio Bermudez.

THE PLATFORM

FOJUBE - A PLACE FOR JUST BEING

ABIGAIL BRADY

We live in a time when access to all forms of information is sitting in our pockets. Our news and information has been perfectly curated to fit our interests and values. What has been lost in this personalization is the connection to the human being. The platform is a culminating point of discussion. Travelers from various countries and cultural backgrounds come together in an effort to expose themselves to a variety of beliefs. The interaction between two people is integral for the ability to understand the importance of empathy. The journey begins on either end of the city block. The beginning points of entries act as the gathering space for groups of people to begin their path inside. The groups walk along winding paths to enter the towers from the center of the building. With the gradual inclusion of nature, the journey becomes distant from the surrounding city, and the focus turns internally. The visitors begin their ascension upwards to the bars, wherein there lies exhibitions and lectures dedicated to the current topic on display. This space does not aim to change the minds of those that visit, but rather allow them the opportunity to be able to learn from the main sources.

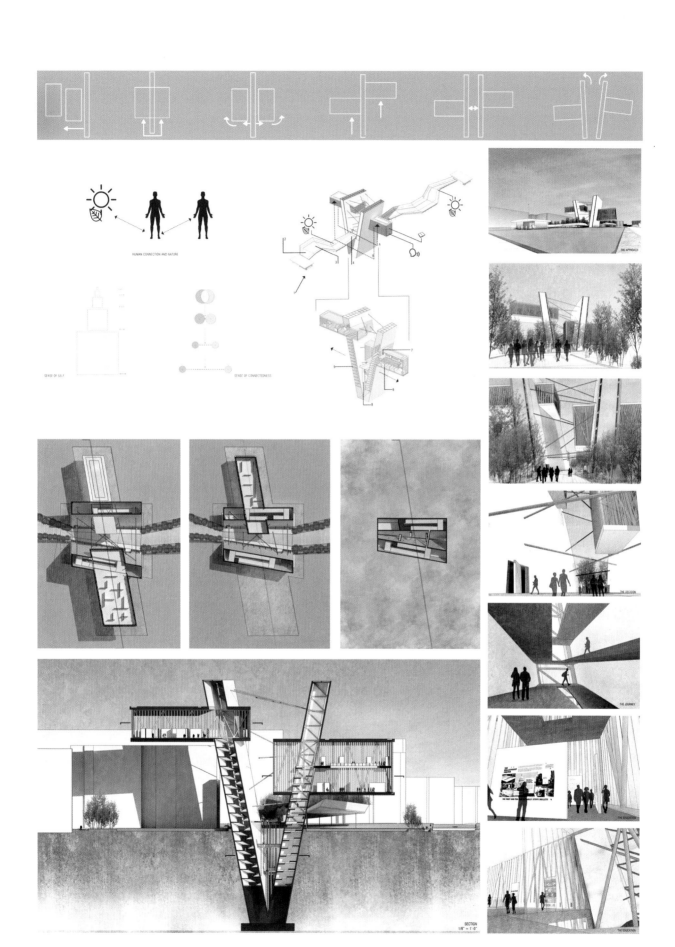

THE UNEXPECTED OF BEING

WHERE ARE YOU TODAY?

ANA GARCIA

While life is an unstoppable journey, we find ourselves constantly in different situations that make us reach a higher consciousness, unexpected events where BEING helps us decipher our real purpose in life.
These unexpected events of life strike us like lightning either in a positive or negative way:

- Life is for us
- Life happens by us
- Life happens to us
- Life happens through us
- Life happens in us
- Life is us

The purpose of this project is to bring the community together by making them realize that no matter what stage in life we are in, we are going through this journey together.

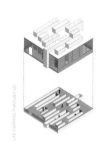

THE UNEXPECTED OF BEING
(where are you today)

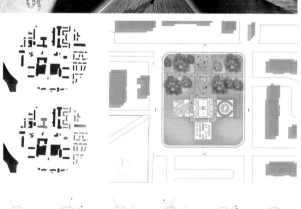

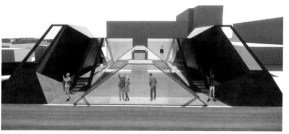

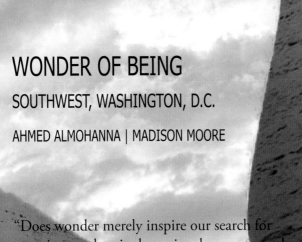

WONDER OF BEING

SOUTHWEST, WASHINGTON, D.C.

AHMED ALMOHANNA | MADISON MOORE

"Does wonder merely inspire our search for meaning, or does it also point the way towards meaning?"—Anders Schinkel, (Wonder, Mystery, and Meaning.) Being is explored through the mystery of wonder. Breaking the cycle of life into different paths, wonder and mystery are showcased through different experiential moments that help one detach from the attentiveness of life and celebrate their being. Upon approach, two large curved walls funnel visitors into a reflective space to discover seven paths to choose from; each invokes wonderment driven by mystery. There are three paths that slope into the earth: "Balance Through Light," "Mystery of Existence," and "Time and Place." The unique formation of the travertine walls and the curvilinear paths invokes a feeling of being in a quiet, contemplative, constantly moving space. "Balance through Light" exhibits a candlelit space where visitors light a candle for a lost memory. "Mystery of Existence" holds glass panels attached to the walls where visitors can leave behind handwritten notes. Finally, "Time and Place" is a narrow path aligned with a reflective pool representing the motion of time. Two paths sloping upward lead to nondenominational chapels, providing a sense of communal and spiritual being filled with light. This sculptural architecture provides a sense of place and being through wonderment for those who wish to reconcile a certain state of mind.

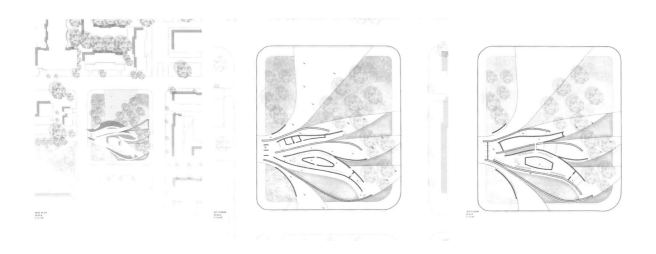

Figure 4-7. Studio Libeskind. National Holocaust Museum, Ottawa — Canada. Photograph by Doublespace.

"ARCHITECTURE IS DEEPLY SPIRITUAL":
in conversation with Daniel Libeskind

BERMUDEZ: Your architecture challenges conventions. Is this action an effort to give users and visitors access to something 'transcendent'? Transcendent in the sense of pushing them beyond social, cultural, disciplinary, and even spiritual values, expectations, beliefs, practices? Am I reading your intentions correctly?

LIBESKIND: I think the quest of architecture is really a quest for something more and rather different than the material presence of architecture. Architecture is obviously built out of physical materials. It is part of the concrete world. But to me the actual architecture is not at all the walls, the materials and the quantifiable or measurable in the building. It is really more about a spiritual atmosphere or spirit of the space. Architecture involves something rather different than the obvious interrogation of the so-called objective reality. Here lies the essence of design, of architecture itself. It is in the material world but responds to us who are not really material beings at all. We live on our dreams. We live on our ideas of our future, of our past. We worry about mortality. We know we are going to die. We wonder about the meaning of the place in which we exist and why we are here at all. So you are right, there is a quest in my work to go beyond what is given in the apparent reality of architecture, something beyond the walls.

BERMUDEZ: Do you see a need for the sacred in our secular, relativistic, cynical, multicultural, multi-ethnic multi-religious age? In fact, is there anything sacred left?

LIBESKIND: Oh, yes. I think some people would pretend that nothing is sacred. We hear people saying that we live in a so-called secular era, but this is a little bit too simple. I can here quote one of my favorite rabbinical authorities from the 18th century, Menachem Mendel of Kotzk who said, *"There is nothing more whole than a broken heart. There is nothing more straight than a leaning ladder and there is nothing more crooked than a straight line."* This is an insightful statement because it summarizes the banality of understanding the world as some sort of transactional condition, politics, or ethics. It's not about transaction at all. It is about the spirit of the human soul and that hasn't aged, no matter how much people would like to get rid of it. In this era of information technology, we might actually be realizing that the sacred is more important than we thought before, during the industrial age. The spiritual is actually more apparent now than it has ever been as we get rid of language, we get rid of almost everything.

BERMUDEZ: Are you talking about the digital revolution and its virtualization of most of our human activities by migrating them into the cloud of cyberspace?

LIBESKIND: What I am saying is that what appears to be something negative about the information age might be in reality bringing us closer to a spiritual era. It invites a realization that all these things that are being virtualized don't really matter at all, and that there is something else that grounds our understanding of things, our knowledge, our lives.

BERMUDEZ: Our mutual friend Finish architect Juhani Pallasmaa often talks about a 'sacred task of architecture,' that is, a profound duty that we architects have with our society and fellow human beings. I sometimes think of this task as an 11th commandment but another way of thinking about it is in relation to the Hippocratic oath in medicine. Perhaps we should ask our architecture graduates to take an oath before entering professional practice. Do you think that there is such a thing as a sacred task of architecture? is there a sacred dimension to what we do?

LIBESKIND: There has to be. Only people who want to understand our world as a result of zoological factors and reduce dwelling to simple habitation would see the task of architecture as being solely materialistic. But knowing the history of architecture, we understand that it is always about the sacred because it is always about others. It is not about ourselves. It's about the door, the window, the passage, the journey, and the thresholds. These are all really references to someone else who is kind of imposing on our space. Not us, somebody who is entering it. Reference to a transcendent dimension of reality (and therefore of architecture) is probably best expressed in Hamlet when Hamlet says to Horatio *"There are more things in heaven and earth, Horatio, Than are dreamt of in your philosophy."* Shakespeare's masterpiece is pointing to the fact that there is more in heaven and earth than in our very limited understanding of reality. So whatever we think of heaven and earth, it doesn't encompass them. The world of heaven and earth is not the world we know and comprehend. There's a whole lot more to them. This is a sim-

ple, almost intuitive, way of understanding our limitations in grasping reality, isn't it? Anybody from a child onto an old person realizes that there is more to heaven and earth than we grasp.

BERMUDEZ: Some philosophers put what you're saying like this: reality exceeds us by its superabundance. Reality constantly overpasses us. Our incomplete cognitive and emotional framings are the only way we manage such exuberance. But in our limited grasp we intuit that there is always this other (perhaps sacred) dimension just looming behind and, if we could just get to it, transcendence might be revealed.

LIBESKIND: Yes. I think you can understand this situation in Husserl's phenomenology of time. There is always that one interval, the microsecond that we don't have and that is coming towards us. It is not coming from us. It is coming towards us from the unknown. And it is no other than the breath that we take. This phenomenological analysis is fantastic because you don't need to believe in God or anything. It makes you understand that you are, we are continuously dependent on that interval, in something coming from beyond us!

BERMUDEZ: The liminal condition between the present moment and when the next temporal interval hits us reminds me of your latest book *"Edge of Order."* [1] If I understand it correctly, you are saying that new insights and the very possibility of creativity are at that very edge of experience. I can see why you would like to put yourself in such liminal condition while designing architecture. But, would you also want to push the inhabitant or visitor to such state as they experience architecture? In other words, do you want to enact such 'edge' phenomenology during both architectural production and reception?

LIBESKIND: We are shackled by our habits. The habits really blind us. We are most insensitive to the world because we are so used to it. It often takes some sort of an accident or disconnection for people to realize where they really are. Such sudden awareness is brought on not by intention but by an unexpected situation. It is hard for architecture to accomplish this feat because architecture is to a large extent built into that habitual world. And it needs to be because it has to reaffirm or support all these activities of the past. But as I discuss in the book and explained at your school last fall, I try to create an edge to that habit where the habit suddenly falls off. Of course, this is not really a one-way street. It also has to come from the person who is experiencing the building. Not me, not the architect. The expression does not come from the architect. It comes from the architecture and from people who in some moment are able to step into something that releases them from their habits and allows them to see the space in a way that is true. This is certainly part of the task of architecture. How much is the index of habits inevitable in a building? You know, we expect the door, expect the door handle, you expect it to open. The amazing thing about the world is that the expected actually happens. It is truly miraculous. The expected is the shock which people mostly miss. Opening a door every day might seem to be nothing but the fact that it actually opens just one more time, just as you expected it is a miracle! It really is. There is something transcendental about that. And that's how I try to approach the prosaic aspects of architecture, which are overwhelming.

BERMUDEZ: When you taught here, you gave the students three artworks (a music composition, two engravings, and a poem) to launch their architectural meditations. Of course, your own work and life demonstrate your profound interest and commitment to the arts. Is an artistic consciousness or sensibility what makes us/you experience the ordinary as extraordinary, turning the opening of a door into a miracle?

LIBESKIND: The arts provide an essential check on architecture narrow-mindedness. You can be asphyxiated by architecture. The whole history of looking at buildings as buildings proves it. But buildings are not really buildings at all. They are something else. They are spaces and situations that unfold with or without our consent and they involve so much more and beyond what we usually think of 'architecture.' In fact, whether it is poetry, arts, science, or mathematics, all that is really part of architecture. That is what architecture is. Architecture is not about building walls and foundations. All that stuff that is in books has actually nothing to do with architecture. It's a kind of catalog of statistical phenomena, which have very little to do with the atmosphere that a building creates or that which we call home instead of prison. Indeed, I have often wondered what the difference between a prisoner's cell and the cell of a saint is. They look to me almost the same from the outside. They both have the walls and a little window, maybe a desk or piece of furniture and a closed door but they are completely different. In one case, take the picture of Saint Jerome for example, a saint sitting in a room, you have total freedom in every way. In a prisoner's cell with the same physical conditions you are shackled, full of despair and lonely. I once read a Spanish story in which a prisoner after years of incarceration walks to the door and pushes it…it was never locked in the first place. So what is the kingdom between these two poles of freedom and oppression? It is architecture on the edge.

BERMUDEZ: I am trying to feel (not think) what you are talking about in actual architectural examples. Concretely, I am thinking of your art museums of Toronto and Denver. In those places, I felt that my traditional habits of appreciating art were challenged. In some way, you freed me from having to follow a prescribed way of enjoying art but, on the other hand, you 'forced' such different attitude into me. Was that 'oppression'? Don't take me wrong, the experiences were positive.

LIBESKIND: Let me answer your question using those museums. To me, a museum is the exact opposite of a container for art. Most people think, let's put the art into formaldehyde. Let's protect it. Let's put it in a vault. That is how most of our white wall museums are created. My idea is very different. My idea is that the museum was born out of the wonder of art. What was originally in them was something miraculous, something that went beyond anything that you ever saw or experienced. It is strange that museums of art have become conventions that make the art in many ways die, because the art is suffocated by that space. Actually, none of the artists thought of this or that museum wall as the final destiny of their artwork. But it is not only me thinking this way. It is also the curators, the directors of the museums who don't want those kinds of spaces. They told me that they would have gone to another architect if they wanted that. They requested a different attitude towards their collections, a unique experience inviting visitors to see and question. I think that's a good word because the words question, request, and quest have a common etymology. Science is based on questions. Art is based on questions. Why should architecture be built on habits? It should also question those aspects that we take for granted in architecture.

BERMUDEZ: Speaking of which, I would like to have my last questions about architectural education. If you were a full-time academic right now, what kind of agenda, pedagogy, or curriculum would you put forward? Would/should they have a spiritual dimension? What would you recommend the academy to take on?

LIBESKIND: It is a very important question. As you know, I spent many years of my life in the academy, in the Cranbrook Academy of Art but also in other really wonderful institutions. Ever since then my thought has been that architectural education needs a major change, away from the formalistic studies of architectures as objects and toward the cultural world that produces architecture in the first place; the humanistic world that includes science, mathematics, poetry,

tragedy, comedy, and the stars. The real root of architecture is not just building, not at all. That would be a total abomination of what architecture is. Architecture was made for the gods in the first place. It wasn't made for people, as the first building we have record of at Gobekli Tepe in Turkey demonstrates. We know that they built it far away. There were no urban environments back then. There were no villages. They went far away to create something else for something totally different. This shows that our long held idea that urbanization came from people wanting or needing to live together may not be true at all. Rather, people built something amazing and then moved together into cities. So there first was the amazement and the door to the spirits, which had nothing to do with the everyday prosaic life. How strange it is that this is the beginning of our work and not what Sigfried Giedion, Kenneth Frampton, or any of those smart historians proposed — but none of them had this very recent piece of information coming from archeology. So, architecture is deeply spiritual. This is number one. Architecture is based on nothing physical, nothing related to the construction of dwelling for us as we have been told. It is based on something completely different. And it is for someone else, for others, not for us! It is in some way a messianic art because the future is coming into it from somewhere we don't know and for someone we don't know.

BERMUDEZ: I'm glad that you mentioned the ancient temple in Turkey. People came together for spiritual reasons and not out of market, defensive, or other practical needs. The polis emerged out of spiritual longing. How beautiful! And here is my last question for you: What would you tell your twenty-year-old self if he lived in this day and age?

LIBESKIND: I would say don't believe so much in what you have been taught. Don't believe so much in the practical experience that others bring to you. Go off beyond the tangent. Don't take the highway. Take the path that hasn't been walked upon. There is so much to be found that is not in the focus of society today. We are focusing on particular things and think that they are what matters, but the truth might be completely elsewhere, not at all on this track that w see on the internet, the news, politics, or social worlds. What is happening might be happening on a very, very different register of events that we don't have that much information about, but we can discover by putting ourselves at risk.

BERMUDEZ: does this have to do with vocation? Each of us is said to have an unique inner call that demands attention. Is the path you recommend to follow one informed or directed by vocation?

LIBESKIND: I think it does. What we want to do is often against the current and might really be what you call vocation. And I say that if somebody has a dream, a desire to do something, they should not be scared. They should not think it is a failure if they fail. In fact, it is the other way around. I would advise against going for success. Don't follow the big crowds, the big flags. Stay away from them.

BERMUDEZ: Is it then about the quest, the question?

LIBESKIND: That is right. It is a quest. Architecture is a quest. This is what makes it spiritual because that's the definition of the spirit. The spirit is not just waiting around, it is not waiting for you. You can't just get it. The spirit moves where it wants to move and you have to follow it.

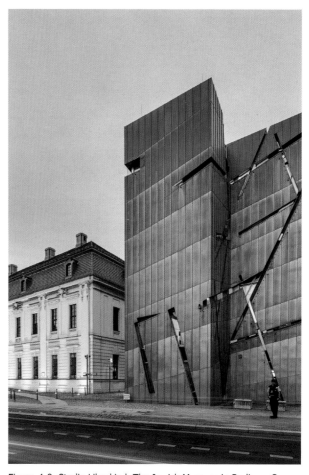

Figure 4-8. Studio Libeskind. The Jewish Museum in Berlin — Germany. Photograph by Huffon+Crow.

Figure 4-9. Daniel Libeskind. Photograph by Stefan Ruiz.

Figure 4-10. Libeskind Studio. Occitanie Tower, Toulouse — France. Rendering by Luxigon.

EMOTIONAL AND MATERIAL FOUNDATIONS OF ARCHITECTURE

SUSAN JONES

2018 WALTON CRITIC

EMOTIONAL AND MATERIAL FOUNDATIONS OF ARCHITECTURE
2018 Walton Studio
Walton Critic: Susan Jones

STUDIO TOPIC

Over the last 70 years, the American celebration of death has become highly institutionalized, sanitized, and commercialized. The 2018 Walton Studio invited students to reflect on this situation through the lenses of architecture. How does architectural design, address grief and mourning, the celebration of one's life, religious teachings, the soul? How do ceremony and symbolism play a part in our culture's historical celebration of death? Should a new perception of the earth and its final limitations induced by climate change affect how we understand death and the funeral industry? How can sacred space intersect all this? These and other questions demanded the consideration of building types that go back deep in history, as well as the existential and spiritual sense of transition and insecurity that death and loss bring up for every individual, family, and community. The topic was studied through the design of a 30,000 sq. ft. funerary complex located in the Washington Bonney Watson Memorial Park in Seattle, WA. This project involved dealing with an existing building, and a program that Walton Critic Susan Jones' office had dealt with in the past. A unique design methodology enabled the students to approach the problem open-mindedly, and thus find intriguing solutions. The studio started with series of readings, precedents study, and site analysis. Once this familiarization phase ended, Jones deployed an unusual pedagogy: students were to conduct a qualitative study of the most fundamental experiences to take place in the building vis-à-vis architectural qualities. Emotions and sensations used as the gateway to envision architectural tectonics, and the way to materialize them. This translated into making quick, simple, and intuitive physical models on 3"x12" base that addressed various experiences of the grieving process. In the next step, students photographed their models, as if they were inhabiting them from a variety of perspectives and light conditions, and then print the photos in a large format. These atmospheric images were beautiful, touching, and quickened the architectural search. Emotion was the entry point to the making process, and then seeing the models reframed became design revelations of scale, space, light and materials. This effort is appreciated in the first two pages of students' work following this introduction. This intense warm-up led to decisions about site, program, experiences, and even building details, and gave birth to advanced architectural schemes. The narrative nature of architecture and funerary rituals, an emphasis on simplicity, and the demand of an overall encompassing concept were utilized to stitch together the key architectural moments discovered in the emotion-driven making process.

Figure 5-2. Susan Jones first meeting with studio (top) and reviewing research studies by one student group (bottom).

Figure 5-3. Susan Jones in a desk crit with Antonio Ugarte. Fai Almahmoud is waiting for her turn.

Figure 5-4. Jones giving instructions during studio (top). Jones reviewing design work by Caroline Winn (bottom).

Figure 5-5. First day of class. Susan Jones informally talks with students.

Figure 5-6. *Faculty:* Susan Jones and Julio Bermudez.
Graduate Students: Alexandra Garner, Odette Leal, Jazzmin Redi, and Caroline Winn.
Undergraduate students: Fai Almahmoud, Gino-Angelo Bretana, Silvia Elias, Melissa Lacayo, Tanya Rivera-Diaz, Antonio Ugarte, and Federico Witzke. Photograph by Julio Bermudez.

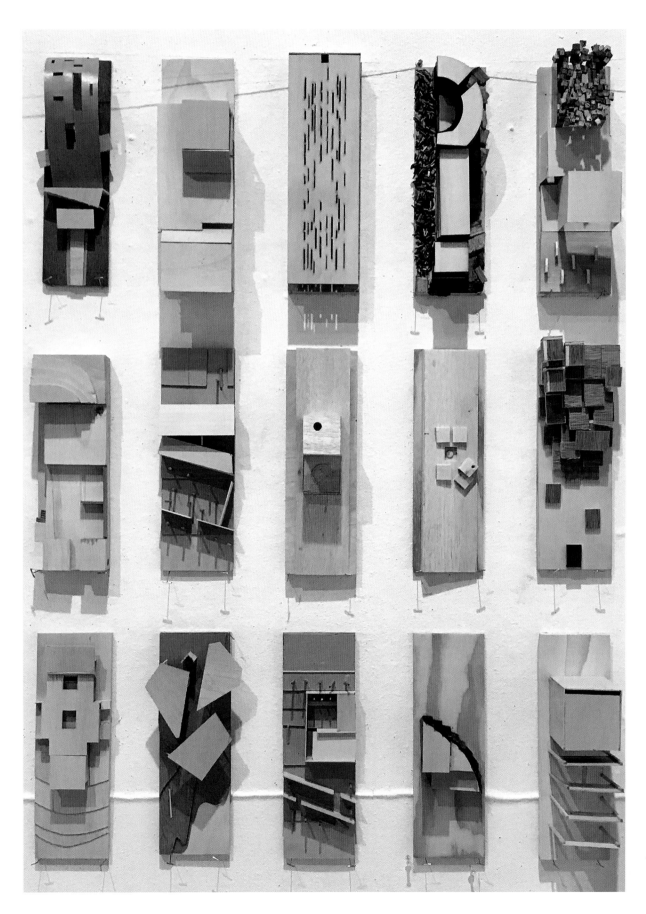

CELEBRATION OF LIFE

SEATTLE, WASHINGTON

ODETTE LEAL

It is difficult to escape the emotional turmoil one experiences when thinking of a funeral. Many people cling to their faith as a way to ease the pain they feel for themselves, their loved ones, and the ones they have lost. However, for many believers, death is only the beginning to an eternity with God. Instead of approaching the project through the memory of one's death, this funeral complex celebrates the life of the deceased through the use of light, nature, and the emotions they can incite. An abstract model was created with the purpose of exploring the emotions a person could experience. Three cubes address light similarly and differently. One of them is punctured by a circular opening, allowed light to enter as the only source of illumination. The circle is viewed in many cultures and religions as sacred. The abstract model was successfully integrated in the chapel, where visitors are encouraged to look up at the gleam of light with the goal of instilling peace and hope in their hearts. It is important for a funeral complex to be welcoming and beautiful for the guest. Although the reason for their visit is to celebrate and bury loved ones, the building must cater to the needs of the living, with the goal of helping them realize that their loved one is finally resting in peace.

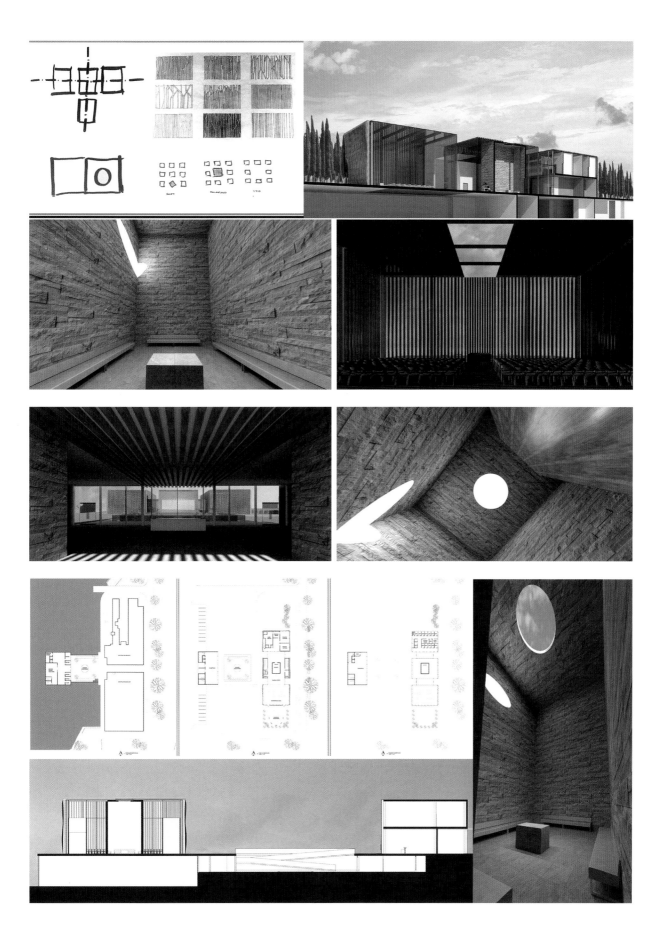

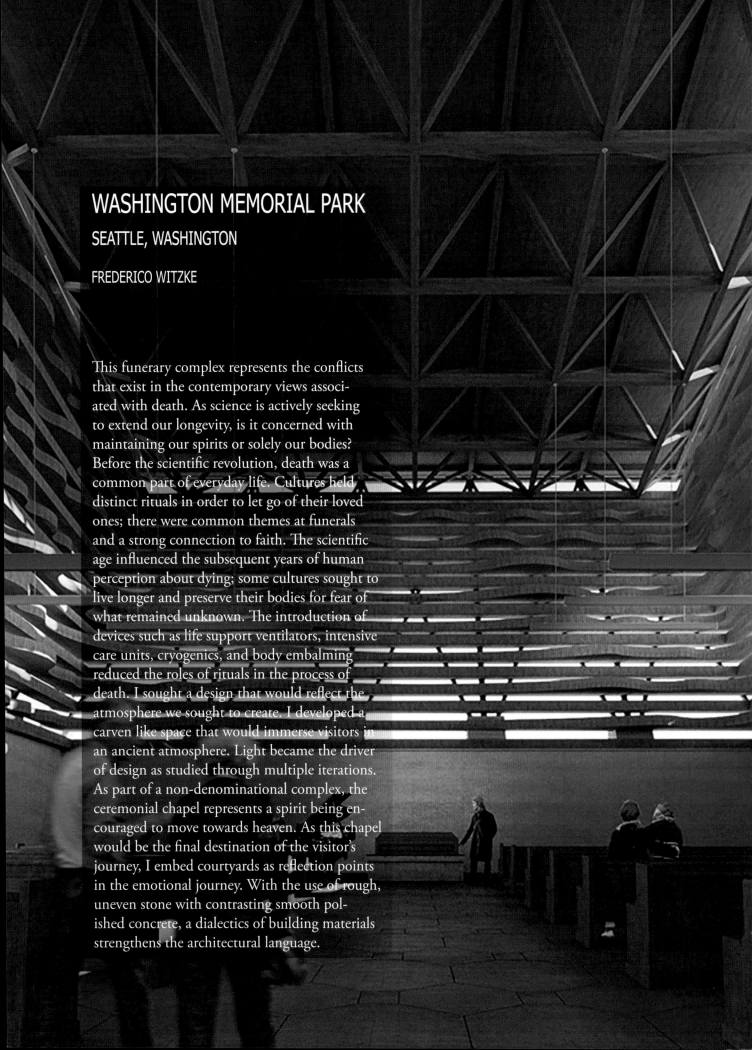

WASHINGTON MEMORIAL PARK
SEATTLE, WASHINGTON

FREDERICO WITZKE

This funerary complex represents the conflicts that exist in the contemporary views associated with death. As science is actively seeking to extend our longevity, is it concerned with maintaining our spirits or solely our bodies? Before the scientific revolution, death was a common part of everyday life. Cultures held distinct rituals in order to let go of their loved ones; there were common themes at funerals and a strong connection to faith. The scientific age influenced the subsequent years of human perception about dying; some cultures sought to live longer and preserve their bodies for fear of what remained unknown. The introduction of devices such as life support ventilators, intensive care units, cryogenics, and body embalming reduced the roles of rituals in the process of death. I sought a design that would reflect the atmosphere we sought to create. I developed a carven like space that would immerse visitors in an ancient atmosphere. Light became the driver of design as studied through multiple iterations. As part of a non-denominational complex, the ceremonial chapel represents a spirit being encouraged to move towards heaven. As this chapel would be the final destination of the visitor's journey, I embed courtyards as reflection points in the emotional journey. With the use of rough, uneven stone with contrasting smooth polished concrete, a dialectics of building materials strengthens the architectural language.

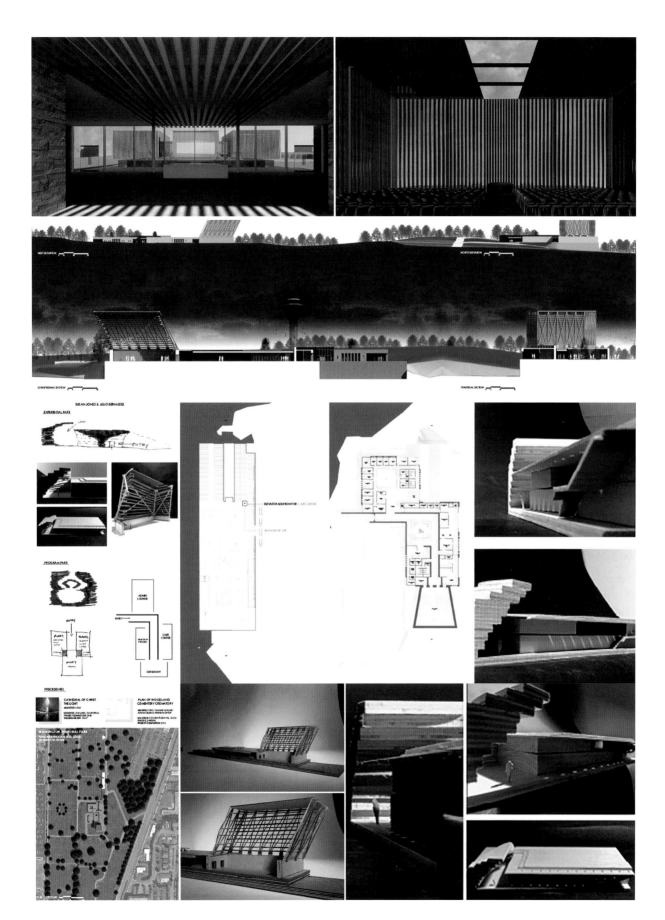

Figure 5-7. atelierjones, Marian Chapel, St. James Cathedral in Seattle — Washington. Photograph by Susan Jones.

TECTONICALLY EMOTIVE
SUSAN JONES

EMOTION AS OPENING

The studio was grounded in the emotion of grief. Initially, asked to register the site, the program as a path, process, journey of grief, the students responded from very deep personal places of their own experiences of grief. Their rough, hand-made, expressions of a site or building – *maquettes, models, gestures* – were released from the presence or need for scale, specifics of program or site dimensions. Instead, they were asked to create, or better, *re-present* experiences of grief that they had had. Not as a single moment, not as a completed resilient hurdle, but as a journey through their own experiences, raw, wild and harrowing.

Using grief as the entry point was a risk unto itself. Several students were drawn to the studio beforehand but had let the instructor know that they felt unable to participate in the studio, given the too personal nature of the topic. At least one student articulated that following the initial three weeks of concept design work, the student felt that she needed to step back from the studio, and process, as yet, still raw grief from a recent grandmother's death, that the studio's conceptual design process evoked. Another struggled, as she was dealing with depression and anxiety issues in real time, and while the chance to process them through building models evoked tremendous therapeutic opportunities, it also left her drained and exhausted. Some students reveled in

the pairing between and seemed to touch deeper aspects of their creative work than ever imagined.

PHENOMENAL MAKING

Grounded in making, the physical act of selecting materials, as real and weighted with texture, weight, color, light, scent as possible was the first engagement with the act of making a model. The power of real materials, of holding, touching, feeling them, seeing them transform through the act of cutting, molding. Watching and feeling a material transform, from hot to cold, in the case of machine worked wood, or from cold to warm, in the case of working with plaster or concrete, was in itself a phenomenal experience, one that evoked raw touch and vivid smells and sounds. The second was risk. Several of the students had not worked with wood, plaster or concrete, and the act of pouring plaster into molds, using the metallic noise of bandsaws or the guttural whirr of table saws, the rattling of drill presses or other digital fabrication tools was a risk that engendered different emotions and phenomenal experiences. From fear to excitement, from excitement to pride, to the thrill of seeing spaces realized that began to evoke emotions of hope, darkness and peace, the process of making the models began to parallel their emotional paths of grief overlaid upon them. The act of making became a way to touch, identify with the representation of the grieving process. Risk, or the ability to face fears, became a parallel strategy for evoking the emotion required for new architectural spaces to emerge.

SHARING TOGETHER

The small models were humble, even crude in some cases. But as presented by each of their makers, they evoked deep emotions and recalled trauma, vulnerability and led to a strong sense of sharing with the community that was now created within the studio. Even after just two weeks, the students felt the shared sense of risk they were all taking together and supported each other as much as possible. Emotions were both high and deep, as students sought to hear each other, see each other's built connections, support each other in personal journeys. The best of the students flew higher, creating multiple iterations, faster, with a higher command of the building process. Possessing the craft to create a conceptual underpinning for their emotions and created a clearer path to work their way through them, whether in wood, plaster, concrete or paper. The less experienced students found breakthroughs in the emotional approach; they were creating architecture through a different processing pathway than before, and it opened up creative channels, some hitherto unknown. All students became highly attached to their models and began to guard the conceptual rigor and beauty contained with them, with loyalty, vigor and depth.

SCALELESS WAYS OF SEEING

The small models were all built on a similar base, of 3" x 12" - an assimilation both of the site plan, and the existing building plan – and they lined up within the studio concept model review, dozens of them. Seen together they made a prodigious grid, of materials evoking emotions, known primarily only to their makers. While some were highly crafted, others, most, were

crude and not obviously recognizable as site, a building, or even a space. But as we broke them all open, and heard their stories, as told by their makers, the stories and then the spaces, began to come alive. We collectively began to see the models through the words and emotions of the students; the spaces of their crafted efforts began to take shape and begin to evoke architectures. Our seeing, hearing and most importantly, feelings, transcended the small crafted models, and began to reveal different scales, once observed very carefully, through the heart of the models. *Seeing with heart* began to shape the crafted efforts. Suddenly buildings, spaces, light came into focus, without reference to scale or place. The abstract leap from object to words, to the emotional heart of the project to space, light, wall, aperture, and even tectonic detail in some cases was at times breathtaking.

CAPTURING SPACE

To capture the transformations of the models, from emotion to space, each student was asked then to photograph them, at very closeup scales at often very different places within the tiny models. Sometimes spaces were captured, sometimes wall sections, sometimes light openings, sometimes façade or interior elevation details were focused on. Depending upon the focal length of each photograph, even the same area of the model could represent different aspects of a potential project. The process of looking, touching, sensing and feeling ourselves through each model was one of true discovery, as the students began to see their own work in entirely different lights, far different than the initial emotional narratives that they had created for the models. While the emotion had been the gateway to the process, the seeing and feeling the models themselves became the guide for the process, full of discovery. The photographs were then enlarged, often greatly enlarged, up to three to ten feet square in some cases. Mostly in black and white; the light quality of each of the spaces was intensified by the scale, and the absence of color. Sometimes a scale figure was introduced, sometimes a single photograph could evoke a detail, or a cathedral-like space. The photographs of the spaces then became the architecture, the idea often even, the tectonic of the project. Strategies were introduced about how to integrate the sequence of spaces introduced by the students' narratives of grief, into the spaces as built and perceived by them, through the larger photographs. The photographs with their revelations of scale, space, light and tectonics became the portal upon which to craft the site approach, program, and architectural detail. Drawings, sketches, scale figures sketched onto the photographs themselves, wall sections, details, texture was sometimes added as an overlay to the enlarged photographs to clarify the intent.

RISK

The studio, like all searches for architecture, felt like a beginning. Explorations of spaces to experience grief, to say goodbye, to create connections between this tangible world, and some kind of afterworld, regardless of belief system, are almost by nature going to feel incomplete for almost any architect: student or master. The early models, photographs and sketches were a window into the possible, a fragment of what-might-be, not necessarily what is possible. The power of the typologically rich and transcendent funerary program allowed a deeper engagement with our very human emotions of loss, grief and peace that became a powerful foundation on which to explore a complex program, site and building tectonics. Being able to take such essential risks beginning with the deep emotive foundation, then enabled an intense studio experience throughout the semester. Revealing emotions, then seeking ways to transform those emotions was a unique opportunity to experience the transformative power of architecture to create spaces that attempted to touch, another, deeper level of experience and awareness.

CLARITY

The supportive structure of the Walton Studio experience provided a level of comfort or safety for the studio and its instructors, to explore architectural issues at such a personal level. I am not sure that the students would have been able to engage so deeply, nor would they have been comfortable to speak so openly. The resulting clarity of the experience was extreme. This compelling level of risk that the Walton Studio engages at – both as a structure within The Catholic University of America's School of Architecture, but as well, within architectural pedagogy as a whole, within the US, certainly, is unusual, and inspiring. I am deeply grateful to have had the opportunity to stand as the Walton Critic of 2018, to teach with Professor Julio Bermudez, and to represent 2018 in the illustrious ten-year anniversary of the Walton Critic program.

Figure 5-8. atelierjones, detail of the Bellevue First Congregational Church in Bellevue —Washington. Photograph by Susan Jones.

Figure 5-9. atelierjones, skylights and ceiling of the Bellevue First Congregational Church in Bellevue — Washington. Photograph by Susan Jones.

PHYSICAL, EXISTENTIAL, AND SPIRITUAL HOME

RICK JOY   2017 WALTON CRITIC

PHYSICAL, EXISTENTIAL, AND SPIRITUAL HOME
2017 Walton Studio
Walton Critic: Rick Joy

STUDIO TOPIC

The 2017 Walton Studio considered the interactions between inhabitation, place, and transcendence within the architecturally, spiritually and culturally concentrated condition of a single-family home. A *house* has the ability to "compress" form, space, site, program, culture, faith, technology, and society in an economically affordable format. This has given architects the opportunity to explore and advance architectural ideas in ways otherwise impossible using other building types. Due to its scale and our familiarity with home dwellings, a house enables an understanding and experiential encounter that are hard to falsify. Not surprising, the roots of house and dwelling go all the way back to the primordial sacredness of *home*. In short, the design of a single-family house requires architects to ask fundamental questions: what kind of life does a home put forward (or critique)? What is it that we-the-architect profess? Walton Critic Rick Joy used these reflections to guide the students in designing a 5,000 square foot home for a middle-age couple with three children between 7 and 22 years of age. The spaces and forms that served the family were defined in relation to their particular attitude towards reality and included practical considerations. Each student was given by lottery one of the following five families: (1) Religious/Faithful, (2) Political refugee, (3) Fortune 500, (4) World-class artist, or (5) Nobel

Prize scientist. The building was to be placed in a spectacular, wooded, and sloped site overslooking the Potomac River in Bethesda, MD. Unlike other Walton Studios when projects are done in teams, the scale and nature of this architectural task was better addressed by individuals working alone. After unpacking their client's worldview along with its implications, architect Joy directed students to consider living rituals that probed existential and transcendental dimensions of family living. The power of the site became the next driver of the architectural conversation. He asked students to deploy a combination of mindfulness and intuition toward finding a synthesis of the logical aspects of the project and a visceral understanding of the experiences afforded. Although Joy always kept bringing students into the narrative, sensual, and emotional nature of architecture, he was adamant that everything should be subordinated to architectural ideas. He kept pushing for fundamental architectural clarity/simplicity along with its phenomenological expression and response to the site. Concept (idea, position) and experience had to be married into an indivisible unity. Unlike most studios in contemporary schools of architecture where single-family dwellings are seldom studied, this Walton Studio capitalized on this age-old problem to strike at the very core of the most profound architectural concerns.

Figure 6-2. Emily Oldham in conversation with Rick Joy during a desk crit.

Figure 6-3. Rick Joy discussing Caroline Winn's design work.

Figure 6-4. Rick Joy in a desk crit with Alex Garner (left) and reviewing the work of Madeline Amhurst (Right).

Figure 6-5. Rick Joy giving instruction to the whole studio.

Figure 6-6. *Faculty:* Rick Joy and Julio Bermudez.
Graduate Students: Alexandra Garner, Anh-Tu Nguyen, Gabrielle Oakes, Emily Oldham, Madeline Amhurst, Ian Walker, and Caroline Winn.
Undergraduate students: Bridget Farley, Sandra Guillen, Ngan Nguyen, Julianne Petrillo, Sabryna Tristan, and Gabby Vera. Photograph by Julio Bermudez.

EXPLORATION HOUSE

BETHESDA, MARYLAND

AHN-TU NGUYEN

At the end of a cul-de-sac, on top of a wooded hill, overlooking the Potomac River, a Physicist arrives home. At work, he acquires knowledge by examining the world, experimenting, and collaborating. At home, he and his family probe the transcendent mysteries of life that lead towards personal enlightenment. Their home fosters all manner of this exploration; a laboratory for learning, a library for research, a kitchen for testing, a den for debate, and a lens for observation. Every discovery brings them closer together and closer to the elusive meaning of life. Through the entrance at the top of the hill, inside, the reverse telescoping volume expands their gaze through the interconnected common spaces and to the view of the river beyond. A tiered staircase stretches down the length of the volume and stops at three levels. To the north, glimpses out force the scientist to extrapolate what's happening outside, and it entices them to walk out to the terraces. Along the south wall, portals at each level branch off to the bedrooms. Retaining the hill and full glass on either side, the hallways transition past pocket gardens to individual retreats. Here they have isolation, intimacy, and a new perspective. The maple floors, walls, and ceilings insulate the interior with warmth while the exterior stacked stone grounds the building into the site like a boulder gently settled into the hillside. Skylights and a roof terrace expand their exploration to the stars and galaxies beyond.

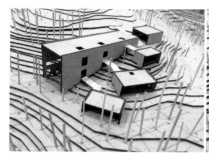

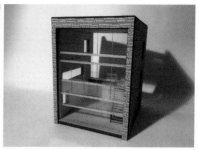

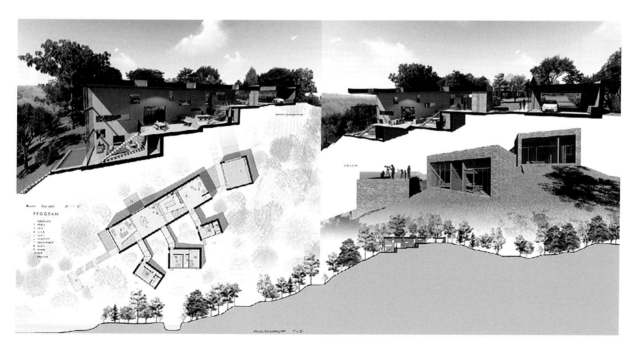

FIELD IN THE FOREST

BETHESDA, MARYLAND

MADELINE AMHURST

The Byrne residence is a 6,000 sf. private home with a 900 sf. public gallery at the entrance to the site. The home is sculpted out of 950 salvaged utility poles on a cliff site overlooking the Potomac River in Bethesda, Maryland. The field of poles participates in a constant dialogue with its context as it functions as environmental art, security, and structure for the house. Within the field itself there are collections of sculptures that the owner, David Byrne, has collected over time that one can approach using the bridge that leads to the residence. Living within this sculpture provides a unique retreat from the city of Washington for the family to enjoy with one another.

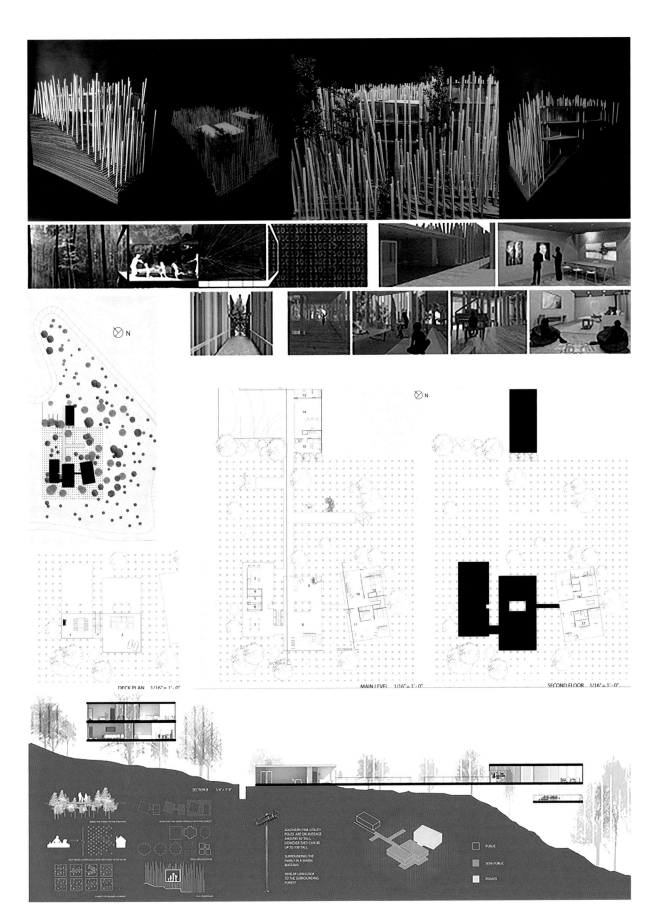

SEEKING HARMONY: A HOME FOR A MUSICAL FAMILY

BETHESDA, MARYLAND

EMILY OLDHAM

A home is a building unlike any other. It exists as both a physical element, and as a powerful psychological manifestation. Humanity seeks to understand the world and to find meaning in it. The importance of the home is related to this desire for meaning. Building a home is about more than finding a safe place to sleep. It is about creating a fixed point in the world from which we can contemplate our place and purpose. Without a home, we are lost wherever we are. Our homes have power over us. They are the stages on which we play out our daily rituals. No other building type has the same ability to influence our thought and actions.

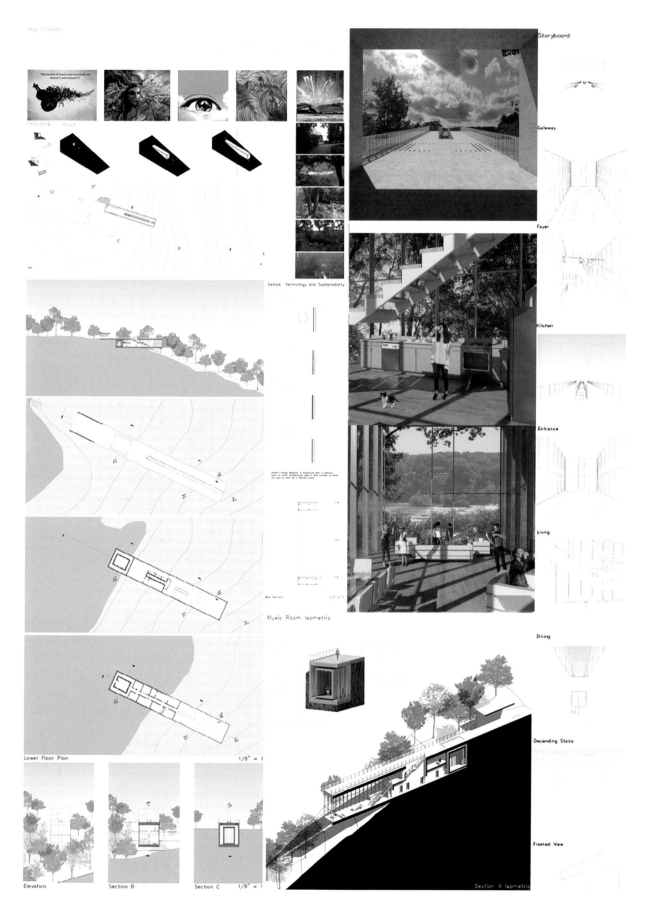

The Clients:

Process: Diart

Details Technology and Sustainability

Storyboard

Gateway

Foyer

Kitchen

Entrance

Living

Music Room Isometric

Dining

Descending Stairs

Lower Floor Plan   1/8" = 1

Elevation   Section B   Section C   1/8" = 1

Framed View

Section A Isometric

Figure 6-7. Rick Joy Architects, Sun Valley House — Idaho. Photograph by Joe Fletcher.

NEW WORLDS
RICK JOY

It truly remains an honor to have been invited to be a visiting professor and co-teach with Professor Julio Bermudez at Catholic University of America in Washington D.C. in the fall of 2017. In Julio I found a special kindred spirit and we made a fast and lasting friendship. He invited me to help bring the topic of designing a home to the Walton Studio and indicated that I could readily share from my practice and experience the role of "spirituality in architecture."

Today our Studio Rick Joy team members are safely harbored in our homes in Tucson, Arizona due to the current Coronavirus pandemic. As we currently rethink our interactions within public and communal spaces, I am channeling my solid life-long belief in home combined with nature as the source of luxury and of spiritual guidance and hope in my life and work. I'm guided by the power of earth's groundedness (cities included) but also from the skies by day and celestial connections by night, and by my personally curated beliefs and most certainly by evolutionary science.

And while spirituality certainly occurs and exists within each individual's soul and mind, we can definitely experience it while being drawn out into our vast Sonoran Desert to feel the quality of its air and brilliant, silent beauty. Yet for others spirituality is a continuous search to be with or serve other human beings. In fact, we usually join others in one set of beliefs to practice and worship a higher being that exists beyond ourselves.

Teaching graduate architecture students about designing a house, with no client involved, is of course challenging. Julio's Idea. Usually, engaging with client dimensions makes the challenge much more of a holistic cooperation. Without such, our students were required to develop a client persona and script through a rather sophisticated script, full of remarkable personalities and scenarios. That brought high spirits to the studio exchanges and, eventually, strong design work.

Teaching at CUA in Washington D.C. was meaningful to me and I'll finish with the following quote from the book Twelve Steps to a Compassionate Life by author Karen Armstrong :

> *Tragic drama reminds us of the role that art can play in expanding our sympathies. Plays, films, and novels all enable us to enter imaginatively into other lives and make an empathetic identification with people whose experiences are entirely different from our own. They can give us moments of compassionate EKSTASIS, and we should resolve, during this step, to allow art to unsettle us and make us question ingrained preconceptions. Imagination is crucial to the compassionate life. A uniquely human quality, it enables the artist to create entirely new worlds and give a strong semblance of reality to events.*[2]

Figure 6-8. Rick Joy Architects, Princeton University Transit Station with Nakashima benches. Photograph by Jeff Goldberg (Esto).

Figure 6-9. Rick Joy Architects, Tubac House, Tubac — Arizona. Photograph by Jeff Goldberg (Esto).

Figure 6-10. Rick Joy Architects. La Cabanon — Turks and Caicos. Photograph by Joe Fletcher.

VOCATION AND THE DEEP SELF: TEACHING THE VOICE WITHIN

2016 WALTON CRITIC PREM CHANDAVARKAR

VOCATION AND THE DEEP SELF: TEACHING THE VOICE WITHIN
2016 Walton Studio
Walton Critic: Prem Chandavarkar

STUDIO TOPIC

The 2016 Walton Studio examined architectural responses to social and spiritual practices dedicated to fostering human vocation and its development in everyday life. Since "vocation" (from the old Latin 'vocare' —voice) ultimately refers to following a deep calling from another (whether God, the true self, a loved one, or a situation), the studio sought to make students sensible to recognize how one is always being summoned by such other. This translated into a working methodology of teams of two students who were expected to listen and respond to each other's calls. Walton Critic Prem Chandavarkar started the studio by asking participants to read, reflect, and discuss the implications and meanings of personal growth, approached from a variety of perspectives including philosophical, religious, and psychological. This happened in relation to four warm-up assignments. The first exercise consisted in sensing and depicting the 'life' or 'aura' of/in inanimate objects (facilitated by reading poet Pablo Neruda's odes to ordinary things). The second task was to develop an "emotional experience map" of ordinary homely spaces (e.g., living room, bedroom, kitchen) to realize the serious limitations of conventional 'functionalism.' Lastly, students were to list things that strongly moved them, consider the greater realm from which these things came, and then design a one-room house for a person

possessed by that transcendental realm. After this initial preparation, the studio shifted towards the design of a building termed *"The House of Sources,"* located in a triangle-shaped urban lot in the Takoma neighborhood in Washington DC. This 25,000 square feet institution was to function as a support structure to help people (half resident and half daily visitors) find their vocation through hearing and following (i.e., practicing) their calling. The building site was not to be thought of as an empty vessel waiting to be filled up. This meant to ask not only *"what is this site?"* but more significantly *"who is this site?"* Although the House of Sources had to address four realms (the senses, knowing, love, and the void), how such areas manifested was up to the students and demanded the consideration and design of a particular *"pedagogy of vocation."* Conceptual and metaphoric approaches were encouraged to facilitate such meditations but it was in its phenomenological performance that the building's educational programming was to be defined and tested. The architecture had to evoke a sense of realms that are beyond the ordinary so that its inhabitants could recognize both the source of the voice that called them, as well as the spiritual message the voice was conveying. Emphasis was put in architectural simplicity and clarity. The studio environment proactively supported risk-taking, questioning, and probing.

Figure 7-2. Final Jury of the 2016 Walton Studio in December.

Figure 7-3. Billy Wantz presenting his group's design proposal.

Figure 7-4. Chandavarkar giving summary remarks (left) and the jurors for the final studio review (right).

Figure 7-5. Chandavarkar reviewing the design work of Tatiana Amundsen and Billy Wantz.

Figure 7-6. *Faculty:* Prem Chandavarkar, Julio Bermudez, Lavinia Fici Pasquina, and Ana Maria Roman Andrino.
Graduate Students: Fatma Al Mulla, Aishah Albader,Faisal Alhassani, Elham Alikhani, Rajih Alshareif, Leyda Tatiana Woodard Freeman, Hisham Khafaji, Anh-Tu Nguyen, Planel Nyontyen, Amanda Ocello, Emily Oldham, , Ian Walker, and Madeline Wentzell
Undergraduate Students: Tatiana Amundsen, Matthew Barton, Andrew Cahill, Felipe Prellezo, Adrienne Rejano, Andrew Santiano, Daeyah Tayeb, and Billy Wantz. Photograph by Julio Bermudez.

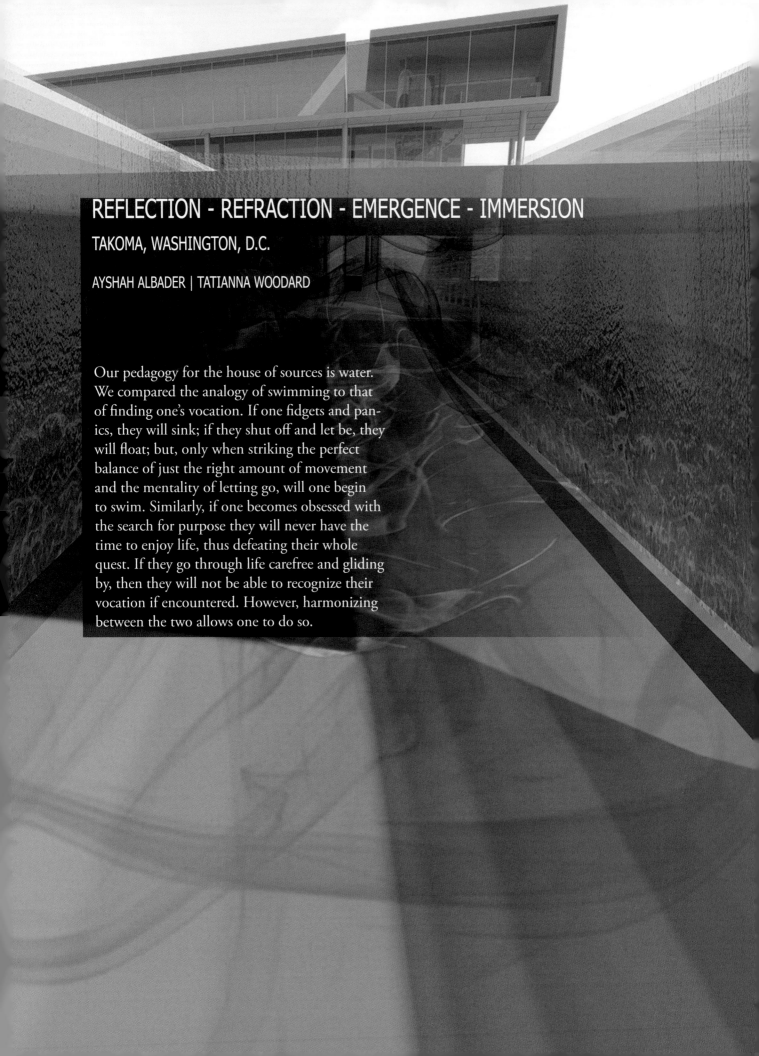

REFLECTION - REFRACTION - EMERGENCE - IMMERSION

TAKOMA, WASHINGTON, D.C.

AYSHAH ALBADER | TATIANNA WOODARD

Our pedagogy for the house of sources is water.
We compared the analogy of swimming to that
of finding one's vocation. If one fidgets and pan-
ics, they will sink; if they shut off and let be, they
will float; but, only when striking the perfect
balance of just the right amount of movement
and the mentality of letting go, will one begin
to swim. Similarly, if one becomes obsessed with
the search for purpose they will never have the
time to enjoy life, thus defeating their whole
quest. If they go through life carefree and gliding
by, then they will not be able to recognize their
vocation if encountered. However, harmonizing
between the two allows one to do so.

Parti Model

Metaphor Diagram

Parti Diagrams

Realm Distribution Diagram

Screenshot

Section B - 1/4th Scale

Glass Bottom Cafe - Floating Experience

Screenshot

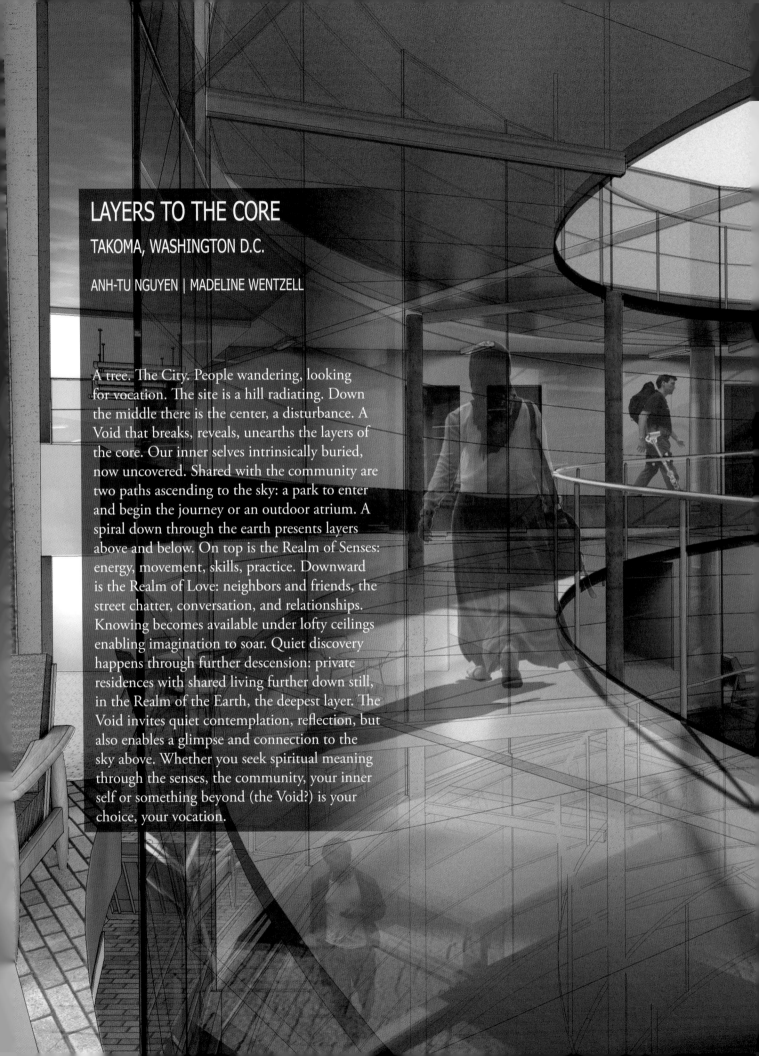

LAYERS TO THE CORE

TAKOMA, WASHINGTON D.C.

ANH-TU NGUYEN | MADELINE WENTZELL

A tree. The City. People wandering, looking for vocation. The site is a hill radiating. Down the middle there is the center, a disturbance. A Void that breaks, reveals, unearths the layers of the core. Our inner selves intrinsically buried, now uncovered. Shared with the community are two paths ascending to the sky: a park to enter and begin the journey or an outdoor atrium. A spiral down through the earth presents layers above and below. On top is the Realm of Senses: energy, movement, skills, practice. Downward is the Realm of Love: neighbors and friends, the street chatter, conversation, and relationships. Knowing becomes available under lofty ceilings enabling imagination to soar. Quiet discovery happens through further descension: private residences with shared living further down still, in the Realm of the Earth, the deepest layer. The Void invites quiet contemplation, reflection, but also enables a glimpse and connection to the sky above. Whether you seek spiritual meaning through the senses, the community, your inner self or something beyond (the Void?) is your choice, your vocation.

Top of Void

Middle

Bottom

Section Looking East   3/16"=1-0"

Section Looking West   3/16"=1-0"

The House of Sources

TAKOMA, WASHINGTON D.C.

HISHAM KHAFAJI | EMILY OLDHAM

Finding your vocation is an iterative exercise of looking in and looking out. By looking in, you discover your sense of self and begin to answer the question, "Who am I?" By looking out, you come to understand the subjectivity of selfhood. You will know your true purpose in life when you accept the apparent contradiction of individual and collective consciousness existing simultaneously. At the House of Sources, students practice the act of looking out and looking in as they traverse through the various realms via a series of ramps. The ramps sit between a courtyard, which contains the realm of the void, a space of quiet reflection, and the learning and residential realms. The exterior walls are substantial, creating a feeling of enclosure with controlled glimpses of the surrounding area.

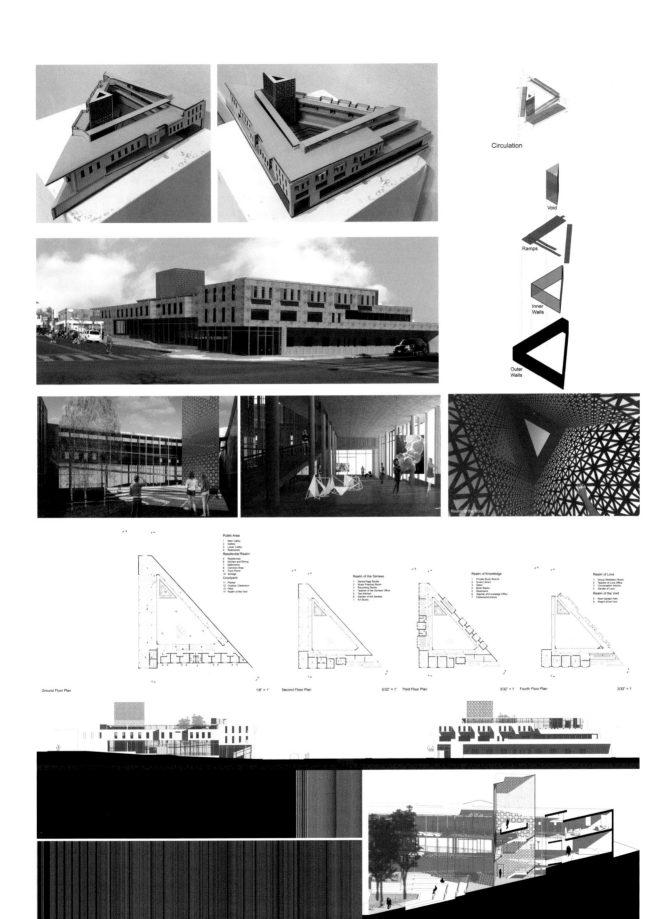

Figure 7-7. CnT Architects, Tata Dhan Academy in Madurai — India.
Photograph by Mehul Patel.

TEACHING THE VOICE WITHIN
PREM CHANDAVARKAR

MODERNITY AND THE SACRED

In sharing my reflections as the 2016 Walton Critic on the occasion of the tenth anniversary of the Walton Critic Program, I find it necessary to begin with emphasizing the significance of the graduate concentration in 'Sacred Space/Cultural Studies' at the School of Architecture and Planning at The Catholic University of America (CUA), within which the Walton Critic Program is a key part. The very existence of this program is significant for it is extremely rare to come across any program in architectural education anywhere in the world that grants magnitude to 'the sacred': an important fact that lies at the core of what we mean when we call ourselves 'modern.' The term 'modern' has a broad usage and was first established as a descriptor of architecture in the late 19th and early 20th centuries. While the ideology of architecture has changed significantly since then, the core ethic of claiming modernity still remains. This ethic has its philosophical roots in the Age of Enlightenment in Europe which rebelled against the exploitative and constraining chains of traditional authority to posit a moral argument that humanity should place its foundations on the creative freedom and autonomy of individual will. Modernity, thus defined, has a political dimension that led to democracy as a system of political organization, and an artistic dimension where art is envisioned as a progressive form of thought that can lead

society forward in its historical development. Modern architecture emerged from an ideal of the avant-garde artist whose creativity, empowered by the individualistic emancipation granted to him/her, paves the path of progress. While the social idealism of early modern architecture is no longer a central tenet, modernity per se remains at the core of the current ideology of architecture which continues to hold the freedom and autonomy of the individual architect as key. This freedom is suspicious of any intervening authority. Given that it was initially won by a rebellion against traditional authority, and one of the primary forms of traditional authority is established religion, modernity has always been suspicious of the sacred. Consequently, the claim to modernity rests on the premise of secularism, and if faith and the sacred are to be allowed at all they are seen as a part of the private realm, and therefore to be kept distant from professional education and practice. It could be argued that constraining the sacred to established religion is a narrow view, and a conflict with the premises of modernity could be avoided through a broader view that recognizes it as a primordial dimension of life transcending the canon of any orthodox faith tradition. But even here there is a clash, for modernity's central premise of freedom grants primacy to individualistic human agency, which entails a substantive degree of derecognition or devaluation of other forms of agency. Modernity involves an objectification of nature, which is why ecological crises are one of the most pressing issues we face. Pre-modern cultures were enchanted by the world they inhabited, seeing it as an animated realm of spirits and magic that the self must adjust to, whereas modernity's axiom of maximizing individual freedom implies a disenchantment of the world that leaves no room for the sacred. To see oneself as a part of a larger world that is sacred and enchanted invokes an ethic of humility, and modernity views such a call for humility with suspicion, treating it as an attempt through the backdoor to reduce personal freedom. The possibility of this broader view of the sacred is consequently rejected by the conventions of current professional culture in academia as well as practice.

However, a proposal that the sacred is a higher realm of significance one must submit to, whose sanction cannot be granted by reason alone, would also be applicable to the aesthetic dimension of architecture. To deny the sacred is tantamount to a strategy of rejection that would also imply an inadmissible denial of architectural aesthetics. This paradox is resolved by treating such higher realms as the tacit possession of individual genius, and where such a realm's existence is recognized it is treated as a product of the creative personality. By casting it as a personality-centric product, it is restored as an individual's possession, and therefore does not threaten the sense of freedom and control we are schooled to believe in.

This perception of modernity is false and fragile, for it assumes that the joy we seek in being alive can only come from a freedom premised on an ideology of individualized liberation. It promotes a culture of isolation and loneliness, failing to acknowledge the deeper joy we feel when our consciousness achieves a harmony with consciousness beyond ourselves. We know this on a routine basis, such as the joy we gain from a loving relationship, yet we forget it because of a training that persuades us to derecognize it with-

in our intellectual and professional worldviews. Even within the loving relationship, our schooling in an ideology of isolation often intervenes to seek the false freedom of control that makes our love self-centered and possessive, losing sight of the generosity and gratitude that is the hallmark of true love. A relationship of love thrives on harmony rather than control, gaining purpose and joy from the resonance felt with a world beyond the self. The sacred is the awe felt when this harmony is recognized as pervading the universe, the self, and other beings. A broad view of the sacred requires jettisoning modernity's illusion that equates freedom with personal willfulness. It is the way forward to re-enchanting the world with purpose, community and ecology at its center, rather than the individualistic materialism we are currently obsessed with.

The CUA program on sacred space offers a rare island of opportunity to explore a reinterpreted modernity by which architecture can explore and reveal the sacred realm. A design studio within this program calls for a shift in emphasis, away from a sole focus on training the individual student's personal creativity toward a recognition that personal creativity is enhanced when the student learns to hear voices larger than the self: voices of an enchanted world.

THE 2016 WALTON STUDIO: THE HOUSE OF SOURCES

The specter of a larger voice was raised in the 2016 Walton Studio through a challenge to design 'The House of Sources': an institution that offers a focused support structure to help people find their vocation. In today's parlance, choosing a 'vocation' means choosing a trade or profession, a field within which one's job will lie. This is typically construed as a choice whose central challenge requires resolving the tension between a personal and practical point of view. The personal viewpoint asks that you choose your vocation on the basis of what you find interesting: in other words, your vocation should indulge your desire. The practical viewpoint asks that you choose your vocation on the basis of the scope it offers to earn and live well: in other words, your vocation should facilitate your living a good life. Both viewpoints begin and end with the autonomous self, and once the choice is made the only question is how one acquires the necessary knowledge and skills to practice one's vocation.

We have lost sight of the deeper root of the word 'vocation', for it involves something greater than one's self-absorbed choices. It derives from the Middle English and Old French word *vocare* which means 'to call': to find a vocation is to find a calling. A calling is much more than your interests or your yearning for a good life; to find a calling means that the voice that calls you springs from a realm that is far greater than you. Every person does not hear the same voice: the voice you hear is unique to the kind of person you are. The central challenge in finding a vocation lies in acquiring the discernment to recognize and hear the voice that calls you. To hear your calling is to know your purpose and place in the world.

Students were assigned to work in pairs, and after a set of warm-up exercises in the first three weeks, designed to provoke the necessary mind-set, the bulk of the semester was spent on The House of Sources, which was located on a site in the neighborhood of Takoma Park in Washington DC. The space program was loosely specified, and each pair of students was encouraged to develop their own interpretation of the possibilities. The overall built-up area needed to be between 20,000 and 25,000 square feet, and the institution was divided into three realms:

- **The Residential Realm**: Rooms where people could stay for a period of two or three weeks to spend focused time within the institution to find their calling. Shared amenities for eating, cooking and gathering formed a part of this realm.
- **The Learning Realm:** This was the space where focused time in search of a calling would be spent. It was divided into three

sub-realms, each representing a mode by which one would carry out one's search:
  - The Realm of the Senses.
  - The Realm of Knowing.
  - The Realm of Love.
- **The Realm of the Void:** This is the anchor around which all spaces center. It is a space of silence and infinity.

As is the pattern in most design studios, the quality of the final designs varied. Most of the projects did get into the spirit of seeking a higher voice, and a few of the schemes were truly evocative and powerful. The experience of conducting this studio lingered in my memory and thoughts for long after. Given that it was my first experience in teaching a design studio focused on a sacred realm of higher voices, the question began to preoccupy me of whether more needs to be done to teach such a studio so that it lives up to the potential of its theme.

HINDSIGHT FROM TWO YEARS LATER

Given that recognizing sacredness as a core dimension of life requires a fundamental rethinking of the very question of modernity, it is necessary to be clear about what is involved when we bring this recognition into a school of architecture curriculum. Is it something we add to a prevailing structure, with the only question being the significance we grant to this new addition? Or does it require a radical overhaul of teaching as an activity?

I had an opportunity for focused hindsight of the 2016 studio when I revisited CUA on the tenth anniversary of the Walton Critic Program. The Walton Critics who participated in that event were also asked to review work of ongoing studios through the school. In some of those reviews, I saw work by graduate students who had been given an opportunity to participate in the concentration on sacred space while they were undergraduates. I noticed that the work they produced could be good, but it was very similar in approach to other students in the studio who had not been exposed to the sacred space concentration. One would expect that an exposure to, and acceptance of, the sacred in one's work would be transformative, resulting in a distinctive approach. While the number of such students reviewed in 2018 does not constitute a statistically significant sample, it was sufficient to provoke critical reflection within me. Does a recognition of sacred higher voices in one design studio provoke an interest restricted to that specific studio, only to be distracted by other themes in subsequent studios? How should one teach so that the sacred is internalized to be consistently evoked in all subsequent work?

TEACHING THE VOICE WITHIN

Modernity privileged instrumental reason, arguing that the justification for individual freedom is that every person possesses the capacity for reason, and we can thus transcend our own self-absorption and subjectivity by deducing a truth that can be known as a thing in itself, apart from any individual. The sacred, when recognized within an enchanted world, does not separate truth from the individual, for rather than a truth that can only be known externally through reason or language, in its recognition of harmony between self and world it posits a truth that must finally be known internally through experience.

The 2016 Walton Studio provoked students into listening for a higher voice, but it must also be recognized that there is a voice within each student, which could have received greater emphasis. Knowing the sacred is to know that this inner voice, the inner voice of others, and the higher voices of the world, all spring from the same source. In placing faith in external truth, we unwittingly deafen ourselves to the key role played by one's internal voice. Once this voice is awakened and stimulated, it will provide consequent consistency in the student. Teachings on the sacred must also account for recognition of the voice within; the teacher must know how to speak directly to this voice. This voice

is experiential and embodied, and thus rests to a great deal on tacit knowledge that is beyond our capacity to explain it. It cannot be invoked through external references; it must be invoked through a direct personal connection between teacher and student within the studio or classroom. This calls for a radical change in emphasis within our models of school curriculum.

The architecture curriculum is usually treated as being made up of the following components:

- Content: The structure of courses, including the focus and subject matter of each course.
- Competence: The knowledge and skills reflected in work product of the students, measured through a defined procedure of assessment.
- Pedagogy: The practices and methods of teaching within the classroom/studio.
- Values: The ethical and epistemological principles that guide the overall curricular structure.

Values are beacons that are periodically sighted to ensure that curriculum is on track, but it is content, competence and pedagogy that constitute the day-to-day protocols of education. In the modern intellectual system that currently prevails, the standard of external truth leads to an emphasis on content and competence, and pedagogy is treated as an instrumental means by which content is translated into competence. A curriculum that privileges the sacred will center on an embodied truth known by the student through her/his inner voice. The recognition of this inner voice can only happen through personal contact between teacher and student, and in this model pedagogy should form the core of education, supported by content and competence.

My first job out of architecture school involved working with Morad Chowdhury, an architect in New Delhi who was also a teacher of architecture. One afternoon in the office, talking about his experiences as a teacher, he remarked, *"I cannot teach architecture, for architecture is not* teachable in that sense. *What I can do is go to the college and communicate my passion for architecture, and if a student gets infected by that passion, that student will learn architecture."* Chowdhury's statement captures the spirit of a pedagogy centered curriculum, where the teacher's spark of passion sets the student's inner voice alight. But passion alone is not sufficient, for passion can be aggressive and can create asymmetries of power. To complete the picture, passion must be present along with her twin sister compassion, who will ensure the necessary symmetry cementing the personal bond between teacher and student.

The role of the teacher becomes different from the conventional model of one who transfers expertise and knowledge to the student. The focus shifts from the subject matter being taught to the self being educated. The teacher's role is to:

- Awaken the inner voice of the student by bringing passion and compassion into the classroom/studio.
- Provide guidance to the way this inner voice can discover and learn.
- Given that this path of discovery is slow and rigorous, the teacher must offer his/her passion and personal mastery as the light at the end of the tunnel, so that the student has the faith to persist.

A pedagogy centered curriculum will require a major rethink of the products that reflect student competence, as well as restructuring systems of assessment. This is beyond the scope of this essay, but this task must be taken up if we wish to privilege the sacred in education and rethink our notion of modernity within a re-enchanted world.

THE INTIMACY OF TEACHING

India's tradition contains a set of ancient Hindu texts known as The Upanishads. There are over two hundred Upanishads, but the first dozen or so are the earliest and most significant. They are known as the principal (mukhya) Upanishads, and all of them predate the Common Era. Their core message is far from the liturgical or ritualistic prescriptions that underpin many of the faith traditions, and centers on the claim that the ultimate sacred reality (Brahman) and the inner self or soul (Atman) are one and the same. The second oldest of the Upanishads, the Chandogya Upanishad, captures this in the aphorism Tat Tvam Asi (Thou Art That), stating that in searching for the sacred one must realize that one is already what one is seeking: you only need to acquire the discernment that allows you to recognize it within you.

This reflects the broad view of the sacred presented here. What is most interesting is the etymology of the word 'Upanishad'. It derives from 'Upa' which means 'close', 'ni' which means 'down', and 'shad' which means 'sit'. 'Upanishad' means 'sit down close'. This refers to the relationship between guru and disciple as being one of intimacy, and the primary means by which one can know sacred truth.

The conventional model entrenched within modern education sees teaching as an act of knowledge. To teach the sacred will require recasting the act of teaching, where it still valorizes knowledge, but is primarily an act of love.

Figure 7-8. CnT Architects. Brigade Courtyard Apartments in Bangalore — India. Photograph by Koteswara Rao.

Figure 7-9. CnT Architects. Ramaiah House in Bangalore — India. Photograph by Amit Rastogi.

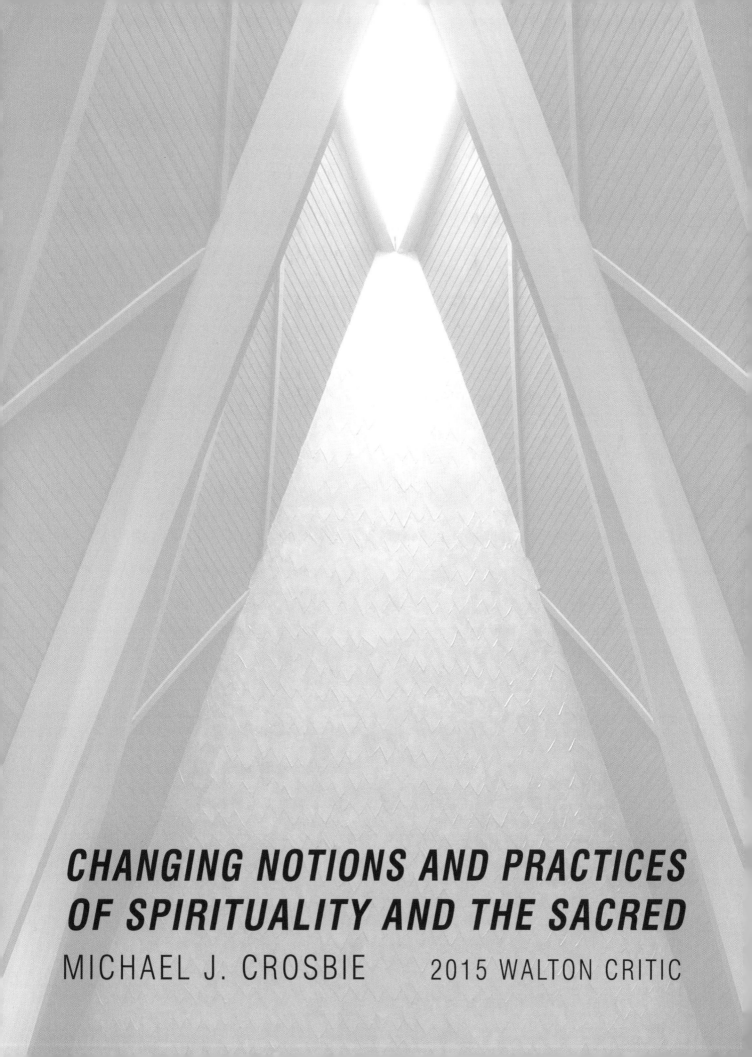

CHANGING NOTIONS AND PRACTICES OF SPIRITUALITY AND THE SACRED

MICHAEL J. CROSBIE   2015 WALTON CRITIC

CHANGING NOTIONS AND PRACTICES OF SPIRITUALITY AND THE SACRED
2015 Walton Studio
Walton Critic: Michael J. Crosbie

STUDIO TOPIC

The 2015 Walton Studio was an invitation to learn about the shifting landscape of spirituality taking place in the U.S. and abroad, and to reflect on what it means for the future of sacred space. Perhaps, it was proposed, there is a need for a new type of sacred space — one that serves dimensions of life currently not addressed by traditional faith practices. Many questions were advanced such as: what are the relationships between contemporary attitudes and directions in religious and spiritual belief?; is the notion of sacredness changing and, if so, how?; what is the importance of sustainability as reflected in the Papal Encyclical *Laudato Si*? Since many of the demographic changes in spiritual belief are being led by Millennials —that is, people of the same age as the studio participants, Walton Critic Michael J. Crosbie asked the students to consider their own experiences regarding organized religion, the contours of their own spiritual life, and the "search for the transcendent" they may be engaged in with others. In order to facilitate such inquiry, the studio was declared as a *"safe place"* in which to present views about how to respond architecturally to these societal changes in organized religion and spirituality. The investigation started through readings, discussions, and a provocative two-week sketch problem to design a *"situational"* sacred space structure on a busy urban corner in Washington DC's Petworth neighborhood. The project asked for a transitory space/object suitable for a sacred purpose (the disposition of ashes on Ash Wednesday in the Christian faith tradition).

Once this work had been completed, the studio turned to the main task of the semester: to design a 25-40,000 square feet *Place for Spirit and Wellbeing* in the same neighborhood. This building included a variety of indoor and outdoor spaces for spiritual and social pursuits as they relate to today's evolving ideas of religion and sacredness. The program was flexible. Students had to use 8 spaces selected (based on the students' intentions) from a longer program list that included places for the spirit, social outreach, creativity, worship, giving and receiving, community engagement, and so on. These spaces could be conceived as situational and substantive sacred environments.[3] The work of this Walton Studio was significant for two reasons. First because it invited students to address their own faith vis-à-vis new attitudes about spirituality held by their own generation. And second because it explored a design realm that has few if any architectural precedents— to consider and give form to a new frontier of belief.

Figure 8-2. Crosbie and Soranno talking to students Joe Barrick, Ariadne Cerritelli, Emily O'Laughlin, and Megan Gregory.

Figure 8-3. Passeri and Hoffman presenting their architectural work during the final jury.

Figure 8-4. Susan Jones gives a crit during her week-long visit to the studio.

Figure 8-5. Michael J. Crosbie and Susan Jones giving a crit to Sina Moayedi and Ugo Nnebue.

Figure 8-6. Devon Brophy sharing her and Madeline Wentzell's architectural proposal.

Figure 8-7. Sina Moayedi and Ugo Nnebue explaining their design during the final review.

Figure 8-8. *Faculty:* Michael J. Crosbie and Julio Bermudez (with Susan Jones and Joan Soranno as guest critics)
Graduate Students: Joseph Barrick, Devon Brophy, Ariadne Cerritelli, Kathleen Crowle, Megan Gregory, Shawandra Herry, Matthew Hoffman, Sina Moayedi, Ugo Nnebue, Emily O'Loughlin, Lisa Passeri, and Madeline Wentzell. Photograph by Julio Bermudez.

HER HOME
Statement of Spiritual Direction

EMILY O'LOUGHLIN | MEGAN GREGORY

Before one can foster spirituality, they must first take care of their own basic needs. To want to get closer to God or a higher power, one must feel safe and cared for with the basic human necessities.

This space is therefore for the socially under-served, women, and the homeless. We have created a shelter for women, including a wom-en's reproductive health center. Starting from the bottom, this building addresses each of the tiers of the Maslow's Pyramid of Needs. We want women, homeless, single parents, or those that need a little extra help, to have a sanctuary.

Our project is about fostering spirituality through connections. This building encourages community while also offering a safe space for women in need. There is a fundamental human need to connect to others, and sometimes, a higher power. By reestablishing a link to society and the surrounding community, we give these women an opportunity to feel whole again. Spir-ituality and self-actualization are thus facilitated by supporting their basic physiological needs and security.

The communal and public spaces are located on the east side of the building. These spaces can begin to reconnect women to daily life, while also giving assistance.

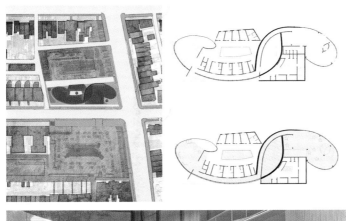

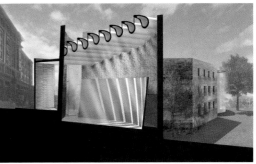

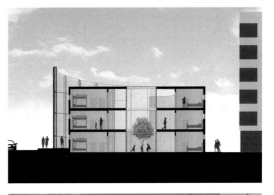

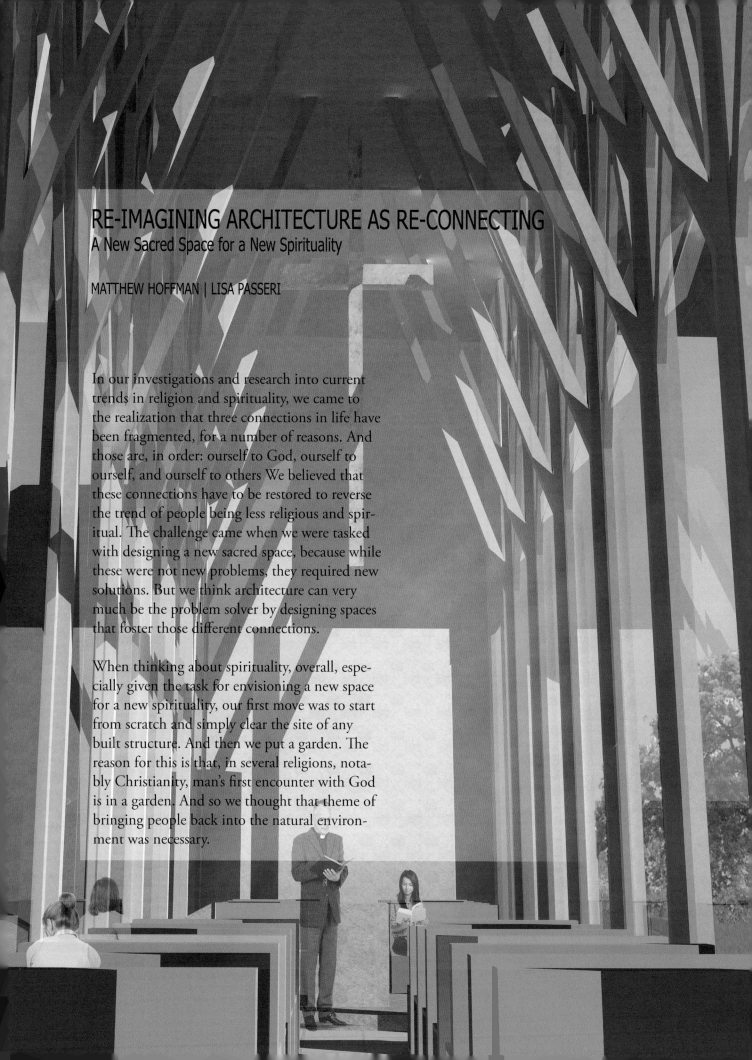

RE-IMAGINING ARCHITECTURE AS RE-CONNECTING
A New Sacred Space for a New Spirituality

MATTHEW HOFFMAN | LISA PASSERI

In our investigations and research into current trends in religion and spirituality, we came to the realization that three connections in life have been fragmented, for a number of reasons. And those are, in order: ourself to God, ourself to ourself, and ourself to others We believed that these connections have to be restored to reverse the trend of people being less religious and spiritual. The challenge came when we were tasked with designing a new sacred space, because while these were not new problems, they required new solutions. But we think architecture can very much be the problem solver by designing spaces that foster those different connections.

When thinking about spirituality, overall, especially given the task for envisioning a new space for a new spirituality, our first move was to start from scratch and simply clear the site of any built structure. And then we put a garden. The reason for this is that, in several religions, notably Christianity, man's first encounter with God is in a garden. And so we thought that theme of bringing people back into the natural environment was necessary.

MAIN FLOOR PLAN
SCALE 1/8" = 1'-0"

HOUSE OF ALL

PETWORTH, WASHINGTON, D.C.

SINA MOAYEDI | UGO NNEBUE

As people are leaving organized religions, and fanatical sects are growing here and there, it becomes pertinent to investigate how a new sacred architecture may help to bring today's society back to faith and belief. Our project is an attempt to architecturally address this problem. Contemporary sacred space should not only be a place of worship, where individuals seek the presence and intervention of the divine, but also where to strengthen the ties and relationship between people. It should serve as a gathering point, and a place that encourages communication and community. We understand the sacred as always involving an act of love, which is physically manifested by giving and receiving. Human beings receive from one another and also give out to one another. This giving and receiving usually creates a ripple effect where we get and, in turn, give thanks by giving back. When it comes to our relationship with the divine, it is us who receive and the divine who is always the ultimate giver. The form of our project is an effort to represent this giving and receiving interaction among people and also between God and humanity. Structural supports for the ramps have become points along the ramp to pause, meditate and appreciate a deity. The bigger ramp journey terminates on to the roof top garden where one can appreciate sunrise. Contemplation and zen gardens in the rear are open for community use and offer a place of quiet and appreciation of nature.

Figure 8-9. Larkin Architect Limited. St. Gabriel's Passionist Parish Church in Toronto — Canada. Photograph by Roberto Chiotti.

SEARCHING FOR A NEW SACRED SPACE
MICHAEL J. CROSBIE

Since its founding over a decade ago, the Walton Critic Studio has presented a sterling opportunity for students, architects, and faculty to explore the contours of sacred space. This is particularly relevant today because the definition of sacred space is in a great state of flux. Thus, the Walton Studio has the potential to be a forum of questioning what sacred space is right now, and how sacred space speaks to both students and the architecture discipline.

During my residence as the 2015 Walton Critic, in collaboration with CUA Professor Julio Bermudez, I led a studio considering this very topic. We asked students about how sacred space is changing, and how we might define it in a new chapter in history. This new chapter is seeing great upheavals in organized religion about what sacred space is, what its potential can be. At the same time, it appears that we are in a time of great questioning about sacred space and its definition. Many of these questions are directed at the essence of being human and being spiritual, questions that have been pondered for millennia.

EXPLORING QUESTIONS THROUGH DESIGN

Over the past few decades, particularly in the West, the concept of sacred space as a setting for the rituals of organized religion has been changing, some might even say radically transforming. Surveys by such esteemed groups as Pew Research and the Trinity College Survey on Religious Identity have shown a precipitous drop in people who belong to organized religions, particularly in the Christian and Jewish faiths and among those under 35. Membership in mainline faith traditions has and continues to decline. Today the largest single segment of the population in the U.S. describes itself as "Nones": affiliated with no organized religious group. People of all ages are turning away from organized religion, but not all of them are choosing to be atheists. Rather, they are looking for a more genuine, personal experience of the spiritual in their lives.

More people today describe themselves as "SBNR": spiritual but not religious. They are suspicious of the institutional power of all religions, no matter what the faith tradition. And they are searching for an expression of that spirituality. The idea that you need a building or a space as the place to practice your religion or to be spiritual is being questioned. What does it mean for religious architecture and sacred space when you ask these questions: Do we need a building at all in order to be religious, to be spiritual, to practice our beliefs? Does the changing nature of how we identify ourselves as spiritual open a new realm of what a sacred space can be? Is there a future for religious architecture?

These are some of the questions that we were eager to explore in the 2015 Walton Studio. The studio's dozen graduate students were invited to learn about the shifting landscape of spirituality taking place in the U.S. and abroad, and to reflect on what it means for the future of sacred space. In the first part of the studio we shared statistical data on people's changing attitudes toward organized religion, how these changes are expressed in personal ideas concerning spirituality, and the effect that these social shifts might be having on the creation of sacred space. In the context of these cultural developments we included two other factors: the connection between spirituality and sustainability (seeing the stewardship of the Earth as an element of belief, expressed by Pope Francis in his encyclical, *Laudato Si*), and the urban concentration of the world's population. This social and intellectual context were prompts for the students to design two studio projects: a quick sketch problem dealing with the concept of "situational" sacred space; and a longer, multi-month design problem about the creation of a sacred place outside of the conventional notions of a "religious" building. Both design problems were set within an evolving, thriving urban neighborhood. This chapter focuses on the larger project.

We provided the students with a range of readings on these topics (a partial list is found in the bibliography at the end of this article): the shifting landscape of spirituality; ideas about "situational" and "substantive" sacred space; demographic changes in organized religion; the place of the city as the context for sacred space; the creation of "safe places" for exploring one's spirituality beyond the walls of religious buildings; the notion of living "in cathedral" within a city. It was noted that many of the changes in spiritual belief are being led by Millennials, those between the ages of 18 and 34, the demographic that included most of the studio's students. We asked the students to reflect upon their own experiences regarding organized religion, the contours of their own spiritual lives, and the spiritual "search" that they might be engaged in. We told the students to consider the studio itself as a "safe place" where they could present their views on religion and spirituality. Working

in teams, the students made short presentations reflecting on the readings, their own beliefs, and how architecture might respond to these new circumstances. How might they address new attitudes about belief that are being led by their own generation, and how could they explore a realm of design that has few architectural precedents to give form to these new frontiers of belief?

The student presentations regarding their reflections on the reading material and their own attitudes about spirituality revealed a willingness to greatly broaden the realm of the sacred. Students found new opportunities to define the sacred in such activities as musical performance; in moving their bodies through space through the medium of dance; in digitally connecting with people and events around the globe; in sharing with and caring for other human beings by "giving and receiving"; in the creation of a safe place for women who are victims of domestic violence; in landscape and nature serving as a setting for contemplation, reflection, and celebration; in providing support to those seeking to strengthen their bodies and spirits through nutrition and exercise. What these presentations revealed to us studio critics is that we needed to carefully consider how to define the design problem we were to assign. Conventional notions of sacred place and space would not do.

DEFINING NEW SACRED PLACE

The students' wide range of attitudes about what the sacred might be and how architecture could respond to it prompted us to make the design assignment more fluid than a typical program list of required spaces with certain sizes and adjacencies. We identified a site in the Petworth neighborhood of Northwest Washington, D.C., not far from the Catholic University campus. The students' site analysis would include not only the physical neighborhood but also the historical/social/economic changes that this neighbor is experiencing, as shifts in population, property development, and social class change the face of this historically African-American neighborhood. We identified an under-developed site at the northwest corner of Georgia Avenue and Randolph Street. We encouraged close observation of the character of the neighborhood, its people, and its assets, and encouraged students to talk with residents and business operators. We wanted students to note the neighborhood's existing sacred spaces and its potential as a setting for contemporary sacred space. We also encouraged them to pay particular attention to the message of *Laudato Si*, Pope Francis's recent encyclical, about our estrangement from the natural world and the ecological and spiritual consequences of that distancing.

The program for the design problem essentially evolved from the student presentations about the readings we had assigned and their own ideas about where the sacred might be found. The "Petworth Place for Spirit and Wellbeing" should reflect some of the elements of contemporary ideas about spirituality, along with some recognition of traditional sacred spaces. Petworth Place was to be between 25,000 and 40,000 square feet, with a combination of places for the spirit, places to share community, places for outreach, places for creation, places for worship. Then we gave the students a program list of the kinds of spaces/places that they might consider in the design of Petworth Place:

Program List
A place to pray, to leave a prayer and to take a prayer.
A place to serve meals to those in need.
An outdoor space that has some privacy.
A place devoted just to viewing the moon and stars.
A place where young people and old people can share.
A traditional worship space.
A place where items and non-perishable food can be deposited by neighbors for those in need.
A place to cry and grieve a loss.

A program element that is "Your Thing."
A place where one can obtain information and guidance on health and nutrition.
A pub or coffeehouse, with a place for groups to share conversation on spirituality/religion.
A place to slow down and appreciate the wonders of nature.
A place where art can be made, displayed, or performed.
A place to find, experience, and practice silence.
A place to house or attend to those in need
A spiritual home for those feeling spiritually homeless
A place to give or receive.

Figure 8-10. Anonymous. God as Architect/Builder/Geometer/Craftsman, The Frontipiece of Bible Moralisee. Illumination on parchment (circa 1220-1230). Work in the public domain.

students had to address eight spaces/places from the program list: the four bold items were required in every design, and four were chosen by the students. It was up to the designer to decide how much space should be allotted to successfully serve their function. The program element identified as "Your Thing" could be defined as a space that a student was particularly interested in exploring as a new kind of sacred space.

Because this was not a single-use building, but multifaceted in its spaces and functions, it should offer opportunities to design "in cathedral." The term "in cathedral" was coined by author and educator Elizabeth Drescher and explored by Keith Anderson in his book, The Digital Cathedral. "In cathedral" recognizes the sacred in everyday life, in everyday places, the network of relationships among neighbors and even strangers, and the witness of believers beyond the confines of an enclosed sacred space. Petworth Place should be "in cathedral" with the surrounding neighborhood and the people who live there.

Related to this fluid sense of the sacred was sacred space, which students were encouraged to consider. Religion historian Jeanne Halgren Kilde notes that "substantive" sacred space is that in which a divine presence is believed to reside, and which makes the space sacred. This view posits "sacredness" inherent in objects, including buildings. But another orientation sees sacredness as "situational": any place can be sacred or holy depending on the presence, location, and actions of human beings. "Situational" sacred space or place is suggested in Matthew 18:20, in which Christ says: "For where two or three are gathered together in my name, there am I in the midst of them." The verse describes a relational aspect to the sacred among people in community. Petworth Place presented opportunities to design this kind of "situational" sacred space.

THE SEARCH FOR THE SACRED

The search for the sacred through the design studio assignment of Petworth Place resulted in some provocative, challenging schemes. But the design process seemed at times frustrating. We asked the students to take on a design project that had no clearly defined expectations—studio critics as well as students were in the search together, which at times made it difficult to provide guidance through studio critiques and to help the students to move forward. However, the changing nature of sacred space right now is a question without ready answers and no clear solutions. In fact, we as design critics might not be ready to accept the visions of new kinds of sacred places and spaces that students might develop. This became apparent during some of the formal design studio reviews, when questions about what could or should be considered sacred, and architecture's role in defining it, was intensely debated by reviewers and students. We then realized that the 2015 Walton Studio had achieved a measure of success: to broaden, challenge, confront, and consider the fact that a sense of the sacred is not static and unchanging, and that every age needs to ask and try to answer what it is.

Figure 8-11. Joan Soranno,HGA, Bigelow Chapel at the United Theological Seminary of the Twin Cities, New Brighton — Minnesota. Photograph by Joan Soranno.

Figure 8-12. Joan Soranno, HGA, Lakewood Cemetery Garden Mausoleum in Minneapolis — Minnesota. Photograph by Joan Soranno.

DESIGNING EXPERIENCES: RITUAL, NARRATIVE, AND EMBODIMENT

ELIANA BORMIDA   2014 WALTON CRITIC

DESIGNING EXPERIENCES: RITUAL, NARRATIVE, AND EMBODIMENT
2014 Walton Studio
Walton Critic: Eliana Bórmida

STUDIO TOPIC

The 2014 Walton Studio inquired about the relationships between nature, everyday life, and spirituality as foundations of architecture. This translated into the experiential consideration of daily rituals and locality (culture, history, landscape). Narrative and storytelling were central tools to approach the site, programmatic responses, the poetics of space and form, and tectonic development. The design class invited a contemplative exploration and discernment of embodied, emotional, social, and intellectual experiences. These intentions guided the design of a 25,000 square feet *Spiritual Retreat in Nature* located in the Shenandoah mountains of Northern Virginia. From the beginning, architect Eliana Bórmida instructed students to avoid 'designing objects' or 'housing functions.' Instead, the task was to design experiences so that the building's inhabitants would awaken from their unconscious slumber into existential awareness. Once there, spiritual sensibility, questioning and realization would naturally follow.

Bórmida kicked off the design process by asking students to develop the retreat's program through a personal, in-depth experiential study of six fundamental daily rituals: awakening, cleansing, nourishment, prayer/meditation, socializing, and sleeping. This work continued over the following week by students attentively noticing their routine activities. The result was

that conventional programmatic responses were revealed in all their stereotypical superficiality. More significantly, students understood the potential that each habit has to reveal their life, nature, and spirit. Bórmida constantly reminded the studio how today's culture has generated an unbalanced relationship between nature and us. But she was quick to point out that while going back to the wilderness facilitates such realignment, paying attention to the deep forces governing our bodies, hearts and spirit already moves us in that direction.

It was fascinating to observe the whole studio adopting a temporal, existential, and ultimately spiritual position toward daily life and nature through this architectural inquiry. Design became assisting, framing, encouraging, and/or celebrating human life in the midst of nature. Experiential simulations, empathy, listening, and authenticity became essential tools to make and critique architectural decisions. This meant the use of graphic and modeling tools facilitating the study and design of experiences such as sketching, storyboards and keyframes, digital animation, gestural models, video capture, and more. In other words, the design process took a decisively bottom-up approach that considered larger compositional, conceptual, and planning issues afterwards.

Figure 9-2. Gregory and Wallace explaining their project to Bórmida.

Figure 9-3. Eliana Bórmida responding to Gregory and Wallace presentation.

Figure 9-4. Eliana Bórmida reviewing the design work of Claudia Jean.

Figure 9-5. Eliana Bórmida in a desk crit with Silvia Ivanova.

Figure 9-6. Eliana Bórmida listening to Emily O'Loughlin during a desk crit.

Figure 9-7. Eliana Bórmida lecturing at the Embassy of Argentina.

Figure 9-8. *Faculty:* Eliana Bórmida, Julio Bermudez, and Matthew Geiss.
Graduate Students: John Allen, Megan Gregory, Silvia Ivanova, Claudia Jean, Sina Moayedi, Ugo Nnebue, Emily O'Loughlin, Ayman Sheshtawy, and Victoria Wallace.
Undergraduate students: Peter Alcivar, Joe Binck, Matt Dougherty, Mike Egnor, Tim FIco, Kelly Foley, Ryan Hall, Daniel Hinchcliff, Michael Klucsik, Isabel Lopez, Mariah Maloy, Narmeen Marafi, Juan Munoz, Miguel Novillo, and Alba Quintanilla.
Photograph by Julio Bermudez.

A RETREAT IN NATURE
SHENANDOAH NATIONAL PARK, VIRGINIA

CLAUDIA JEAN

The retreat focuses on creating a healthy balance of mind, body and spirit. This is achieved through a diverse program that promotes awareness of the senses as you interact with nature: touch, sight, hearing, smell and taste. Throughout the retreat, there are spaces for the visitor to practice meditation and mindfulness, connecting directly with the elements: earth, water, fire and air. A lap pool and a yoga studio help encourage physical movement and strengthen the mind-body connection. A kitchen with fresh produce and hanging nest-like seating activates the sense of taste and promote mindful eating. A sauna and fireplace allow for individual or communal moments of reflection. A long, linear bridge hovering above the trees provides a platform for a walking meditation which activates the sense of sight and touch with the wind and the surrounding landscape. Through a deep study of phenomenological concepts in architectural design, we were able to develop a unique and memorable encounter through an impact on the human senses, which resulted in this floating retreat in the Shenandoah Valley.

REBIRTH, RENEW, REVIVE

SHENANDOAH NATIONAL PARK, VIRGINIA

MEGAN GREGORY | VICTORIA WALLACE

We began our design process by first identifying our goal for our retreat center; a place that would renew and refresh the visitor. We had focused on trying to understand the fundamentals of experiential design – how designing for certain stimuli can heighten spatial experience. We used this knowledge to design a space where architecture responded to a curated sensory-based daily ritual. With the given site of the Shenandoah Valley, we chose a location that was far from the only access road, and close to a level point of the Piney River. The visitor first began their retreat by journeying away from their car and finding an immersion in the sights, smells, and sounds of the forest as they trekked to the entry point. Upon arrival, the visitor passes through a heavy stone façade to have a clear view of the spaces that house their daily routines: stone-enclosed individual rooms surrounding a lush flower-filled courtyard, a minimal, glass-enclosed pool house that overlooks the Piney River, and on the other side of the river - seen through the pool house - a dining hall and small chapel/meditation space. Traversing between each of these spaces forms the visitor's daily ritual, but crossing over the Piney River serves to symbolically cleanse and renew visitors before coming together for evening meals and meditation. Heavy natural materials, minimal fenestration, and expansive skylights are incorporated to appeal to the senses and view of the dramatic natural surroundings.

TRANSFORMATION IN THE CROSSING

REBIRTH, RENEW, REVIVE
SHENANDOAH NATIONAL PARK, VIRGINIA

AYMAN SHESHTAWY

The soul is our real Self, which has become dormant with our everyday life. We have to awaken it, through feeding our body and brain. Only then, can we get to know what the soul is. If we know the soul, if we are enlightened, if we know the connection with our nature, we are always right there. We were never born, we are only reborn and then will never die. The concept for the awakening is rooted in the sacred journey of rituals, namely the pilgrimage to Mecca. The pilgrimage begins with the start at holy Mecca, then prayers at Arafat, sleeping at Muzdalifah, stoning evil (Jamarat), and finally returning to Mecca after being reborn through the pilgrimage process. The building is located deep into the woods of the Shenandoah National Park. In order to access the entrance, the user must stop at 4 markers along the path, each speaking to a different activity. Following similar steps, this building brings the user through 5 distinct spaces. Finding Soul, Feeding Mind, Feeding Body, and Rebirth. Each step of the building focuses on separate stimuli for the mind, body, and soul.

SITE MAP

FINDING
SOUL

Garden of
heaven Chapel

FEEDING
MIND

Library
yoga
Aroma
therapy

FEEDING
BODY

Kitchen
Dining

REBIRTH

Housing
Cleansing
Sleeping
Bathing

MAIN FLOOR PLAN   SCALE 1/16"=1'-0"

SECOND FLOOR PLAN   SCALE 1/16"=1'-0"

SLEEPING EXPERIENCE

BATHING EXPERIENCE

FEEDING BODY AND MIND

SECTION   SCALE 1/16"=1'-0"

Figure 9-9. Bórmida & Yanzón Arquitectos, Interior of the Diamandes Winery in Tunuyán — Mendoza, Argentina. Photograph by Bórmida & Yanzón Arquitectos.

ARCHITECTURE AS EXPERIENCE
ELIANA BÓRMIDA

This article reflects on the role of architecture as experience. Firstly, I consider the professional practice that led my office to steer towards this fundamental phenomenological understanding, explaining how our design paradigms shifted, distinct criteria and value systems emerged, and new working methodologies were developed and tested. In the second section of this essay I theorize on experiential architecture, focusing on basic aspects derived from applying such a design approach. Finally, practical recommendations are offered to direct the design process toward generating an experiential architecture. It was this design philosophy and methodology of architecture as experience that I taught in the Walton Studio I led in 2014.

WINE ARCHITECTURE AND EXPERIENCE
Our office has been developing projects for the wine industry for 20 years. Everything started when wineries in Mendoza decided to open their doors to the public and become places to visit, socialize, and tell stories. Wine needed to recover its appeal, lost at that time to the ferocious competition of other beverages which, supported by a strong marketing campaign, created imaginary stimulants and strong, contagious magnets for the overall consumer population. At the end of the 1990s, we were charged with a series of winery projects devoted to make wine and to attract the public toward wine. Pioneer entrepreneurs

were interested in opening their production plants to wine tasting in situ and to intentionally communicate their brands' quality and identity. There were not many precedents in Argentina for building architectures of wine aimed at attracting, communicating, gaining customer loyalty, and entertaining. In those days, wineries were conceived as wine factories, focused on quantity, technology, and engineering.

The first commissions came because our office was known for understanding the region's cultural heritage, history, architecture, and landscape. These initial jobs were ephemeral and relatively trivial but taught us invaluable lessons on the sociability of wine. They involved designing the settings for the meetings of entrepreneurs, journalists, and trend setters, where wine was sometimes the great protagonist and, on other occasions, an indirect host still supporting people's experiences albeit from the backstage. It was particularly illuminating to create those first spaces that were 'only' atmospheres to stimulate an exciting social experience of wine. We were able to successfully design those environments by the careful use of the most basic resources. For example, comfort and intimacy were attained by modulating the intensity of light, sounds, and a few other sensory stimuli. The result was magical moments of empathy, communication and enjoyment that highlighted the values of wine. Later on we received commissions to remodel existing wineries in order to update them to new wine making techniques and visiting tours, generally geared to journalists. When the first significant project arrived, we were already clear on the importance of creating atmospheres through the use of the senses and the design of visit itineraries. We thus started to implement a design approach that was quite different from the ordinary. The method unfolded out of simple but poignant questions such as this: was the architectural goal to create productive, rational, and efficient spaces in which to insert visitors? Was the building only about drinking, entertaining, and shopping? We didn't think that this was the whole story. Rather, we saw our design task as going one step further: to tell the story of wine, to give it its value and place so that it could be felt without the need for words, just through the pure experience of its architecture.

A first paradigm proved revealing: modern wine making declares that wine is born out of good soil and taking great care of the grape. This led us to become interested in open spaces and nature, to understand the landscape of viticulture as inseparable from wine architecture and to integrate nature and architecture in projects that value both. At the same time, we discovered that interior spaces where wine is elaborated are rich in certain sensory qualities: shape and dimensions, cool temperature, darkness, silence, varied materials, typical equipment, aromas, and sounds. We also discovered that the wine making process is done through different spaces that allow for the creation of sequential circuits with great architectural potential.

Besides becoming aware of the values related to the physical conditions of spaces, we also reflected on the immaterial values of wine; about its meanings and associations that encompass different spaces and scales such as intimacy, family and friends, sociability, parties, representations, and rituals. Finally, we reflected on the realms of genealogy and affiliation, which make wine enter the great world of cultural history. It is here where wine reveals itself as a fine cultural asset on its own and at the same time as social and transcendental. It is here where wine appears in its ineffable dimension.

CONCEPTS ABOUT EXPERIENTIAL ARCHITECTURE

The use of architectural experience to communicate programmatic meaning was still a research topic in academia in the 1990s. Without even knowing it, this is what we were doing then while working in wine architecture. The keys to this mode of designing were centered in the architectural utilization of the senses and mnemonic associations, both important factors in the mechanisms of perception. As architects, we had to learn how to express the values and qualities of the region where the wineries were located since the relationship between brands and their geographic region was important when communicating a winery's identity and authenticity. In this regard, we determined that there were four essential factors to be considered in Mendoza: the Andes, the desert, the pure melting water from the high peaks, and the irrigated oasis. These elements of the natural landscape became the key to the design of our exterior spaces. We associated them to particular experiences of scale, shapes, dimensions, elements, materials, colors, aromas, textures, sounds, and memories. Their interaction holistically stimulates human perception and makes us feel the unique natural personality of the place, its genius-loci.

In the same way, the interior spaces of wineries have their own general qualities, derived from oenological requirements such as asepsis, temperature and sun light control, space dimensions related to wine barrel positions, and the sequence required for the wine making process. There are noisy areas and others in absolute silence, some busy with human labor and others monotonous and mechanical. While some are technically interesting, others can awaken poetic feelings and romantic evocations. Still respecting oenological needs, interior spaces allow for the design of an experiential architecture that contributes to telling the story of wine and also expresses the intrinsic values of the architectural work.

FINDINGS ABOUT EXPERIENTIAL ARCHITECTURE

In experiential architecture, it is key to focus on the design of space as experience. This asks us to focus and understand the human body in space, not only in terms of scale and function, but also in relation to a sensitive and emotional subject that perceives, reacts, feels, evokes, and creates their own version, their own image of the reality they experience. And in order to do this,

The architect must be aware of their own sensitive body in the space they design. This is not usually taught in architecture schools that are more interested in the creation of architectural objects. However, one goal does not exclude the other. They are complementary and, in many cases indispensable. The architect ought to help the users, visitors, and inhabitants of a building to become aware that they themselves are subjects of the architectural space; they are part of the architectural narrative. This means to design for people that move in the space and interact with the stimuli that the architect proposes in their work. These stimuli (or architectural properties) are incitements or provocations to react to. And although each individual will have their own way to act, it is also true that we all tend to respond following a general pattern. This ability to awaken particular reactions in people that experience architecture is a critical value to add to the consideration of the work itself, both in terms of its intrinsic architectural attributes and its communication power.

In my opinion, it is imperative to define the character and atmosphere of architecture during the conceptual stage of the project. This allows us to direct the design process toward generating an architectural identity that is immediately experienced as authentic and does not need to be figured out intellectually. While this may disappoint some professionals who get enjoyment out of the critical analysis of buildings, it is clear to me that the ultimate dimension of architecture transcends the intellectual.

When the character of the work is envisioned beforehand by the designing architect, it stimulates aspirations and suggestions that open remarkable creative opportunities without losing focus. In this process, evocations, memories, tastes, preferences, relations as well as images, feelings, and emotions emerge out of the subjectivity of the designer. The creative moment when the intuition of what is to be achieved is reached is very intense. Then the path to the "design-how" is open. This "design-how" uses architectural qualities but it is not a rigid and infallible mechanism of translation from the intuitive to the concrete. There are no recipes. There is only research, study, and design work. After applying this method in wine architecture for over two decades, I am happy to share some general findings. The selection of experiential properties to incorporate in a project is an open process with multiple variables. Some of them come from external conditions and may be either inescapable or fairly manageable, as is the case of local climate or the building site. Other architectural properties come from the specific building program, local construction traditions, or the culture of the place. But a large number comes from the architect's own subjectivity or the interaction of intersubjectivities when there is a working team.

At any rate, these experiential stimuli act as a guide or "trigger" of ideas in the design process. Although the rational and poetic qualities appear mixed at the beginning, all of them must be identified so as to be incorporated and be part, at the appropriate time, in the design decision making process. For this reason and in order to be useful, it is necessary to organize the group of architectural properties systematically and relate them to the experience of a subject that moves in space. In our office, we generally employ the following categories in this order:

- Scale
- Movement (linear, labyrinthine, centrifugal/centripetal, aleatory…)
- Spatial sequence (fluency, diaphragm, articulation, perspective…)
- Stimuli:
  - Light and shadow: discover materials, colors, brightness, shapes, textures, movements, dimensions, give orientation to space.
  - Sounds: give orientation to space, suggest distances, denote materials and elements, stimulate associations.
  - Smells: give orientation to space, suggest distances, stimulate associations
  - Touch: gives orientation in the space and reveals textures, shapes, dimensions, temperatures, breeze.
  - Haptics: creates awareness of our own body situated in the space, parts of our body, of movement, weight, the context surrounding us, emotions we feel through physical reactions (in the skin, breathing, heartbeat, stomach).

This guide has the sole practical purpose of enabling experiential awareness during the design process, especially when we do not have the habit of designing in this way or when working in teams that are not homogeneous and/or involve several disciplines.

The understanding of architecture as experience comprises two complementary paths. On the one hand, the designer should be open to broader methodological and design horizons that incorporate the building user as a sensory and emotional subject who is going to construct their own perception of the work, invariably utilizing three instruments of their own: reason, sensations, and emotions. On the other hand, it is fundamental to help the layperson (i.e., the real recipient of architecture) to access and manage these three instruments so that they enjoy the intrinsic qualities of architecture while being receptive to its semiotic content. Without doubt,

designing architecture as experience would require new critical reflections in architectural education regarding its curricular and pedagogic implications.

Figure 9-10. Bórmida & Yanzón Arquitectos, courtyard of the visiting center, Salentein Winery in Tunuyán — Mendoza, Argentina. Photograph by Bórmida & Yanzón Arquitectos.

Figure 9-11. Bórmida & Yanzón Arquitectos, central courtyard of the visiting center, Salentein Winery in Tunuyán — Mendoza, Argentina. Photograph by Bórmida & Yanzón Arquitectos.

Figure 9-12. Bórmida & Yanzón Arquitectos, entry way to the visitor center (the Killka), Salentein Winery in Tunuyán — Mendoza, Argentina. Photograph by Bórmida & Yanzón Arquitectos.

Figure 9-13. Bórmida & Yanzón Arquitectos, main public entry to Séptima Winery in Luján de Cuyo — Mendoza, Argentina. Photograph by Bórmida & Yanzón Arquitectos

CONTEMPLATIVE AND NON-EGOTISTICAL IMPROVISATION

CLAUDIO SILVESTRIN   2013 WALTON CRITIC

CONTEMPLATIVE AND NON-EGOTISTICAL IMPROVISATION
2013 Walton Studio
Walton Critic: Claudio Silvestrin

STUDIO TOPIC

Guided by architect Claudio Silvestrin, the 2013 Walton Studio approached the design process as an intuition-building, contemplative, and non-egotistical method for questioning, critiquing, and offering essential architectural solutions to contemporary society. This stance was inspired by the fact that new approaches are necessary to resolve today's completely novel challenges, and the need for students to gain confidence in their instinctive (but not selfish) design capabilities that have been often repressed or unacknowledged by formal professional education. Additionally, pedagogic studies have shown that creativity, new ideas, and inspiration are facilitated by letting go of preconceptions, rationality, and criticism. Surrealist automatism, lateral thinking, jazz improvisation, meditation, and 'flow' states describe conditions in which our ordinary mind is put in parenthesis so that we may operate more attentively, spontaneously, and successfully. In order to prepare to work with Silvestrin, students were asked to engage in a series of readings, discussions, and studies. Once on campus, Silvestrin launched the studio with a succession of three design improvisations in response to provocative aphorisms — a signature of his architectural approach[4]: a first "take" had to be produced in 45 minutes time; a second expression was to follow within the next 45 hours; and a third and final take 45 hours later. By requiring nearly immediate response to complex problems, students were forced to surrender their normal ways of thinking and doing, and adopt a more open and experimental approach. This jump-start into design action proved to be an elightnening and useful way to immediately get to the task at hand: the design of one of three projects in Washington DC: *a National Immigration Museum on the Mall, a Homeless Shelter in Chinatown, and a Nursery/Kindergarten in Downtown.* The premise for the museum project was to consider the architectural and cultural implications of a very large building dedicated to a quintessentially (but usually insufficiently told) American story, in a space that many deem sacred like the National Mall. The Homeless Shelter project aimed to support the multi-functional needs of the homeless and other at-risk persons. The Nursery/Kindergarten project addressed the educational needs of young learners in the most comprehensive way through enlightened and thoughtful design strategies. Despite the obvious differences among these projects, students were instructed to design buildings that *"uplift our spirit and prevent the weight of materialism from crushing us ... to create temples for the spirit and silence."* Architect Silvestrin demanded high levels of clarity and simplicity in the architectural ideas and design as well as in how such work was developed, executed, and communicated.

Figure 10-3. Silvestrin in a desk crit with Lillian Heryak and Lisa Nucera.

Figure 10-4. Silvestrin checking the work of Marisa Aschettino and Erica Donnelly.

Figure 10-2. Claudio Silvestrin examining the design proposal of Emily O'Loughlin.

Figure 10-5. Silvestrin teaching while Toni Lem works in the foreground.

Figure 10-6. Interim review of students' work by Silvestrin and faculty.

Figure 10-7. *Faculty:* Claudio Silvestrin, Julio Bermudez, and Randall Ott.
Graduate Students: John Allen, Marisa Aschettino, Erica Donnelly, Amirali Ebadi, Lillian Heryak, Eric Hofman, Christopher Motley, Robin Munoz Valencia, Lisa Nucera, Tomi Lem, Christine Parisi, Ana Roman Andrino, Matthew Schmalzel, and Kristen Weller.
Undergraduate Students: Jorge Cornet, Nicholas Darin, Christopher Derks, Pamela Eggerton, Christie Melgar, Emily O'Loughlin, Timothy Rutten, Adam Schroth, and Chris Urban. Photograph by Julio Bermudez.

REVEALING AMERICAN ROOTS
IMMIGRATION MUSEUM

MARISA ASCHETTINO | ERICA DONNELLY

Immigration is the foundation of America. The museum was designed to embrace this concept. It is meant to lift back the earth and reveal the different cultures that make up this nation. The museum burst out of the land, lifting up towards the light, to symbolize the immigrants' hopeful journey.

The building program is organized in a system of layers, similar to layers of dirt and soil that make up the earth's foundation. After entering the building, a series of elevators take you to the bottom most level. This is where the museum's 'Origin Exploration Gallery' is located. From there, a center circulation and exhibition ramp known as 'The Walk of Memories' brings you back to ground level, where a cafe and museum shop are located.

The interactive gallery is the main feature of the museum. It is a place where one can discover their individual origins in the United States of America. The museum works off a private data base that is continuously growing. Visitor immigrants are able to input their personal experiences into the database to share their stories with other visitors. You can then print the stories of your American roots to display throughout the museum.

CULMINATION OF COMMONALITY
IMMIGRATION MUSEUM

CHRIS MOTLEY | KRISTEN WELLER

Our task was to create an architecture that channels the spirit and fortitude of those who leave all they know behind them, yearning to reach the fullest human potential. To always strive for a better life, disrupt the given circumstances, and become a unique piece of the American Mosaic. Allowing the hope of the future to guide the way and the shadows of the past to fall behind. A place to facilitate an understanding of United States policies with regard to immigration and how these policies shape the past, present, and future. An interactive, democratic space where education and contribution can occur; a Living Museum.

SITE PLAN

LEVEL 1

LEVEL 1

DEPTHS OF DISCOVERY
IMMIGRATION MUSEUM

ERIC HOFMANN | MATTHEW SCHMALZEL

The design for a National Museum of Immigration seeks to reconcile two distinct, yet related, experiences. The first is that of the immigrant in history. The progression from the known, through the depths of uncertainty, to a life in a new place. The second is the experience of the visitor who is seeking knowledge of the past. The visitor too must descend from what is obvious, through the many layers of stories of the immigrant experience before reaching a moment of enlightenment. The brief description above poetically describes the tension between individual and communal experience as well as between despair and hope. These are the forces that gave form to this design. The museum is largely subterranean, and it is experienced through a meditative descent through the myriad layers of the history of immigration to the United States of America. Beginning in a gallery devoted to contemporary issues of immigration, visitors descend through a series of spaces that depict stories and artifacts from various time periods, as the gently sloping floor spirals into the earth. The galleries are undefined rooms, walls that show the layers of time with their stone interrupt and wander through the sloping exhibit spaces. After journeying through the depths of discovery, the visitor's experience ends in the lowest level of the open air courtyard. This is a place for meditation on the idealistic unity of the American people and on the sacrifices made by those who have journeyed seeking a better life.

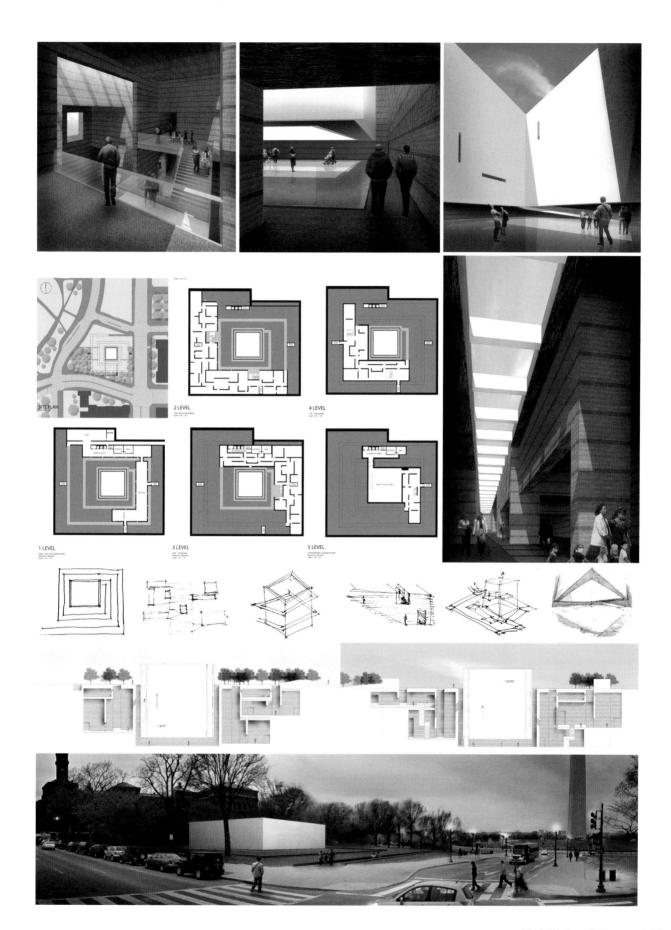

Figure 10-8. Claudio Silvestrin Architects, Neuendorf Villa in Majorca —
Spain. Photograph by Claudio Silvestrin Architects

SPIRITUALITY AND DESIGNING A SACRED SPACE
CLAUDIO SILVESTRIN

As far as I am concerned, the co-creation of sacred places in which to feel the presence and the force of the divine is the highest measure of our human evolution. This responsibility is immense. The design of skyscrapers, airports, resorts, and housing mainly satisfies our material-self and our ego. But the design of sacred spaces feeds our spiritual-hunger and invites our higher-being to come forth.

From a materialistic point of view, designing a sacred building may seem equivalent to working on a villa or a shopping mall. But such understanding is fundamentally flawed. I recall a couple of years ago visiting a new chapel in Europe designed by a most prestigious architect. I was enthusiastic and drove for miles and miles to reach its remote location only to be disappointed. All that was offered to me by this building was the sight of good design. There was no spiritual presence and no sacred impression afforded by what should have been a holy construction. One thing is for a work of architecture to be admired for its outstanding design quality but another thing is to manifest the Divine. When design comes first the Divine spirit cannot feel welcome. When design comes first, it creates an ego-trip and fuels the dominance of materiality, idolatry, wealth and power.

WHAT DO WE MEAN BY 'SPIRITUALITY'?

Certainly, we should not confuse spirituality with religion. Spiritual knowledge does not belong to any religion. Religion is built on and depends on tradition in the form of an institution, temple, church, cult or sect (ritual, scriptures, law, dogma, attachments and convictions that, if improperly interpreted, may lead to fanaticism). Spirituality is immaterial vibration, pure and uncorrupted ethereal thought. Spirituality is the energy of the invisible and of the unseeable beings alive in our inner self as well as in the cosmos but (potentially) accessible via our heart, feelings and esoteric knowledge. By allowing us to directly perceive the transcendent invisible in the immanent visible, spirituality encourages us to question what our raw perception can merely see. Going beyond our physical and intellectual limits opens us to faith, to believe and to experience the thirst of spiritual knowledge. It is here where we are free and detached from intellectual and materialistic dogma, able to contemplate and build a cathedral in our inner self. It is here where we understand why Jesus Christ says *"come to me and you shall see"* and not *"see me first and then come to me."*

Saint Paul stressed the importance of being capable of "discerning the spirits," the most recognizable to us being the Holy Spirit, although you may call this what you wish: the manifestation of the Divine, the Primordial Sound, the Eternal, the life-Creator or God. But there are other spirits too, some of which are spirits of darkness, hence the importance of discernment.

In the Gospel, the word 'spirit' continuously repeats in order to bring home God's message. For example, in Luke 11:24 we read *"when an unclean spirit goes out of someone, it roams through arid regions searching for rest but, finding none, it says, 'I shall return to my home from which I came.'"* In Mark 14:38 we find, *"watch and pray that you may not undergo the test. The spirit is willing but the flesh is weak."* And in John 1:32 and 3:6, *"I saw the Spirit come down like a dove from the sky and remain upon him,"* as well as *"what is born of flesh is flesh and what is born of spirit is spirit."*

It is also in the Gospel that we find Jesus Christ giving us a hint as to how to give a physical home to the Holy Spirit. This would be a place in which our Divine-self or spiritual-self feels awake, attentive, meditative —be it alone or in the company of others. In Luke 19:45-46 we read,

> *Then Jesus entered the temple area* and proceeded to drive out those who were selling things, saying to them, "It is written, 'My house shall be a house of prayer, but you have made it a den of thieves'.*

If we wish to design and build with the true intention to house the Celestial Spirit and be re-united with the Divine, we must be humble and put aside our school teaching, our degrees, our professional habits, and our self-referential ego to start afresh with a new mind. This will allow us to design and build a bridge between Earth and Heaven, divinities and mortals and at the same time, make ourselves feel like we can be both citizens of the material world and the spiritual world.

Spirit cannot be measured. Spirit does not respond to mechanical numbers and calculation but it does respond to quality. We ought to acquire knowledge of sacred geometry from the dawn of humanity when the bond with the Divine was immense and the circle was the

form manifesting the spiritual world. We must harbor understanding of the mysterious gifts of the ground on which to build, knowledge of the golden proportions as well as the divine proportions. We must know the Bovis scale, the ethereal forces of the natural materials, and astronomy as the construction ought to be in alignment with the stars. We must grasp how to create harmony between all the elements of our composition. We need to bring forth the essence and quality of natural light and reveal pure space and its eternal void-ness. The sacredness of water, earth, wind and fire must be communicated and in doing so, express the material beauty when erecting an edifice.

Finally, our heart must be the driving force behind it all. We must think with our heart (something we are not used to) to design and build a sacred place in which the Divine (our spiritual-self and the eternal celestial Holy Spirit) may feel at home.

Figure 10-9. Claudio Silvestrin Architects, Neuendorf Villa in Majorca — Spain. Photograph by Claudio Silvestrin Architects

Figure 10-9. Claudio Silvestrin Architects, Neuendorf Villa De Wec, in front of the Lemanus Lake in Geneva — Switzerland. Rendering by Claudio Silvestrin Architects

BUILDING ESSENTIAL IDEAS

ALBERTO CAMPO BAEZA   2012 WALTON CRITIC

BUILDING ESSENTIAL IDEAS
2012 Walton Studio
Walton Critic: Alberto Campo Baeza

STUDIO TOPIC

Since time immemorial, peoples across Earth have counted on the unfathomable capacity of architecture to envision and build sacred place in order to invoke the presence of God. They have generally achieved it by resorting to very simple spaces, forms, and materials. Architect Alberto Campo Baeza often refers to this historical fact and a short text written by Le Corbusier to illustrate the miraculous possibilities afforded by the simplest architectural geometry: a box.[5] With this vision at heart in the context of his professional work and writings,[6] the 2012 Walton Studio directed students to imagine what a *21st Century Catholic Monastery* could be like. The site chosen for this inquiry was a beautiful lot next to the Potomac River in Northwest Washington DC. The 5,000 square foot building program called for a facility supporting the monastic life and practice of 12 monks. Answering this challenge first demanded students to study precedents: the monastery has always been a key topic in architecture throughout history. Once the lessons of the past were learned, students were to seek design solutions with an attitude of simplicity and beauty that supported and celebrated the monks' daily contemplative practices. Upon arrival and most dramatically, Campo Baeza asked students to produce 20 small scale models in a couple of days. The purpose was to rapidly and holistically respond to the design challenge,

something that proved to be a very successful teaching technique. He advised students to approach the monastery like a city, that is, like a complex organism with cells, chapel, refectory, deambulatory, library, grove and services — each space inviting an unique experience, reflection, and expression. Thus cells were to be felt as existential habitats for one person. The Chapel was where to ponder the temporal, luminous and spatial embodiment of the transcendental; the Refectory where the experience of service, sustenance, and multiple uses is met; the Library where memory and faith entered in conversation, and the Deambulatory and Grove called for an exploration of the relation between architecture and nature. All these parts of the 'city-monastery' had to come together under the auspices of a simple architectural idea that not only provided a sense of unity but also spoke of the plight of monastic life in a new millennium. Campo Baeza taught students that architectural design is building essential ideas; the result of applying intellectual rigor and clarity during a design process informed by form, hand, and geometry as much as by philosophy, faith, and architectural history. He explained that developing fundamental ideas never comes at the cost of beauty. On the contrary, an idea is good if and only if it could be beautifully embodied as architecture.

Figure 11-2. Alberto Campo Baeza giving a desk crit to Christopher Motley. Corey August is in the background.

Image 11-3. Campo Baeza commenting on the project of Vanessa Hostick and Ana Roman Andrino.

Figure 11-4. Munoz Valencia, Parisi, and Bollino presenting their design proposal during the final review.

Figure 11-5. Campo Baeza and Bermudez giving instructions to students after Alberto's first day at CUA.

Figure 11-6. *Faculty:* Alberto Campo Baeza, Julio Bermudez, and Luis Boza.
Graduate Students: Corey August, Michael Bollino, Yousef Bushehri, Patrick Digiovanni, Amirali Ebadi, Vanessa Hostick, Toni Lem, Robin Munoz Valencia, Christine Parisi, Alex Parzych, Brandon Ro, Ana Román Andrino, and Mandira Sareen.
Undergraduate students: Anthony Andrews, Kara Borton, April Despeaux, Samantha Giangiuli, Eric Hofmann, Robert Lang, Christopher Motley, William Sergison, Anthony Stoffella, and Claudia Wainer. Photograph by Julio Bermudez.

TURRIS EBURNA

WASHINGTON, D.C.

Turris Eburna, the Ivory Tower for the Virgin Mary, explores the vertical gradient of dark to light in a monastery. The building is accessible through a path in the forest that connects the monastery to the river and the canal. The living cells of the monks are burrowed into the earth beneath the deep shadows of the trees. As one moves up through the building, toward the chapel, the building becomes progressively lighter moving through space lit by transparent and translucent glass. Finally, one arrives at the chapel, the highest space. The chapel is flooded with light and the white structure melts into the atmosphere. The intent is to bring the occupants closer to heaven, and closer to the God of light.

IMMERSION

WASHINGTON, D.C.

KARA BORTON | CHRIS MOTLEY

When design meets the realm of the sacred, simplicity and restraint become necessary qualities for architecture to embody. The sacred-ness of space emerges. The design of this monastery employs a reductive approach that addresses form, nature, and light with clarity and order to achieve a quiet space for one to reflect. This is a place for 12 monks to go about their ordered life in a simple manner. A stark concrete mass, formed in layers of concrete, sits boldly on the site clearly displaying its presence in contrast to the natural surroundings while subtly making a relationship to the horizontality of the landscape around it. Minimalist attitudes toward the use of geometry, proportion, material, and light interplay with each other to create a space of pensive reflection grounded within the earth and sky. Spaces are placed adjacent to the planar faces of the mass in order to reinforce various experiential and sacred conditions found within the surroundings. Spaces which connect the sacred and the profane are dimly lit, creating an experiential threshold between the two and reinforcing the notion of the struggle in one's inner journey to their final destination.

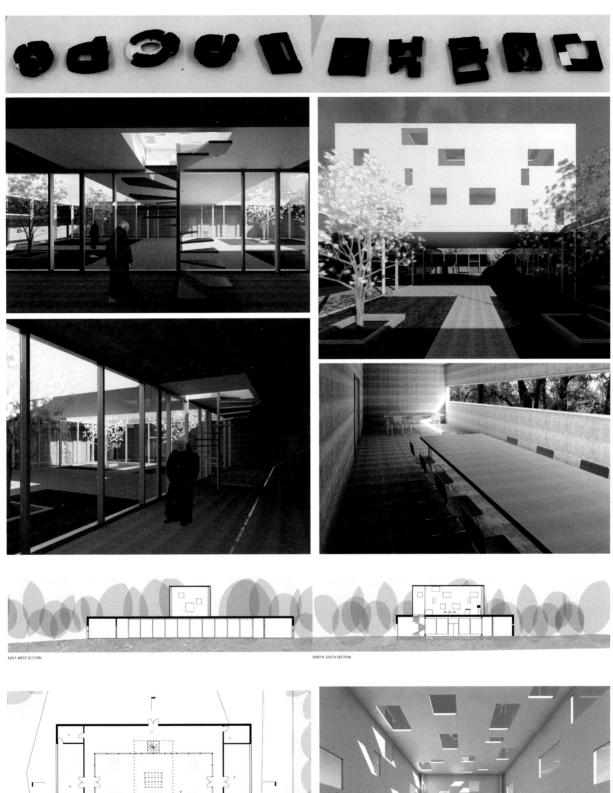

EAST-WEST SECTION

NORTH-SOUTH SECTION

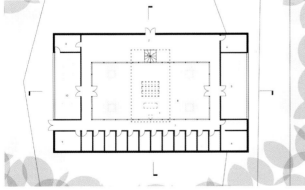

OUR LADY OF THE SKY

WASHINGTON, D.C.

TONI LEM | ALEX PARZYCH

The main architectural idea of the monastery is to have a floating chapel of light expressing the difference between the sacred and the profane. The solid heavy base made out of reinforced concrete contrasts with the light steel frame and skin of the chapel that floats above the court-yard, like a cloud placed delicately upon four white columns. The earthly realm of the base is characterized by its introspective and supporting nature. The short, wide windows in the Chapel are located high along the exterior walls to allow for light to access the room, but minimize dis-tractions. The glazed walls of the courtyard space are related to history, ritual, and Catholic beliefs. They define the open side of a covered walkway defining the traditional monastic ambulato-ry. The whole building is far enough from the Potomac River's edge to provide glimpses of its shimmering waters, while still keeping its inhabi-tants separated from any noise and activity

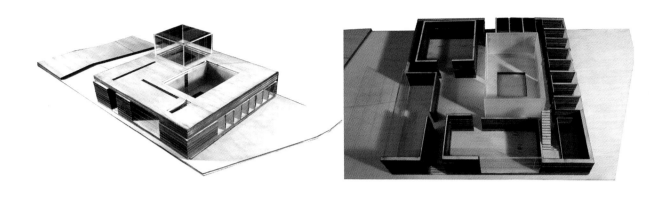

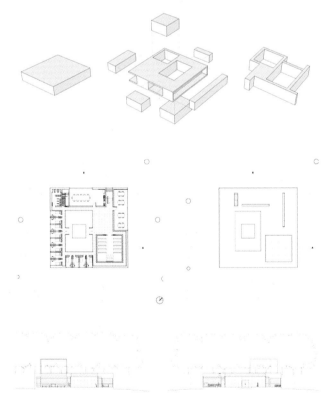

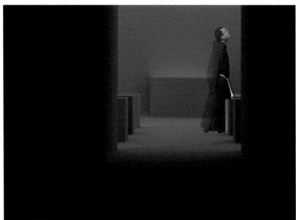

Figure 11-7. Alberto Campo Baeza. Casa Moliner in Zaragoza — Spain. Photograph by Javier Callejas

AT HOME
ALBERTO CAMPO BAEZA

If I should summarize my experience as a Walton Critic at CUA, I must say I was at home.

SEPTEMBER 2012

I warmly remember my first visit to the School of Architecture and Planning at the Catholic University of America. It was in September 2012. Julio Bermudez had invited me to be that year's Walton Critic for a month-long residence and I had said yes. I did not start my course at the ETSAM in Madrid until October so I had enough time to come to Washington DC. I was coming to CUA right after spending my 2011-2012 sabbatical year at Columbia University in New York City, where I had also taken my previous sabbatical leave in 2003-2004. I was acquainted with architectural education in the U.S. I had taught at the University of Pennsylvania with professors Adele Naude Santos and Richard Wesley (1999-2000), Virginia Tech University with professor Donna Robertson (1996), and Kansas State University with professor Matthew Knox (2006), not to mention delivering many one-day lectures at many American universities. I was happily surprised to discover that CUA architecture program was strong, possessing a team of very fine professors and an excellent student body. I perfectly recall the experience. We worked on the theme of a monastery and the design work produced by the studio was outstanding.

OCTOBER 2018

It is good to be back in Washington DC to celebrate the 10th Anniversary of the Walton Critic program at CUA School of Architecture and Planning. This second visit has been a true gift. Some of my students from 2012, like Eric Hoffman or Ana Roman Andrino, have come to the event.

There are five other guests with me. They are architects from all the world that served as Walton Critics during the past decade: Juhani Pallasmaa from Helsinki (Finland), Eliana Bórmida from Mendoza (Argentina), Prem Chandavarkar of Bangalore (India), Michael J. Crosbie of Hartford (CT, U.S.), and Susan Jones from Seattle (WA, U.S.). CUA professor Julio Bermudez officiates as the host of this unique gathering. And we also have with us the Canadian architect Roberto Chiotti and my old friend, CUA professor Carlos Reimers. All great people. I will never forget the conversations and exchanges I had with these accomplished people during those five days at CUA. Can you imagine that instead of talking about architecture, we would be talking about poetry and painting and music? Juhani spoke about the poetry of Herbert and I talked about the writings of Szymborska or Mandelstam, recommended by Kenneth Frampton. And if Eliana referred to Borges, I would answer her with Cartarescu. And I shared with everyone the fable of the giraffe and the mouse, of the great Jerez writer Juan Bonilla.

And then we had that wonderful meal in the cafe of the Philips Collection in downtown Washington after enjoying Renoir's Luncheon of the Boating Party, Matisse's work, and especially the fascinating Mark Rothko Room. I still remember my silent time in front of one of his painting in that room, the one in only red and orange. This is the room that really deserves to be called Rothko Chapel. And then there was another meal at the National Gallery of Art on the National Mall, after paying our respects to Picasso's Family of Saltimbanques (a painting surrounded by other pieces of the great artist), appreciating El Greco's Laocoön, and admiring Rembrandt's self-portrait. And, not unexpectedly, our poets came back and joined us during our meal.

During this visit I also learned more about the work of the other Walton Critics. For example, in his lecture Juhani showed some of his built works which I did not know. They were "few and good" which, as we say in my country, is the best way to seek and attain excellence. I found the buildings of Eliana Bórmida very beautiful: wonderful wineries where the wines are doubtlessly happy. And Prem's architecture gave me access to another, quite impressive world of practice. The five days of meetings, conversations, design crits, and lectures celebrating the 10 years of this world-class Walton Critics program at CUA proved to be truly unique and memorable, all weaved by the skillful hands of Julio Bermudez, a wonderful character. This second visit to CUA reaffirmed my original observation of the excellent architectural education offered by this School of Architecture in the heart of Washington DC. So much so that if I had a child I would send him to study architecture at CUA.

Image 11-8. Alberto Campo Baeza. Between Cathedrals in Cádiz — Spain. Photograph by Javier Callejas.

ON SURRENDER AND UNIVERSALITY
ALBERTO CAMPO BAEZA

ON SURRENDER AND UNIVERSALITY

T.S. Eliot, Ortega y Gasset, and Sota. Plus Gombrich and Melnikov. All creative work, including architecture, requires a degree of self-sacrifice, of depersonalization, if one is to achieve greater universality. Or so are we told by our protagonists: a poet, a philosopher and an architect. And you might well ask, what is the connection between a poet, a philosopher and an architect? What does T.S. Eliot have to do with Ortega y Gasset, and Alejandro de la Sota?

T.S. Eliot (1888-1965) was American by birth, became a British citizen and writes poetry like the angels. Ortega y Gasset (1883-1955) is a brilliant philosopher full of practical insights. And Sota (1913-1996) is a Spanish architect with a profound love for Bach. The three could have known one another because they were contemporaries. Had this happened, they would have been surprised to learn how much the poet, the philosopher and the architect had in common. If we were to ascribe a single adjective to each of them, one could call T.S. Eliot transparent, Ortega clear, and Sota laconic. And all three coincide in their respective genres — poetry, philosophy and architecture — in the demand for a certain sobriety of expression, a certain surrender of the individual ego, as a prerequisite for universality.

T.S. ELIOT

In his essays *What is a Classic?* and *Tradition and the Individual Talent,* T.S. Eliot stoutly defends the need to extinguish personality from his work in the interest of greater universality. The first quote comes from a speech he delivered in 1944 as the first President of the Virgil Society of London. The second citations date back to 1919 and present many of the arguments supporting the former.

> *When an author appears, in his love of the elaborate structure, to have lost the ability to say anything simply; when his addiction to pattern becomes such that he says things elaborately which should properly be said simply, and thus limits his range of expression, the process of complexity ceases to be quite healthy, and the writer is losing touch with the spoken language.*
>
> [It is instructive to exchange the words 'author' and 'writer' with the word 'architect.']
>
> *There comes a time when a new simplicity, even a relative crudity, may be the only alternative. Now, to some extent, the sacrifice of some potentialities in order to realize others is a condition of artistic creation, as it is a condition of life in general. In short, without the constant application of the classical measure, we tend to become provincial.*

The fact that T.S. Eliot uses the term provincial is relevant to the discussion. I don't know if the term provincial in English has exactly the same pejorative connotations as the word 'provinciano' in Spanish, but the poet's idea in his search for the universal is very clear.

> But my concern here is only with the corrective to provincialism in literature. [Provincialism involves] a distortion of values … which confounds the contingent with the essential, the ephemeral with the permanent. The progress of an artist is a continual self-sacrifice, a continual extinction of personality. There remains to define this process of depersonalization and its relation to the sense of tradition. It is in this depersonalization that art may be said to approach the condition of science.

Lying on my table, there is a little gem: an original edition in English of *"What is a Classic?"* edited by Faber & Faber and published in London in 1950. The above quotations have been extracted from this edition.

ORTEGA y GASSET

An architectural congress was held in Darmstadt in 1951 which was attended by Ortega y Gasset (it's where he met German philosopher Martin Heidegger). In this event, Ortega said[7]

> Style has a very peculiar role in architecture which doesn't have in other arts, even in the more pure arts. Paradoxical though it may seem, that is how it is. In other arts style is merely a question of the artist : he decides —with all his being and with a level of decision-making that runs deeper than his will and consequently acquires an aspect of necessity rather than free will — for himself and unto himself. His style does not and cannot depend on anyone else but himself. But the same is not true of architecture. If an architect produces a project with an admirable personal style, he is not, strictly speaking, a good architect.

It is very clear that he is directly criticizing any personal style of architecture, which could be called provincial if using Eliot's term. Ortega y Gasset's point reminds me of the work of an extraordinary architect like Antonio Gaudí, and how his excessive personality takes away from the universality that we find in maestros like Mies Van der Rohe or Le Corbusier. Returning to Ortega y Gasset, we are able to better understand what is at stake:

> The architect finds himself in a relationship with his art, very different from the bond formed between other artists and their respective works. The reason for this is obvious: architecture is not, cannot be, must not be an exclusively individual art. It is a collective art. The genuine architect is an entire people, which provides the means of construction, its purpose and its unity. Imagine a city built by "amazing," but dedicated architects, each out for himself, and his own individual style. Each one of these buildings could be magnificent and yet the overall effect would be bizarre and intolerable. In such a scenario, far too much emphasis would be given to an aspect of all art which has not been sufficiently remedied; its capricious element. Its capriciousness would manifest itself naked, cynical, indecent, intolerable. We would not be able to see the building as part of the sovereign objectivity of a great mineral body, but display ing on the contrary the impertinent profile of someone who is doing whatever he feels like.

It would seem that Ortega's words could have been uttered today regarding much of the arbitrary, capricious architecture that we see being built.

SOTA

One tires of seeing beauty and the grace of things (perhaps they are the same) being pursued with added embellishments, knowing the secret is not there. My unforgettable friend J. A. Coderch used to say that ultimate beauty is like a beautiful bald head (Nefertiti, for example), from which one had pulled out each and every hair, lock by lock, with the pain of ripping them out, one by one. Painfully we must tear from our works the hairs which impede us from achieving their simple, simple end.

These expressive words from the Spanish architect Alejandro de la Sota close the book on his work[8] and define so well the views on architecture and life itself of this true maestro, who began each day playing a Bach sonata. Sota's architecture has that extreme elegance of the precise gesture, of the exact phrase, that so accurately touches silence. The silence of his work and his personality is gifted with the difficult capacity to fascinate. So close to poetry, to poetic breath, to hushed music.

Sota's architecture is especially encapsulated in the Maravillas School Gymnasium in Madrid. This extraordinary building is impressive in its terse, absolute simplicity. So much so that it goes unnoticed by non-architects. It may just be hard for the layperson to understand its beauty — not unlike the difficulty that many find in appreciating Mark Rothko's paintings. Sota's simplicity and logical pursuit of architecture led him to say: *"I believe that not making architecture is a way of making it."* And when asked about the Maravillas School Gymnasium he just replied: *"it solved a problem."* We can almost hear Sota saying that architecture *"is not a turning loose of emotion but an escape from emotion,"* which is what T.S. Eliot wrote about poetry.

How could we fail to recognize an identical universal breath in these three creative people? As the years go by, I must acknowledge the great intellectual enjoyment produced by the interaction of these characters and issues in my memory. How great and profitable is the passage of time!

NOTA BENE

And, just when I thought that I had finished writing, Austrian art historian E.H. Gombrich steps forward. Well, it's not as if Gombrich, whose wonderful book *The Preference for the Primitive* I have known for such a long time, has just appeared out of the blue.[9] Rather, it has to do with my periodical rereading of my favorite books that I keep together on a special shelf. I have already mentioned the enormous intellectual enjoyment of returning over the years to one's sources.

Gombrich's book opens with a quotation from Cicero that says it all:

How much more florid, in the gaiety and variety of the colouring, are most objects in modern pictures than in ancient ones; which, however, though they captivate us at first sight, [they] do not afford any lasting pleasure; whereas we are strongly attracted by rough and faded colouring in the paintings of antiquity. And he adds, *"The more the artist knows how to flatter the senses, the more he will mobilize defences against this flattery.*[9]

In the end, this preference for the 'primitive' is a clear expression of the need for personal sacrifice in order to attain universality. Or, as my old friend Russian architect Konstantin Melnikov once said:

Having become my own boss, I entreated Architecture to throw off her gown of marble, remove her make-up and reveal herself as she really is: like a goddess, naked, graceful and young. And to renounce being agreeable and compliant, as befits true Beauty.

Figure 11-9. Alberto Campo Baeza. Andalucia's Museum of Memory in Granada — Spain. Photograph by Javier Callejas.

THE SACRED TASK OF ARCHITECTURE

JUHANI PALLASMAA   2011 WALTON CRITIC

THE SACRED TASK OF ARCHITECTURE
2011 Walton Studio
Walton Critic: Juhani Pallasmaa

STUDIO TOPIC

Today's world threatens the art of architecture in two opposite ways. One reduces buildings to mere utility and economy, whereas the other to pure representation. In these reductions the fundamental historicity as well as mental and affective essence of the architectural impact are lost. When buildings are viewed as aestheticized constructions or pragmatic objects, they lose their emotive, empathetic, and spiritual qualities. This situation has also caused architecture to lose its cosmic, metaphysical, and symbolic content. Yet, a fundamental role of architecture has been to mediate between the cosmic and human realms, Gods and mortals, the transitory and the eternal. In so doing, architectural structures bridged and concretized the deepest emotions: grief and ecstasy, loss and hope, veneration and awe. If architecture is to help alleviate, if not heal the many serious ills affecting our civilization, we need to deepen its commitments to respond to our existential condition as embodied, emotional, social, and spiritual beings. In this sense, the sacred task of architecture goes beyond religious buildings. It is to awaken visitors into true, heart-felt, spirit-developing dwelling by creating spatial frameworks that encourage authentic behaviors, experiences and understanding. This consists of giving even our most mundane acts their just meaning and dignity. It means to participate in the creation of a good, true, and beautiful world. Based on this philosophy

and his writings,[10] 2011 Walton Critic Juhani Pallassmaa asked the studio to probe into human feelings as the central existential conduit to access our incarnated spirituality and, though it, the ineffable. Pallasmaa started by using special exercises, lectures and conversations on the affective and poetic essences of the arts. His objective was to identify how emotions are evoked by the arts and suggest ways in which the architectural language could be emotionally intensified. Using this foundation, the studio then moved to the architectural design of an *urban, non-denominational burial chapel in downtown Washington, D.C.* Students were asked to study, experiment, test, and critique the nuanced relationship between architecture and the subjective, objective, and transcendental dimensions of death. A topic so avoided by contemporary society, but of huge impact in everyone's life. Addressing this building type demanded students to reflect and address the extreme gamut of emotions that death invariably brings: from profound sorrow/sadness and loss/desperation to melancholia/nostalgia, consolation/solace, hope/optimism, God/nothingness, and more. In a design studio investigating the intersection of emotions and architectural design, funerary architecture demanded that students exercise sensitivity, understanding and tact born in *empathy and compassion*, to console without being patronizing.

Figure 12-2. Juhani Pallasmaa participates in Chloe Rice's Master's Thesis review.

Figure 12-3. Juhani Pallasmaa teaches while students Brandon Ro listens and Emily Anderson listen.

Figure 12-4. Pallasmaa shows a possible design path while students Brandon Ro and Matthew Kline observe.

Figure 12-5. Pallasmaa responds to Gina Longo and Amanda Seligman. Ashley Prince pictured in the background.

Figure 12-6. *Faculty:* Juhani Pallasmaa, Julio Bermudez, and Greg Upwall.
Graduate Students: Andrew Baldwin, Scott Gillespie, Gina Longo, Patrick Manning, Ashley Marshall, Brandon Moore, Ashley Prince, Brandon Ro, Mandira Sareen, and Michael Steinmetz.
Undergraduate students: Emily Anderson, Kelly Corcoran, Justin D'Alessandro, Elizabeth Esposito, Matthew Kline, Amanda Seligman, Alecia Wilson, and Brigid Wright. Photograph by Julio Bermudez.

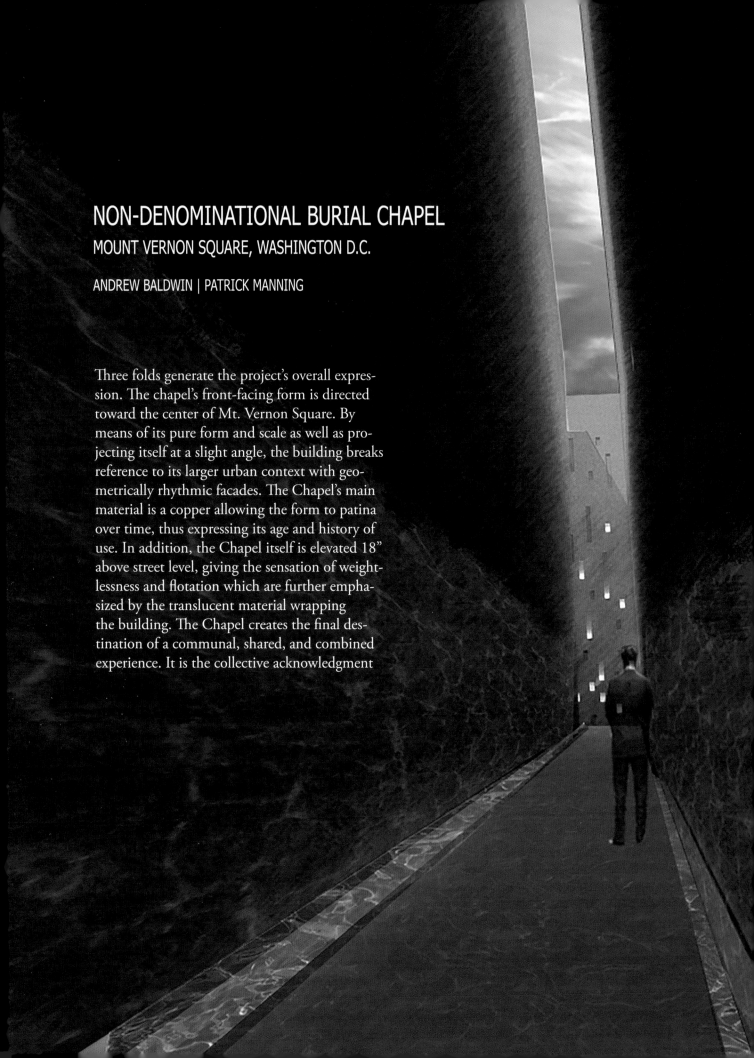

NON-DENOMINATIONAL BURIAL CHAPEL
MOUNT VERNON SQUARE, WASHINGTON D.C.

ANDREW BALDWIN | PATRICK MANNING

Three folds generate the project's overall expression. The chapel's front-facing form is directed toward the center of Mt. Vernon Square. By means of its pure form and scale as well as projecting itself at a slight angle, the building breaks reference to its larger urban context with geometrically rhythmic facades. The Chapel's main material is a copper allowing the form to patina over time, thus expressing its age and history of use. In addition, the Chapel itself is elevated 18" above street level, giving the sensation of weightlessness and flotation which are further emphasized by the translucent material wrapping the building. The Chapel creates the final destination of a communal, shared, and combined experience. It is the collective acknowledgment

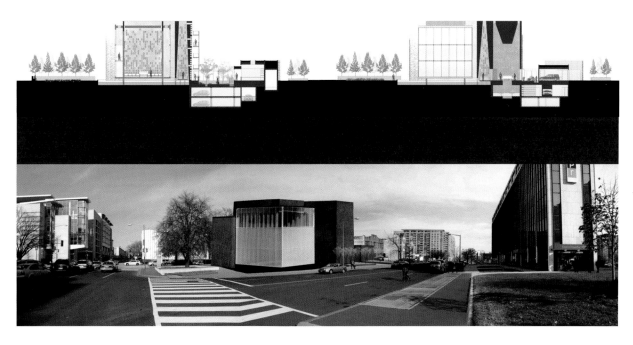

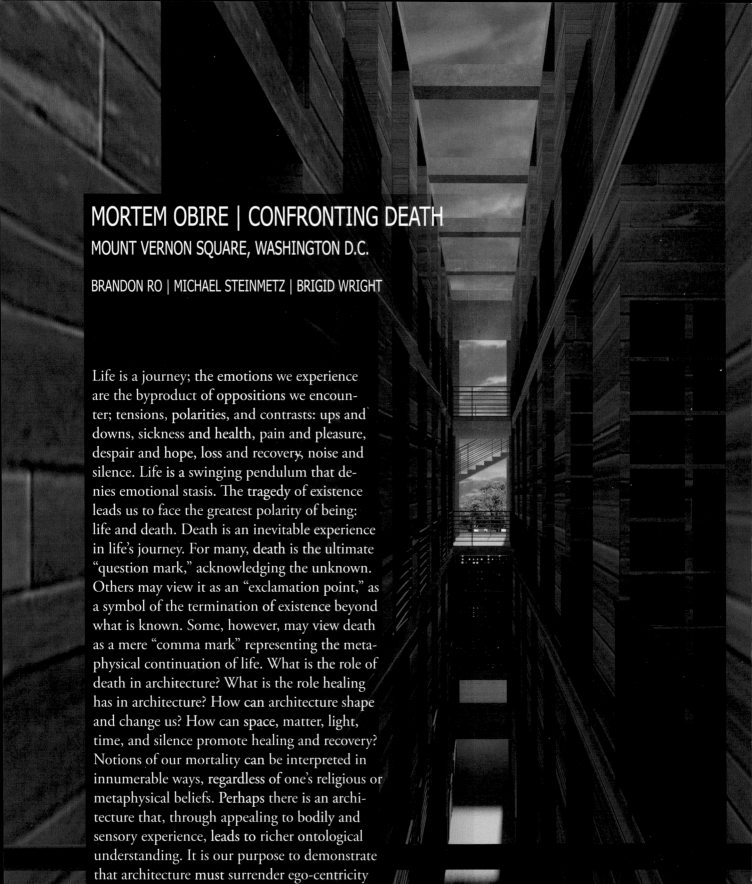

MORTEM OBIRE | CONFRONTING DEATH
MOUNT VERNON SQUARE, WASHINGTON D.C.

BRANDON RO | MICHAEL STEINMETZ | BRIGID WRIGHT

Life is a journey; the emotions we experience
are the byproduct of oppositions we encounter; tensions, polarities, and contrasts: ups and
downs, sickness and health, pain and pleasure,
despair and hope, loss and recovery, noise and
silence. Life is a swinging pendulum that denies emotional stasis. The tragedy of existence
leads us to face the greatest polarity of being:
life and death. Death is an inevitable experience
in life's journey. For many, death is the ultimate
"question mark," acknowledging the unknown.
Others may view it as an "exclamation point," as
a symbol of the termination of existence beyond
what is known. Some, however, may view death
as a mere "comma mark" representing the metaphysical continuation of life. What is the role of
death in architecture? What is the role healing
has in architecture? How can architecture shape
and change us? How can space, matter, light,
time, and silence promote healing and recovery?
Notions of our mortality can be interpreted in
innumerable ways, regardless of one's religious or
metaphysical beliefs. Perhaps there is an architecture that, through appealing to bodily and
sensory experience, leads to richer ontological
understanding. It is our purpose to demonstrate
that architecture must surrender ego-centricity

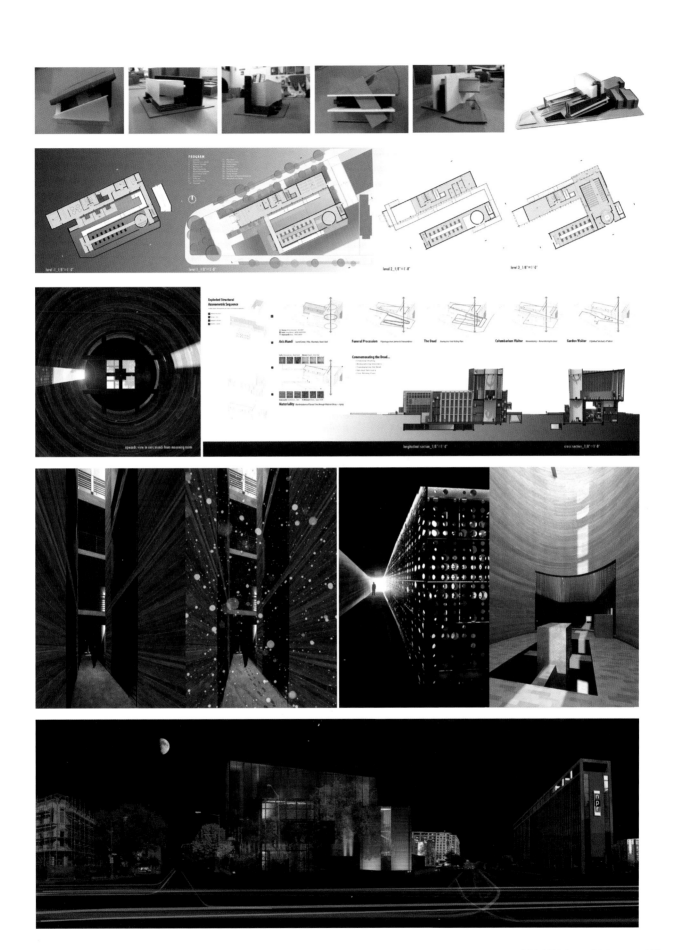

NON-DENOMINATIONAL BURIAL CHAPEL
MOUNT VERNON SQUARE, WASHINGTON D.C.

ASHLEY MARSHALL | ASHLEY PRINCE

Death is the most rational thing that happens in life. The moment we are born, our bodies begin to age and die. This building is not about the rationality. No, instead, this burial chapel seeks to speak to the grief and the mourning that surrounds death. This place is a place to situate the dead because in situating the earthly remains of our loved ones, we situate our grief. This place is about the most irrational thing that happens in life: love; and when the bodies of the ones we love die, the irrationality of grief and ritualization of mourning begin.

"No one ever told me the grief felt so like fear. I am not afraid, but the sensation is like being afraid. The same fluttering in the stomach, the same restlessness, the yearning. I keep on swallowing, at other times it feels like being mildly drunk, or concussed. There is a sort of invisible blanket between the world and me. I find it hard to take in what anyone says. Or perhaps, hard to

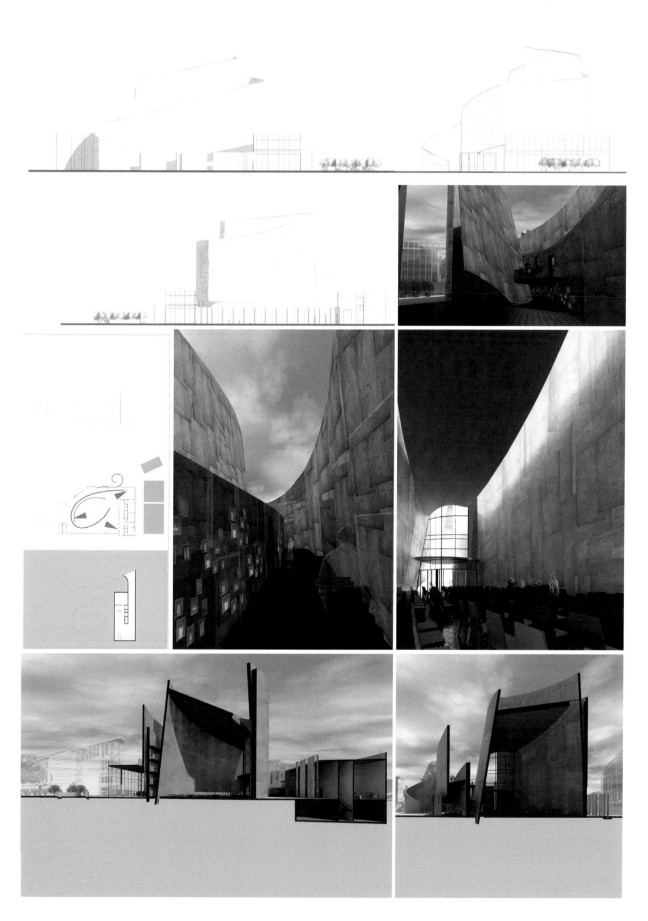

Image 12-7. Juhani Pallasmaa (in collaboration with Kristian Gullichsen), Moduli 225, Prefabricated Vacation House System, Prototype in Finland. Photograph by Kaj Lindholm.

THE ART OF TEACHING:
OBJECTIVES IN MY WALTON STUDIO
JUHANI PALLASMAA

Architectural education has two parallel perspectives and goals: architecture as a historical, cultural, technical, and disciplinary practice, on the one hand, and the sense of self and mental identity of the student, on the other. However, educational philosophies and curricula tend to focus on the external requirements of the architectural practice and undervalue the significance of the individual inner reality of the student. The complex phenomenon of architecture has to be confronted, experienced and internalized through a personal encounter and identification, not as an external objective or a set of facts and rules. Architecture is not a rational, logical or clearly definable discipline; it is an *"impure"* category, which juxtaposes and fuses irreconcilable aspects, such as scientific knowledge and personal beliefs, technicalities and mental realities, logical deduction and imagination, given factual parameters and internal mental and ethical aspirations. The first task of the teacher is to fire the student's passion for architecture and its existential meanings, and to enable the student to see the craft of building in conjunction with the drama of life and her own persona.

The internally conflicting phenomenon of architecture has to be approached and encountered through personal experience and identification, as only the act of experiencing architecture can fuse the irreconcilable dimensions and interactions into a coherent and poetic entity. Only through the individual imaginative experience can an artistic or architectural phenomenon be emotionally grasped in its full essence. Due to its conflicting essence, architectural design cannot be a problem solving task; it is closer to being a personal confession.

Meaningful works of art and architecture are worlds, open and limitless images, probes and mental excavations, which open up entire universes, *"as reflected in a drop of water,"* as the Russian film director Andrey Tarkovsky describes the internal richness of the poetic image in the art of cinema.[11] Also the philosopher Jean-Paul Sartre emphasizes the inherent openness of artistic works: *"If the painter presents us with a field or a vase of flowers, his paintings are windows which are open on the whole world."*[12] A meaningful architectural work is likewise more than the material building; it confronts us with the world and our own existence. It creates frames to perceive and horizons to grasp the world, and it makes us sense our own existence intensely. The artistic image fuses the realms of beauty and truth, aesthetics and ethics. *"Art is not a little selective sample of the world, it is a transformation of the world, an endless transformation towards the good,"* Rainer Maria Rilke, the poet, demands.[13] Deep architectural experiences are not products of rational deduction or mere aesthetic fabrications; they rise from a fundamental existential ground. The craft of building is not merely about the discipline, as it is deeply rooted in our experiences of being. It is a spatial, material and embodied language of its own, an existential language, which cannot be turned into words.

It is crucial in education that the student is, from the very beginning, made to confront experientially authentic phenomena and entities, whether works of visual arts, poetry, literature, and architecture, or authentic and deeply felt human relations. Art and architecture can only be learned through genuine encounter, not through secondary explanation. A true teacher teaches primarily through her authentic persona, her accumulation of lived life, emotive presence, empathy and wisdom, not the collection of facts that she has learned and accumulated. Learning is a collaboration and shared responsibility of the teacher and the student. In meaningful education we shape and mould ourselves, our very personality, character and sense of self, instead of primarily accumulating facts, or even skills. This molding of self takes place predominantly through an unconscious embodied osmosis, or to use the Aristotelian notion, *"mimesis;"* existential mimesis, I wish to add. The essence of learning is the gradual construction of an inner sense of identity, goal, responsibility, empathic imagination, ethical stance, and a combined sense of humility and pride.

In his essay *"What Calls for Thinking?"* philosopher Martin Heidegger makes a remarkable comment on the difficulty of teaching:

> *Teaching is even more difficult than learning. And why is teaching more difficult than learning? Not because the teacher must have a larger store of information, and have it always ready. Teaching is more difficult than learning, because what teaching calls for is this: to let learn. The real teacher, in fact, lets nothing else be learned than – learning. His conduct, therefore, often produces the impression that we really learn nothing from him, if by "learning" we now automatically understand merely*

> *the procurement of useful information. The teacher is ahead of his apprentices in this alone, that he has still more to learn than they – he has to learn to let them learn.* "[14]

This wisdom has never been more important than in the Sargasso Sea of our age of non-contextual, externalized, fragmented and non-hierarchical information.

The very essence of learning in any creative field is embedded more in the student's sense of self and his/her unconsciously internalized image of the world than in detached and external facts. Education and learning has to address the student's individual and unique self, and the meaningful content of education is more existential than factual and related with experiences and values, not information. Education tends to advance from elements towards complexities and larger entities. Yet, there are no meaningful *"elements"* in artistic phenomena, only complete and lived images and experiences. *"[U]nderstanding is derived from the whole, since it is only in the light of the whole that one can truly understand the nature of the parts"*, the philosopher therapist Iain McGilchrist states in his book on the interacting roles of our two brain hemispheres.[15]

Architecture, as all artistic work, is essentially a product of collaboration. It is not only collaboration in the obvious and practical sense of the word, such as the interaction with numerous professionals, workmen and craftsmen, but it is a collaboration with other artists and architects, not only one's own contemporaries and the living, but also with predecessors, who may have been dead for decades or centuries. One's most important teacher of architecture may well have died half a millennium ago. I often instruct my students to be careful and ambitious in choosing their private mentors. You can choose to have Brunelleschi, Michelangelo or Louis Kahn as your mentor, if you have the courage to decide so. The legendary Finnish designer Tapio Wirkkala (1915-1985) told me that his real teacher was Piero della Francesca, the Renaissance painter, although Piero had died in 1492, 423 years before the birth of my friend. During the past few decades architecture has been increasingly rationalized, intellectualized and aestheticized. In our era of obsessive consumerism and aestheticized capitalism,[16] practically everything is being aestheticized: personality, behavior, products and politics. Even beauty has lost its innocence and authenticity through turning into a calculated manipulation of desire and style. However, the environmental and architectural experiences are dominated by unconscious and instinctual atmospheric and emotional reactions. We are unnoticeably in dialogue with our environments on deep ecological and biological levels.

Architecture is not only engaged in utilitarian, functional, technical and aesthetic issues, as it also generates emotions, feelings and existential meanings. The deeper, but hidden task of our buildings is to give us our foothold in the world. Yet, today's design practice tends to give priority to the performative and rational aspects and detach aesthetic objectives from their deep ground in our biological and cultural past. In my teaching, I attempt to guide my students to focus on the experiential, emotional, poetic and existential dimensions of architecture.

These critical views have led me to give studio assignments that cannot easily be dealt with intellectually, stylistically or through precedents, as they require personal, embodied and emotive commitment and reaction. I prefer studio and workshop tasks that are simple enough in their logistical structure not to strengthen the intellectuality of the design approach. I also favor tasks that are engaged in materials, processes and phenomena, rather than formal concepts. Instead of autonomous qualities or direct aesthetic intentions, I emphasize the role of architecture as a mediator of affect and meaning. Architectural meanings do not primarily arise from forms, as they are evoked by our existential experiences. Meaningful architecture always guides our consciousness outside itself. *"We come not to see the work of art, but the world according to the work,"*

as Maurice Merleau-Ponty wisely asserts.[17]

I have also become concerned about the elimination of the reality of death in our culture. Death is suppressed in consciousness and eliminated from experience, as it takes place behind closed doors and outside of individual experience. I have often given my students assignments which concretize the acceptance of death as part of the human reality. My intention is to guide students to acknowledge the significance of human emotions and the subtleties of grief, sorrow and mourning. In the Walton Critic Studio, 2011, my co-teacher Julio Bermudez and I decided on the program of a non-denominational burial chapel located in the central area of Washington, D.C.

We tend to think that emotions are subjective and hence beyond identification, articulation and discussion. Yet, emotions are varied, definite and subtle, and they can be discussed and articulated. Emotions are our primordial mode of relating ourselves with the world, and they are frequently more genuine, true and reliable than our intellectualizations and rationalizations. The entire period of mourning a deceased relative or friend, as well as the funeral process itself, are colored by a dominant feeling of grief and loss, but the various situations and phases of the process project differing emotive situations and subtleties. Grief not so much a singular emotion as it is a process and progression. In the various phases of the burial, very distinct emotions arise and they resonate with equally distinct and purposeful spatial qualities, moods, illuminations, materials and colors. Modern and contemporary architectures emphasize visuality and formal qualities. However, this exaggerated emphasis on visuality tends to create the feeling of outsideness. Spaces of mourning need to have tonal, haptic and material resonances as well as intense tuning through illumination. The spaces should support gently the existential experience and recovery from grief. My studio tasks aim at the identification and understanding of the complexities and subtleties of emotive immersion, atmosphere, mood and architectural attunement. These are all complex mediated experiences.

I begin my studios and workshops with an introductory task which touches upon the basic issues of the assignment proper, and also serves to establish a sense of a shared mission and responsibility. Sometimes the warm-up exercise has been the task of designing an urn for a deceased well-known artist, poet, or writer (as we did in the 2011 Walton Studio at CUA). The task aims to guide the student to define her feeling of the individual and his/her character and mental world, as well as the artist's work. The students are also encouraged to identify their own emotions and to discuss them in the various educational situations. The empathically imaginative criteria for such an exercise is to imagine whether the deceased person herself would have approved the design proposal. Another warm-up exercise I use (which we employed in the Walton Studio) is to find artistic works (paintings, sculptures, poems, films, music, theatre or dance performances and architectural works) to demonstrate given emotions or sentiments, such as grief, sorrow, sadness, melancholy, despair, condolence, happiness and ecstacy.

Learning requires paradoxically the presence of the instructor and the simultaneous individual mental solitude of the student. The instructor has to be both available and absent, and always leave the final decisions to the student. The teacher has to leave each student alone in her personal world and only help her advance in her personal exploration. The teacher can also evoke questions and concerns, but the solution has to be left to the student. A wise teacher can make the student see and feel the phenomena that her working process has brought up. If a student ends up executing ideas and opinions of the teacher, the teaching has failed. When the projects in the studio are similar, the instructor has failed in her task to open up the uniquely individual minds and existential worlds of the students.

Figure 12-8. Juhani Pallasmaa, entrance foyer, Rovaniemi Art Museum and Music Hall in Rovaniemi — Finland. Photograph by Arto Liiti.

Figure 12-9. Juhani Pallasmaa, Sami Lapp Museum in Inari, Lapland — Finland. Photograph by Rauno Träskelin.

CONSUMING CREATION

CRAIG W. HARTMAN 2010 WALTON CRITIC

CONSUMING CREATION: RETHINKING CONSUMPTION AND MATERIALITY
2010 Walton Studio
Walton Critic: Craig W. Hartman

STUDIO TOPIC

The desert has played a central spiritual role in the Abrahamic traditions. It was therefore natural that this Walton Studio invoked its awesome power to reconsider the state of present-day culture vis-à-vis nature, self, and transcendence. The architectural vehicle was a 25,000 square foot *treatment-rehabilitation center for consumption addiction*. Run by Trappist lay and ordained people, this institution followed the order's strict yet liberating living precepts. The building was sited in an isolated area in the beautiful and empty red rock country of southern Utah. The studio commenced by inviting students to become familiar with (1) the philosophy and architecture championing minimal attitudes and responses towards the challenges of today and (2) the central role that spiritual practice and sacred space play in such a plight. More specifically, the studio considered Thomas Merton's Christian teachings in relation to principles of voluntary simplicity advanced by Duane Elgin and implied in minimalism. The objective was for each student to develop their own Architectural Manifesto as a hypothesis (not a dogma) to guide their design process throughout the semester. The VAS (Voluntary Architectural Simplicity) manifesto, included in the last section of this book, was provided as an example to consider. This phase involved research, readings, precedents analysis, discussions, and presentations. Architect Craig

W. Hartman, the 2010 Walton Critic, joined the studio right after this initial phase in order to direct an intense one-week long charrette. He challenged the students to design a relic or ritual space in a pilgrimage route in the red rock desert. The pilgrimage chapel had to be earthbound yet inviting 1-3 individuals to connect to the divine. This work was a perfect starting point for what was to come next: a disciplined, mind-expanding, and exciting exploration based on analog-digital media migrations. Students' stated architectural aspirations/inspirations were expressed, tested, transformed, and reframed time and time again until relevant ideas were found. At that point the effort moved into clarifying and simplifying them in conversation with architectural and spiritual values, vision, and commitments elaborated earlier in the semester (students' written manifestos). Theoretical rigor was important but subservient to experiential authenticity, architectural order, conversation with the larger (natural, cosmic, and 'transcendent') context, and beauty. Ultimately, the success of the proposed buildings (a *Being-affirming Desert Center*) was demonstrated not only by how well the structure responded to the programmatic demands and unique natural conditions but also its therapeutic capacity to treat the consumption additions of its patients by turning their attention to "being."

Figure 13-2. Craig W. Hartman discusses the work of Chloe Rice (pictures) and Paul Baines.

Figure 13-3. Craig W. Hartman (and other reviewers) making final comments after the final studio jury .

Figure 13-4. Val Hawkins and Kevin Thomson presenting their design proposal in the final review.

Figure 13-5. Allison Wood and Shelby Foster share their project for the Rehabilitation Center.

Figure 13-6. *Faculty:* Craig W. Hartman, Julio Bermudez, and Greg Upwall.
Graduate Students: Nina Africa, Travis Akiwowo, Paul Baines, Shelby Foster, Ana Garcia Bilbao, Val Hawkins, Julie Hernandez Gomez, Carrie Kramer, Dan Lucenti, Ashley Marshall, Kristyn McKenzie, Andrew Metzler, Ashley Prince, Chloe Rice, Allie Steimel, Michael Steinmetz, Kevin Thomson, Brittany Vanveen, Evan Wivell, and Allison Wood. Photograph by Julio Bermudez.

ROCK-WALL REHABILITATION CENTER
CASTLE VALLEY, UTAH

DAN LUCENTI | MICHAEL STEINMETZ

In this building the procession through circulation and space is a form of meditation. The straight, continuous halls marked with narrow paths of water, the gentle sl`opes into the earth or toward the sky invite reflection on the nature of the elements and our fundamental appreciation of them. Procession through spaces is demarcated by zones of compression and release. As one proceeds, the wall gently pulls away from the building. Punctuated in the endless, meditative halls are zones of massive decompression; the wells of light that pour into the sleeping quarters and offices, the high ceiling of the bath, or the stairwell that ascends to the open sky. Each space is unique in its section, and is critical in creating a unique sense of place in each environment. The tallest space is the chapel. The narrow opening along the northern wall is made meaningful when the sun setting in the west casts a horizontal beam, creating an ethereal cross of light that is overwhelming in scale. The monumental cross is made powerful by its intangibility; the idea that one can't touch the divine, but can only see its by products.

TIME, SPACE, HORIZON
CASTLE VALLEY, UTAH

ASHLEY MARSHALL | ANDREW METZLER

The building is positioned in a location that can capture the vastness of the site. In the empty desert, the horizon line dominates, something that we did not want to disrupt. As a result, we dug into the earth in order to respond to this architectural challenge. To combat the sheer size of this site and the possibility of getting lost, we decided to make the person aware of their place in space and time. We carved into the ground, keeping the horizon unbroken and forcing movement along the undulating bands created. Our excavation reveals layers of both the site and the self as the user travels along the bands. Approaching the place, a visitor would not know that this building exists until they are right on top of it — as one stumbles across it while passing by. Circulating through the building one essentially travels along the bands to get from one place to another; enjoying a different experience from every point. Once down to the desired level, a person will turn into a walkway allowing them to reach the different spaces. Moving through this building of layers and bands means to have a different perspective of the land while being surrounded by mystery. Submerging into the dark earth, crossing the interface between soil and air, traveling along tight confined areas only to find release at the gathering point. What organizes this project is the experiences that enable people to explore the land and their truest selves.

BEING AFFIRMING DESERT CENTER
CASTLE VALLEY, UTAH

VAL HAWKINS | KEVIN THOMSON

The project takes a conceptual and tectonic approach to respond to site, program, and experiences. A layered and dense set of walls grows out of the soil. Made out of the same red rock permeating its desert context, these walls define narrow, canyon-like environments that are next to each other, yet they remain private and intimate. While seemingly disorienting at first, this organization brings the vastness of the desert into human scale while modulating sunlight, wind, and other extreme climate/weather variables. Their slight non-parallel geometry is a play between manmade and organic orders to infuse vitality to the spaces and experiences that culminated in the center path. Here the two sides of the project, one addressing lodging/individuality and the other multiple therapeutic services, meet and provide people a chance to meet and enjoy unstructured activities. The clouds and sun are invited to circumvallate across it. From this central corridor one is invited to enter/leave the compound into the wilderness. The simplicity and repetitiveness of the architectural gesture along with its unique layout envelop participants in a protective atmosphere of silence and introspection. The result is an architecture that roots people into the desert, inviting them to feel the earth, the sky, the sun, and ultimately the fundamental rhythms of their own lives. The wisdom of the desert meets the spiritual wisdom that each person carries within themselves.

Figure 13-7. Craig W. Hartman, SOM, The Cathedral of Christ the Light in Oakland — California. Photograph by SOM.

FINDING THE ESSENCE : PLACE AND SPIRITUALITY
CRAIG W. HARTMAN

DOMINIUM

The 21st century has revealed new truths about the reciprocal relations of humanity, the planet, the universe. For the first time in planetary history a single species — Homo sapiens — is consciously altering the planet and its long-term ability to support life itself. The biblical account, in which humanity is given dominion over the earth, has now materialized.

Planetary scientists have identified our era as the beginning of a new geological age. The earth is in human hands and we are aware that we are shaping the planet's future. The Anthropocene epoch offers a stark, existential choice; shall we continue to consume the earth's stored finite resources, emitting its residue as life-ending toxicity or shall we direct our newly gained scientific awareness toward living within our planetary means in harmony with the earth?

Emerging simultaneously in this era are new social norms that are weaving an entirely new global social fabric that is a synthetic, digitally enabled, hybrid cultural construct. Even perceptual reality is something conditional and subjective, often defying what our eyes tell us. It is a breathtaking time of self-enabled, hyper-evolution for humanity.

Paralleling a broad, fundamental law of the universe, we have created an entirely new physical and cultural condition of rapidly increasing entropy. Civilization is moving at warp speed toward a high-energy, interwoven, global web of connectivity and complexity, liberating humanity. Distance is being erased and, with it, we are losing physical and intellectual connection to geographic place: we observe places but we do not belong to a place.

And yet we long for, and are preconditioned to be grounded in, specific physical places, as if they were part of our DNA. For millennia — since agriculture enabled collective human settlement — architecture and culture have been inextricably tied to the unique conditions of their localized, physical place. Architecture was built of materials that could be found and gathered locally and erected by hand. Physical distance separating human settlements produced distinctive architectural forms, material expressions for different cultures.

PERMANENCE, MATERIALITY, AND SPIRITUALITY

The underlying ethos of architecture and its pedagogy must be reconsidered in the context of what has been lost and what has been gained as we enter our third millennium. With distance erased, contemporary architecture is made of materials and cultural influences gathered from around the world. But, having shed our dependency on local resources, we have lost the immediacy and specificity of the human relationship with — and spiritual reverence for — the earth beneath our feet and the preciousness of its finite resources.

Architecture is materiality and spirituality — a spirituality that honors the earth, respects and maintains our inherited built environment and cultures while drawing inspiration from the intellectual and physical liberties of our time. Intelligent forms of human settlement must be devised that touch the earth lightly — that consider the limitations of finite planetary resources and the biodiversity necessary to support with equitability the aspirations of a population soon to reach eight billion.

In this fluid, dynamic, and increasingly rootless time, architecture's permanence and its role in sheltering humanity and providing refuge — and its ability to nourish the human spirit — is more important than ever. This is nothing new, of course. In the first century BC Vitruvius observed that architecture must possess firmitas, utilitas and venustas.

Building with strength and utility for the ages is of critical importance today — the world cannot afford to continue to destroy and rebuild. But venustas remains the most elusive, most difficult and most important architectural quality. Beauty and delight elevate architecture beyond mere commodity to the realm of the spirit. With care, architecture can be built to last for the ages, but it is venustas, together with firmitas and utilitas that makes it worthy of doing so.

ESSENCE: ABSTRACTION, SPACE, LIGHT

It is architecture's role as a place of refuge, respite and dwelling that separates it from other art forms; for those reasons architecture is uniquely positioned to elevate and ennoble the human spirit. It is not its aesthetic quality as an object that gives architecture its special ability to engage spirituality. Sculpture's purity of intention can, of course, achieve formal perfection, but architecture alone among the arts creates a space to be occupied, a space for shelter, a space within

which to enact our rituals of life.

The cathedrals of the Middle Ages are among the world's most iconic spaces — their patrons using the most advanced, even experimental, architecture to create awesome, soaring spaces to honor the majesty of God. But spirituality is achieved equally, perhaps more profoundly, in intimate spaces, constructed of modest materials, ennobled by the poetics of light.

The entirety of the Notre-Dame du Haut at Ronchamp would fit comfortably into the great seventeenth century basilica of St. Peter's. Yet Le Corbusier's accomplishment at Ronchamp, a work of great humanity and limited size, arguably speaks more powerfully to today's spiritual sensibilities. In our era of massive public and commercial works — of airports, train stations and even shopping malls— spirituality in architecture isn't gained through grandeur and awe. Rather it is found in the quiet moment within contemplative space, a place to nurture "the still, small voice of calm."

Ronchamp is abstract, free of overt historic quotation, and while it stands apart from its rural setting, it is phenomenologically inseparable from its physical and cultural landscape. Its essence is ineffability, gained through the poetic introduction of light, softly raking its surfaces, its deep voids and the fluid space within. Its spiritual hold on those who enter its space belies the modesty of its scale and materials.

For me, this attention to human experience, spirituality and place is paramount. Works like Eladio Dieste's Church of Christ the Worker in Atlántida, Uruguay, E. Fay Jones' Thorncrown Chapel in Eureka Springs, Arkansas and Peter Zumthor's Bruder Klaus Field Chapel in Mechernich, Germany demonstrate how important this interconnectedness can be. I sought a similar integration of these values in the Cathedral of Christ the Light in Oakland, California. Dieste and Zumthor's works were built by farmers, unskilled in construction. Dieste's church, made of the thinnest layers of hand-cast brick is a work of structural rationalism in which strength is achieved through the union of curved wall forms and vaulted roof. Zumthor's chapel is a simple, crisp, yet irregular exterior form of 24 layers of rammed concrete. Within is a poetic, fluid void formed by Lodgepole Pine tree trunks. The charred surface of concave verticals records the original tree trunk formwork and the fire that removed it. The darkened floor is of poured lead.

Both the Thorncrown Chapel and the Cathedral of Christ the Light are constructed of wood and glass, but there the similarity ends. Jones' Chapel is a delicate intervention within a forest — its structure a literal extension of the surrounding trees; its glass enclosure is meant to disappear, allowing the forest itself to create the space for the congregants. Christ the Light, an urban cathedral adjacent to an estuarial lake connected to the Pacific Ocean, is its antithesis. Like Zumthor's chapel, the heart of the Cathedral of Christ the Light is its interior. Its true spiritual essence is experienced upon crossing the threshold of entry. But unlike the Bruder Klaus chapel, the nature of the Cathedral's internal space is daily concealed and then revealed to the city as day turns to night and the interior is illuminated and visible. Christ the Light's volume is entirely formed by its timber structure; two spherical segments of louvred wood which, in turn, serve as light veils providing reflected, indirect daylight for the interior. The timber spherical segments of Christ the Light are entirely contained within conical walls of glass. The timber and glass forms are separated by several feet of air and are laced together with compressive wooden struts and steel tensile rods. Together, these complementary geometries — the sphere and the cone — create an extremely lightweight and sturdy hybrid form to rest upon a thickened concrete base. This base, a "reliquary wall" is carved, creating darkened voids for shrines and chapels which themselves are punctuated to allow raking light on their internal surfaces.

The Cathedral plan and geometry grow directly from the liturgical precepts of Vatican II; its vertical section expands those precepts into the third dimension with light. Below the sanctuary, altar and reliquary wall rests the mausoleum, embedded in the earth. Above, the sanctuary ascends from darkness to light. The Cathedral of Christ the Light is the spiritual home for an extremely diverse, multicultural congregation — immigrants from many nations for whom the received religious iconography from Europe lacked meaning. As Karsten Harries observes in The Ethical Function of Architecture, we are, today, liberated from place and yet we seek roots. Harries states that: "Human beings belong to both body and spirit – to the earth and to the light."

The Cathedral of Christ the Light seeks to mediate body and spirit through architecture of deep spirituality gained through principles both ancient and contemporary: touching the earth lightly with its materials, and using space, form and the poetics of light to create a modern humanism that serves the culturally diverse Catholic Church of today. Can we turn these values into principles for today's architectural pedagogy? It is time to search the profession and academy for the means to bring a quality of spirituality to our global cities. Architecture is the cultural vessel through which this can happen.

Figure 13-8. Craig W. Hartman, SOM, praying chapel inside the Cathedral of Christ the Light in Oakland — California

Figure 13-9. Craig W. Hartman, SOM, praying chapel inside the Cathedral of Christ the Light in Oakland — California

Figure 13-10. Craig W. Hartman, SOM, main worship space of the Cathedral of Christ the Light in Oakland — California

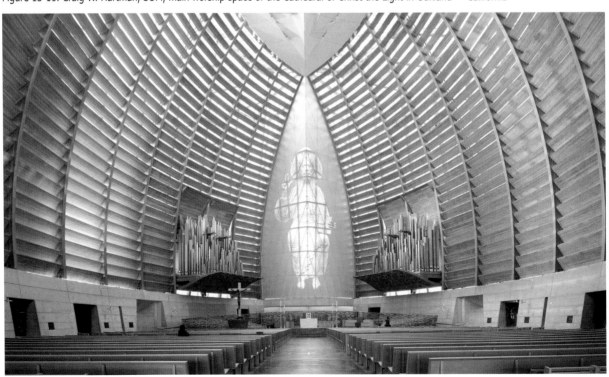

INTUITING SPIRITUALITY THROUGH MAKING, SPACE, AND LIGHT

2009 WALTON CRITIC   ANTOINE PREDOCK

INTUITING SPIRITUALITY THROUGH MAKING, SPACE, AND LIGHT
2009 Walton Studio
Walton Critic: Antoine Predock

STUDIO TOPIC

The semester-long studio project was an ecumenical chapel on the CUA campus. This curriculum included a three-day workshop entitled "Examining Sacred Space in the 21st Century" directed by Antoine Predock, the 2009 Walton Critic. This intense learning experience explored spiritual spaces through the intuitive act of making, paying particular attention to light. A critical component of sacred spaces, light can only be understood, as Predock proposed, through materiality, textures, and haptic practices. In an approach reminiscent of Abstract Expressionism, students were to put aside pre-conceived notions about architectural graphics and explore light through phenomenological representations that involved large bodily gestures, unconventional drawing surfaces, and sensory experiences. The media employed were relief models, charcoal sketches, paintings, physical constructs, installations, and projections. Careful consideration was placed in finding/expressing the depth of emotions associated with architectural environments and the role of hand making and the digital depictions of ideas. Questions were raised about the power of the image: how and when do we enter into an understanding of spiritual spaces through imagery? These words by Predock summarize the approach:

"In my case, whether it is a painting or a clay model or a collage, it becomes the beginning, the source for the project. Rather than being a highly rational methodology, my process remains connected to spirit through the body and to the personal space that the body defines. The trick is getting through the thicket of what Kahn called 'the measurable' in the making of a building to come out the other side with the original content, the original aura intact, for the built work to express that initial physical and spiritual impulse."

The outcomes of this workshop became the impetus informing the schemes of the campus ecumenical chapels that were designed during the rest of the term.

Figure 14-3. Antoine Predock talking to Thomas Walton

Figure 14-2. Antoine Predock considering one of the student's projects produced in his workshop.

Figure 14-4. *Faculty:* Antoine Predock, Luis Boza, Ann Cederna, and Andreea Mihalache.
Graduate Students: Michael Fitzgerald, Gurushabad Khalsa, Nicholas Saylor, Spiro Gianniotis, and John Peragallo IV. Photograph by Ann Cederna and Andreea Mihalache.

Figure 14-5. Student demonstrates the impact of translucency in his design/art effort.

Figure 14-6. Workshop final review. The large Miller room was used as the location of the workshop.

Figure 14-7. Student pinning up his work just before the final workshop review.

Figure 14-8. Antoine Predock with various faculty and friends at CUA, from left to right: Louis Boza, Andreea Mihalache, Kelly Davies, Judith Dwan Hallet, Ann Cederna, AP, and Stanley Hallet. Photograph by Ann Cederna and Andreea Mihalache.

SPIRITUALITY IN ARCHITECTURAL EDUCATION AND PRACTICE

SPIRITUALITY IN ARCHITECTURAL EDUCATION AND PRACTICE
Round-table discussion among 6 Walton Critics

In celebration of the 10th anniversary of the Walton Critic program, the Catholic University of America School of Architecture and Planning hosted a special symposium in October 2018. This event brought together six Walton Critics, namely Juhani Pallasmaa (2011), Alberto Campo Baeza (2012), Eliana Bórmida (2014), Michael J. Crosbie (2015), Prem Chandavarkar (2016), and Susan Jones (2018). This reunion provided an opportunity to assess the work produced over the last decade and consider future directions. The symposium was launched with a round-table discussion on the role of spirituality in architectural education and practice and was moderated by Michael J. Crosbie. Following is the edited record of the conversation that ensued.

MICHAEL J. CROSBIE

Why are we here today? Why have we gathered on this campus and in this place? I want to offer some of my thoughts that might help guide us during this important conference over the next few days.

The Catholic University of America is one of the few places of architectural education in the world, where students and faculty are invited, indeed, encouraged to contemplate the role of not only culture, but also spirituality in the creation of the built environment. This has been primarily accomplished and celebrated over the past decade through the Walton Critic program, established through the generosity of the Wal-

ton family. At most schools of architecture, discussions of the spiritual and the sacred simply do not exist. They are relegated at best to what I call the forbidden zone. But at the Catholic University of America (CUA) School of Architecture and Planning, the Walton Critic program promotes the examination of architecture vis-à-vis spirituality and culture. In our discussion today, we hope to explore this forbidden zone. To reveal what students, as well as faculty, potentially can discover there.

CUA's graduate concentration in sacred space and cultural studies (SSCS) is unique. No other architecture school has a focus like this one, at least none that I am aware of, and I have visited many schools. Several students I have met here and worked with over the past few years have told me that this concentration was the deciding factor for them to study architecture at CUA. The questions that are open to consideration here can be challenging; some might even describe them as difficult. And immersing yourself in such inquiry often pushes you out of your own comfort zone. But isn't that the point of higher education? Over several years, I have spoken with students in the concentration, who have experienced the Walton Studio. One student, Emily, told me that the sacred cultural program was the reason she came to CUA. She wanted to focus on how architecture shapes the human experience, what emotions and perceptions can be elicited by the spiritual in architecture. This line of the inquiry resonated with her. Emily wanted to explore how the spiritual in architecture helps to build community. There is passion at CUA about the spiritual dimension in architecture, but that does not mean it is primarily focused on religious architecture. Any kind of structure, any type of environment for any sort of function, can be spiritual architecture.

Building a bridge between the merely functional and the spiritual imparts architecture with a timeless yet existential dimension. Emily explained to me that she was relieved that the program did not put undue emphasis on religion. She said, *"it is not pushed, but rather there is a space created here for us to investigate architecture's spiritual side, however we might define that."* Defining it is part of the exploration, and creating a space for that inquiry is the essential characteristic of the program. *"In this way,"* Emily told me, *"students and professors learn together."* She described her experience, and her work in the Walton Studio as *"our projects are our journeys."* Another student admitted to me that as awkward and challenging as such journeys

might be, sometimes it is good to be in an uncomfortable area because it can push you a little bit more. You can see how spirituality influences your design. Lisa told me that here at CUA, she felt protected and supported in expressing her faith through her architecture. Andrew revealed that the Walton Studio awakened within him the realization that architecture is not just about works and order, or only about utility. And then there was Andrew, who discovered that part of the architect's role is to create environments that can help one to transcend the everyday. Andrew adopted this role in his life and made it his focus as an intern architect. The studio gave him a chance to rethink who he was. He described the conditions in the SSCS graduate concentration and the Walton Studio as a retreat. It reminded him why he wanted to be an architect, that his primary desire was to create places that give a person a momentary pause, maybe a private haven in which to pray. Places that invite us to do something else with our lives, perhaps to become someone else for just a little while, to leave one's form and space behind and to occupy another, to transform and to transcend. Sina said that his

Figure 15-2. Bórmida & Yanzón Arquitectos, Alfa Crux Wines, San Carlos — Mendoza, Argentina. Photograph by Bórmida & Yanzón Arquitectos.

experiences in the graduate studies at CUA let him conclude that it is architecture's fundamental purpose to do just this, to transform and to transcend. It has the same meaning as spirituality itself. My colleague architect Roberto Chiotti who is seating in the audience today, once told me that he believed we are not human beings trying to discover how to be spiritual. Instead, we are spiritual beings wanting to understand how to be human. This search is fundamental to our lives as architects, and I believe it is the underlying foundation of the Walton Studio and the SSCS concentration to discover how architecture can guide us as spiritual beings in pursuit of our humanity. So, here are some questions about architectural education and spirituality that we might reflect upon and inquire of each other while we are together here this evening and over the next three days.

How do considerations of the spiritual by both students and faculty enrich their architecture education and their role as future professionals? How does the contemplation of such issues and design help us as students and as architects to respond to the full range of human experiences?

What are your own experiences in teaching and learning to create spiritual and cultural resonances in architecture?

How have those experiences changed you not only as an architect or a student, but as a human being?

Is there a driving hunger inside each one of us who enfolds the spiritual into our works, and what does that say about the place and the time that we live in?

As architects and teachers, we create a space for students and colleagues to inhabit this realm, to traverse the forbidden zone. How can we create a welcoming place in which discussion, deliberation, and exploration of the spiritual and the cultural in architecture are promoted and celebrated? And how do we approach the spiritual dimension of architecture in our work and our own lives?

I am asking the participants in this round ta-

ble to talk for about three to five minutes about their perspectives on these questions. Then we will have thirty minutes to have a conversation among the round table participants about the issues raised and my questions. Then we will wrap up tonight's event with fifteen or twenty minutes of open Q&A exchanges with the audience.

SUSAN JONES

I want to start with what teaching means to me. When I think about the spiritual and cultural, it is tough to divide them from the emotion that we feel when we teach, and when we design, when we practice together. I thought about the goal of teaching, and I wanted to focus on this because it is very intimate to me. I am involved now with twelve students in the studio I am teaching here at CUA, most of whom are in this room. I think about the power of teaching throughout my life as an architect. It has been one of the most giving and empathic experiences that I have had in my life, in addition to, perhaps, being a mother. The educational moment when you are giving and sharing, teaching and learning, the thoughts and responses of you and the people around you. So as a young architect, when we are in that very difficult period of growing, maturing, and seeking that pathway to professional competence, teaching became a pathway for me for emotional release and humility. I came to my own maturity, professionally, through teaching. It was through those moments when sitting with students, hundreds and hundreds and hundreds of students, like those in this room today, like the twelve students in my studio. When we are sitting on the desk, it is a great moment to listen to the students trying to express their idea, to try to inhabit their world and investigate what they have to say, and then come back full circle. This process demands to release your ego and be humble. Humility is required to listen to these very young and often vulnerable students. It is a transcendent moment when you are listening. It is a pathway when you are connecting and accessing something far greater than what either the teacher or student does or says. For me, there has always been a very spiritual experience when I just listen and inhabit somebody else's world.

I think the topic of this conversation is fabulous, but I do want to note that it is not only about an educational program focused on the spiritual and the cultural. All of us in this panel and many of us in this room understand that we are talking about a moment of giving, accessibility, and transformation that takes place between our moments of thinking and our moments of working. Moving beyond the teaching, I will say a few words about my practice. I come from a very remote part of this country. I was born in a very remote place, Bellingham. It is not Seattle. It is a tiny little town in the state of Washington. I grew up in the woods and had many, many experiences walking through natural environments. While I was raised a Catholic and still am a devout Catholic, there were lots of journeys and bumps along that way, but what was very constant with me was that experience of nature. I was fifteen when I had a chance to travel abroad and visit the Cologne Cathedral in Germany. We didn't travel a lot when I was young, but I walked through those forests almost every day to go to school. I was eight, nine, ten, eleven, twelve, thirteen. My experience of just watching a house being built in the middle of the woods (that my parents built), and watching the light come down through those bedrooms was memorable. As a five-year-old, I was allowed to go to the new house's three bedrooms and choose which room I wanted. As that young five years old, I intuitively sensed the spatial relationships, the way the light came into those white rooms, the way the mountains stood in the background, and the way the trees and the light filtered through those windows. I noticed the difference between this room and this room and this room. And that power as a five-year-old will never leave me. And that relationship to nature, that relationship to the beauty and purity of ma-

teriality, texture, and light are all things which fill my practice intensely on a day to day basis.

When I think about my architectural practice, I realize how lucky I am to have based it around spiritual practice. I can't think of anything more significant to do as an architect. There was a period in my life when I was in a large corporate firm. This was frankly a dead period of my life as a creative person, but it was then that I had the opportunity to build that small chapel, that Michael Crosbie was gracious enough to recognize twenty, twenty-five years ago now. It was a pro bono project, a volunteer project, something I gave back to the church there. But during that whole time at the corporate office, I didn't have access to that level of emotion. It was only when I started my own practice and began to be formally committed, to working in this realm of the spiritual, that then my gifts as architect grew, gifts as a professional grew, and my gifts as a teacher grew as well.

ALBERTO CAMPO BAEZA
I don't have enough words to say thank you. Thank to every one of you here because I feel like at home. And what could be better than being at home and speaking about exciting things? I will begin by pointing at the importance of teaching and the spiritual dimension of our spaces, of space in architecture. In terms of teaching, and I know that there are many, many professors in the audience, I think they will agree with me that teaching is all about passion. Teaching is a passion. If it is not, then it is not possible to do it well because it is very demanding, exhausting, but of course, tremendously worthwhile. When you can remember the name of all of your students and speak with them one by one, the experience is very fulfilling. When you discover that you are learning more than teaching, you find out the true nature of education.

Before Alzheimer's was a common illness, my father was a surgeon that conducted medical procedures with scissors and scalpels instead of a laser. Back then, it was necessary to sharpen the scalpels continuously to make surgeries very precise and safe. Sometimes I compare doing an excellent job as teachers and architects with always maintaining our instruments sharp so that we can design and make the best buildings, the best architecture. When I am in front of a lot of young people, I know they are the future, and it is very satisfying. At the same time, I wonder what will happen with such a large number of architects. But I don't worry. I know that it will be about what it has always been about: to balance the many things in life wisely.

Is it possible to transmit spiritual feelings in architecture? I would like to remember a passage in the Book of Wisdom of the Holy Bible. It is a beautiful episode where the prophet Elijah is waiting because God promised him that He was coming in the low part of the mountain. So Elijah is waiting for God, and it is raining very, very heavily. But God wasn't in the rain. The earth then trembled, and he thought that God would come, but God did not. And so on with other different physical events. Finally, when he is exhausted, he hears a shuffle of subtle air. Saint Jerome, who translated the Bible into Latin, uses a beautiful expression to describe that subtle shuffle of air: "Sibilus aurae tenuis." And it was in that imperceptible breeze where God manifested. I try to transmit to my students that it is by being sensitive to such subtlety that we can create beautiful architecture because, in the end, it is about beauty. We can do it. Beauty is the splendor of the truth, as Saint Augustine said, although he was really quoting Plato because it was Plato who had said it before. And it is possible to get beauty in our architectural work in the studio. It is not reserved for special architects that go floating or flying. No, no, no! It is possible to be like this group of people in this round table in front of you. It is possible for all of you, for all of us, to get it, to get beauty, and this is the best way to respond to a building's function and construction. Vitruvius expressed it very well long ago, utilitas firmitas venustas. Getting venustas necessitates utilitas and firmitas.

JUHANI PALLASMAA

I have never taken architecture as a profession. Architecture is a privilege and responsibility. It is a privilege in terms of offering an extraordinary position to view human culture and life. I cannot think of any other craft where the story of humanity opens up so widely as in architecture. It is a responsibility in terms of improving the human condition, particularly by bringing existential meaning. We have devised three systems by which to seek meaning. The first one is religion and myth, the second is science, and the third is art. The first is grounded on faith, the second on reason and knowledge, and the third only on emotional experience. These three realms do not easily blend into each other. Our architectural task is to bring existential meaning through emotive experience.

For me, architecture is an art of mediation. Maurice Merleau-Ponty has a beautiful sentence, where he says: "We come not to see the work of art, we come to see the world according to the work." I think this is precisely also a definition of a responsible architecture. It is not the object; it is the way it makes us see the world and possibly even understand the world. Ludwig Wittgenstein, who was one of the philosophers who was very interested in architecture (and actually made some buildings himself), offers us a rather strong statement with a humorous touch. He writes, *Architecture glorifies and eternalizes something. When there is nothing to glorify, there is no architecture.* This is a tough statement, but I must say that we are very quickly approaching the no-architecture situation in our surreal consumer society. I have difficulties understanding that there could be anything worth glorification and eternalization in the ideology and culture of consumerism and superficiality that we are currently living.

The increasing flatness of today's life experience is a consequence of the disappearance of a second dimension of life. It reminds me of Herbert Marcuse's book titled *"One-Dimensional Man."* We are becoming increasingly one-dimensional men and women because our quasi-originality does not accept or acknowledge the second level of reality, which is the level of an elevated or projected perspective of values and life. When this second level of reality (which can also be called the spiritual level) is missing, life flattens, and the prophecy of Wittgenstein is very near. There is nothing to glorify. What can we glorify in architecture today? We can and need to glorify the human narrative. We need to glorify and strengthen tradition, which is a beautiful force for further creativity. I will end by giving a quote from a writer, Edward Edinger, who has written the most significant texts on the importance of metaphor. He says, *"Modern man's most urgent need is to discover the reality and the value of the inner subjective world … to discover the symbolic life … The symbolic life in some form is a prerequisite for psychic health."* I think that this is our task as architecture practitioners and teachers, to support the human experience of another reality, in support of mental health.

PREM CHANDAVARKAR

When we think of spirituality, we think of it as a matter of choice, personal choice. We can choose whether we are an atheist or a believer. We can choose to follow a particular spiritual tradition. So in education, we extend this notion of choice, and in looking at spirituality in architecture education, we perceive it as an option rather than something that lies at the core. And if you want to follow that option, you go to a faith-based university. Because we claim to be modern, we say education must be secular, and spirituality is pushed to the side. And because we claim to be intellectual, we believe that what we do must be underpinned by empirical and logical rigor. So, spirituality is pushed farther out into a forbidden zone. I would argue that this is a significant error as spirituality lies at the core. (Note: I distinguish spirituality from established religious traditions).

In order to make my point, let me articulate the following argument. In the way we currently structure architectural education, there is no con-

nection between the quality of such professional training in that school's region and the quality of architecture around that school's area of influence. Now, this may seem something strange to consider, but it is apparent that one follows from the other. I would observe, for example, that the average level of rigor in a college in the United States is way ahead of the average in India. But walk around a modern American city, look at the buildings designed by professionally trained architects, and you will find the same mix of quality you would find in an Indian city, a dominant majority of mediocre buildings, some that are downright ugly, and a small minority of good architecture. And traveling in many other countries, I have observed the same mixes, whatever the education system may be. Now, this is happening even though students from colleges in the region with differences in quality exist, and a variety of professional offices in the same area with diverse qualities also exist. It is as if the education system has an inbuilt capacity for amnesia. I believe that this is because we define what is worthwhile as something external to the student; because it is not something that is internally embodied. The student is dependent on an external support system to sustain this way of knowing. And that way of thinking continues as long as the surrounding context is maintained, as long as the student remains in that academic context. Move to a different setting, the world of commercial practice, where the language and the priorities change, and a student, like a chameleon, slowly changes color. This strongly suggests that we must start with what lies within us.

Each of us has a source of silent and infinite creativity within. Take the everyday act of speaking. Out of the silence within, we coax words, transform the invisible into the visible. The ordinary act of speaking is an artistic act with immense creative potential. Still, because we are not schooled to think that way, we often speak conditioned either by habit or predetermined expectation, and we lose touch with that artistic spirit within.

John O'Donohue remarks that it is sad to witness so many people today frightened by the wonder of their own presence. In praising academic and abstract intellectualism, we are teaching our students that they should not trust the awe of just being. Some fortunate souls have it within them the capacity to flourish whatever education they receive. Still, we should judge our education systems for what is achieved by the average student, not by what the best student does.

I will end by pointing out two major implications. We should shift our emphasis from abstract definitions of the curriculum to the person being educated, and figure out how we can incorporate the sensitivities of recognition of that person in the way we organize that education. And second, since the curriculum is made from three components –values, content, and pedagogy— we should realize the central importance of pedagogy as the core around which all else revolves. This is the level at which the personal spot between teacher and student flares up. It is the spot that lights the inner fire of that silent infinite creativity between both teacher and student. All else springs from there.

ELIANA BÓRMIDA

My words are going to be very simple because the four previous speakers have been quite eloquent already. I want to start by stating that spirituality and culture are essential dimensions of our existence. And we have to remember this all our lives. When we are students, we should make sure that we are pursuing two parallel educations. One consists of following a formal education at a university. Here, professors are trying to give us the tools to design, which is mainly teaching us the practice of geometry, the practice of creating forms, the practice of representing a future reality of building and spaces into papers or models. Faculty don't have much time to do more. So the other, second education is on our own. We are responsible for maturing in two other fundamental dimensions of our existence: spirituality and culture. That process start started much earlier in our childhood, in what we read, in what we talk about, in what we listen from our parents, and that continues all around and throughout our life, but we are responsible for moving it forward once we reach a certain age. If we do not follow this other learn-

Figure 15-3. Round-table speakers. From left to right: Prem Chandavarkar, Eliana Bórmida, Juhani Pallasmaa, Alberto Campo Baeza, Susan Jones, and MIchael J. Crosbie. Julio Bermudez is in the back. Photograph by Julio Bermudez.

ing path, if it is not in our intention of life, then nobody will ever be able to transmit the power of spirituality to us.

I don't know when I became conscious of this. Perhaps it was when I started studying history at my university or maybe when I decided not to teach design, not to be a design professor. I decided to study the history of culture, the history of architecture, and travel a lot to experience architecture from all periods and regions of the world by myself, with my own body, with my own senses. And I was on the right path, I think. Because afterward, I don't know why, all those experiences arrived when I had to talk to people, to students, or I had to make a project. All those experiences were alive in me.

I come from South America, Argentina, to be precise, which is even farther away because it is at the bottom of South America. It is not in the Caribbean. My home is in northern Patagonia. It is Mendoza, thirty-two-degrees latitude south, and a place where we are very close to nature. Nature is a bright presence to us. It is the most evident sign that life, creation is real. This is a strong belief that gives us a certitude that spirituality is a daily life experience. Transcendence is never felt too far away; it is not difficult to feel. We are spiritual people. We have emotions. We are sensitive to many things. We react with human attitudes towards one another.

So what are we going to do when we design? We are going to do good things for people. We are going to practice geometry and design beautiful artifacts in well-organized spaces. What qualities will those spaces exhibit? What am I going to feel there? How do I feel emotions? I want to feel sensations. I want to recover my memories, my experiences. I want to sense beauty, and I want to enjoy the world with people. And as I do all this, at the same time, I am also trying to grow as a spiritual being. In a way, it is elementary because both are totally related. Try to follow both educational paths in your life. Try to get a formal education in college and a spiritual education on your own, and then go on. It is easy.

QUESTION & ANSWERS

MICHAEL J. CROSBIE: Since the six of us are from four different continents in the world, we come to this question of spirituality and architecture with different cultural and geographic backgrounds. I would like to hear a little bit about your particular perspective on these issues. Does it have to do with the place where you grew up or where you continue to pursue architecture in your part of the world? Juhani, would you like to start? Having been born in Finland, a place that has a very spiritual dimension, in terms of its history and its legend, how do you think that has helped you shape your perspective on the spiritual and architecture?

JUHANI PALLASMAA: I think, as architects, our first task is to create ourselves and the world. This is not really understood in education very much. Both are taken as given, but they are not. The young architect needs to work on this issue for many years. Who am I in this world, and what is my responsibility in this world, and what is the world? There is no self-evident world. It is our own creation, and as architects, we can only work based on this relationship between self-understanding and understanding of the world. That is what works ought to do and something that, according to art critics, Cézanne's paintings achieve: they make us feel how the world touches us. It is a beautiful description that can also be directly applied to architecture. Architecture makes us feel how the world touches us. Still, we are not sensitive enough to those issues without having deliberated a few years, working on our relationship with the world. And in my view, spirituality is not a special category. It is our human understanding of our very human life. It is implicit in the human condition. We are mortal people.

We cannot survive without an understanding and the assumption of another reality. This has been part of humanity throughout history. Our time, as I said earlier, is quasi rational. We believe we are rational, but we are far from rationality. Just look at the world developing today. It is near complete irrationality and madness, in the name of rationality. So, I think we architects should not take our profession as a given defined thing. I am, at least, questioning my position every day. And, when I was a young architect or student, I knew what a window was, and I knew what a door was. Now when I am eighty-two, I don't know anymore because they are not given things. They are specific things. It is the particular apple tree that is seen through that window, and that makes it a window. And that is why there are very few generalizations and why the idea of spirituality should not be generalized. It is in one's personal responsible attitude to life, or it is not, but it is not a subject matter to be taught in school.

ALBERTO CAMPO BAEZA: I think it is evident that spirituality is a feeling. Spirituality is capable of being experienced when architecture moves our heart. But we also need to be capable to sense it. I give a test to my students when they go to visit the Pantheon in Rome. They either cry or not cry when they experience it. If they cry, they are obligated to write a postcard to me. I have a collection of postcards. Some postcards have humility in their letters because they are authentic to what the person experienced. This is spiritual. Some of you may remember a lecture I gave here a few years ago about my bank in Granada and one worker crying the first day he entered the space. When I went to visit my finished building for the first time, I also went to see this man, an office clerk in the bank. I did it to make a point that buildings should not just function and be well-constructed but also bring out emotion, transmit beauty. All this reminds me of an old tale by a Spanish writer that I discovered one month ago. He is speaking about a giraffe and a mouse. What is the difference between a giraffe and a mouse in architecture? The giraffe is an an-

imal that has the brain very far from his heart, and the poor giraffe is incapable of enjoying architecture because its neck is three meters long. But the mouse's brain is very close to the heart, and the mouse is immediately crying! I feel architects should be more like mice and less like giraffes.

MICHAEL J. CROSBIE: Prem, how has your particular situation, place, culture influenced, or awakened within you what is important?

PREM CHANDAVARKAR: In my mid-twenties, I considered myself an agnostic. Then a group of friends, basically four couples, were interested in my and my wife's spiritual tradition. But we didn't know enough and decided to take a weekly class that my wife was keen on going. I went along more with an academic interest. What was helpful for me was that Hinduism is not based on a central book or teaching. Faith is based on a huge multiplicity and possibility of choices. That was very useful for me because I was resistant to religion as I perceived it as an external imposition of dogma. In that discovery, I found things that I was thinking of, words like beauty could be substituted with spiritual value, with very little change, and that slowly started changing my sensibilities. Another thing that was very useful was working my way to transcend Hinduism by finding information not just based on my specific faith. In other words, it has been a journey of self-discovery, although I learned very recently that perhaps this is the wrong way to think about it. According to the 13th-century German mystic Meister Eckhart, we deceive ourselves when we label our spiritual pursuit as a journey, because a journey means that we came from somewhere and are in the process of moving somewhere else.

Actually, we just need to discover that we are already there. So it is not a journey. It is about changing the rhythm of your life so you can realize where you already are. And I found the echo of this in the ancient teachings of Hinduism. In this tradition, a guru plays a remarkable role. The etymology of the word *'guru'* is interesting. It means more than a teacher. It means a *'dispeller of darkness.'* In other words, the role of the guru is to lift off the student's veil of ignorance. And this is what all true teaching is all about: to help the student sense the light that has always been shining inside them.

ELIANA BÓRMIDA: In my case, I go back to my place in South America, where nature is so prevalent. The experience of nature is vital to human beings. It is unavoidable. You must be in nature, and you must also experience solitude. Both things are significant for people who live in western cultures because we are forgetting them. We are increasingly living an artificial way of life, away from nature and with too much company. We are always trying to have things to do, be with people, all but feel yourself. And that is not good at all. Because being with yourself is the best company. You are always going to be in your life with yourself, so try to become your friend. Try to learn how to be in solitude and to feel life. Because that is the only way you will be able to give the best of life to other people. If you don't do that, how can you ever give others what you haven't given to yourself? So go to nature, enjoy solitude, and become an architect naturally, trying to follow your instincts. Try to read, try to understand what other people do, but try to discover your own path. It is essential because subjectivity and spirituality are dimensions of our inner world, and to understand that inner world, the best way to go is through the outer world, the factual world. Reality is always hard, and you still have to make decisions, decisions in life, decisions in projects, and the best way to do it is to know yourself, get self-confidence, and learn the skills to draw and make models. And consider what those drawings and models contain. What they intend to make real is what is behind, the transcendent, and this is coming from your subjectivity, your spirituality.

MICHAEL J. CROSBIE: Also, Oscar Wilde said, *"be yourself because everybody else is taken."*

Susan, can you talk a little bit about the place you grew up in? You shared a couple of experiences about how that shaped your spirit of joy, how it awakened in you this idea of spiritual architecture.

SUSAN JONES: Everybody in this room is a unique individual and has unique personal experiences. We said this here, but you must listen to yourself and give yourself space to process those experiences. For me, it was about transcending a very happy and lucky childhood, full of privilege, and lovely experiences in nature, as I mentioned. It involved a sharp tragedy, a very difficult tragedy, that I probably spent the next twenty years trying to understand myself and my role as to how that tragedy played out in my life. And there were many ways and stages in my path, some incredibly self-destructive, some incredibly destructive to others, but mostly destructive either way. And there was this point in my life where I began to realize that I needed to seek peace, calm myself, and understand the role of these tragedies in my life and how to overcome them and transcend them. Along the way, there were *'bookmarks.'* There were times when I walked through the woods, as I said, and I knew every stone of that trail — a trail that was around a mile long and took about 20 minutes to go from one end to the other. And I can see those stones. I can draw those stones. I can draw the way the muddy path, the way it is in the rain, the way it is in the dry earth. And then when you get to the dark place where you are under the thick woods, and the way the fruit trees and their light falls down on them, I could write a volume about that trail. And that process of walking every day and many years, two to three, when I was, again, a young person, trying to process this somehow before I realized other ways, more self-destructive ways to processing that tragedy. But those were experiences in nature that were indelible in me. They were experiences of space: the way the trees create the space, the way the landscape and the field, the rocks, and the berries, at different times of the year created different areas. There were five different rooms in that little trail, and all of them have their unique indelible experience in my mind.

When you become a *'real'* person and go around the world to places like the Cologne Cathedral (which I keep talking about), you realize that you are walking into a different constructed world — a world constructed by people over centuries. And you realize that there is transcendence in where you are, whether on the dirty ground, even in the pews, trying to make sense of your fifteen-year-old wretchedness (which is what I felt at that time) and the way the light comes down. You realize that there is some relationship between your humanity at this level and the light that is being brought down from that very, very high space down to you. And all of a sudden, the world gets bigger. Your life gets bigger. Your load on your shoulders gets lighter, and it is a connection that is profoundly uplifting. At that time in my life, I was not a religious person, but it was one of the most potent religious experiences I have ever had. It took me another decade to process what I had felt at that time. It was only when I had some consciousness of what that meant that I could become a religious person. I am not telling you about this experience because it is about me. Every single person has had that experience at some level. Every single person has some darkness to be touched upon, to bring about, to be processed so that you can be at peace with it. And I don't say that is an easy process at all. It was a life work of some twenty-plus years for me, and it is never-stopping, but I want to give you faith that it will happen. If you continue to pursue that path, to understand yourself, and to move into the realm of architecture, I can't think of any other gift or better medium to do that. This is why we did those really emotional models in the studio I am teaching this semester here at CUA. We did them to let you touch those places that are dark and that

are hard to access so that you can create something powerful and beautiful and transcend that. Don't stay in that darkness. You don't have to, but you will go through that, move through that part. And I just can't believe how lucky I feel to be, to call myself a practicing architect, not an architect — someone who practices how to reach those places, to make some connection between what we are feeling now, what we are feeling later. And for me, it started with a rock and a forest, but for all of you, it begins from someplace that is very powerful. Follow that path. Follow that path.

Figure 15-4. Claudio Silvestrin, Victoria Miro Private Collection Space, London — England. Photograph by Marina Bolla.

ROUND TABLE CONCLUSION

MICHAEL J. CROSBIE: We have heard this evening of the privilege and the duty of being an architect and also the power and responsibility of being a teacher, and I would like to transition this discussion to everyone in this room. But first, I would like to hear just briefly from each of our presenters what you learned about privilege and responsibility by being a Walton critic. Then I would also like to invite people from the audience to share their experiences in working with students and professors to build trust, which, I think, is very important to accomplish what we are hereafter. Eliana, would you like to start?

ELIANA BÓRMIDA: When you work, when you are a practitioner, as I am, you are not really conscious of what you are doing, particularly in the sense of whether or not it is spiritual. You are just working the way you know how to. It was not until Julio Bermudez went to Mendoza, visited one of our wineries, and afterward asked me to be a Walton Critic that my questioning began. I asked him, *"Why are you interested in our work?"* and he said, *"because it is spiritual and it provokes emotions. It makes you react as a human being."* I then started to analyze my own work, ask people, accompany them, and paid attention to their reactions to my building. Only then, I began to understand that I was doing phenomenology without knowing. This realization was quite a very, very important experience for me.

PREM CHANDAVARKAR: There is a Zen saying that *"before enlightenment it is about carrying water, chopping wood, and that after enlightenment, it is carrying water, chopping wood."* Earlier today, Juhani was asking me how the studio went, and I said that the problem with doing a studio like this in the Walton program is that after you have finished, you realized what else you could have done. I think it is imperative to have these kinds of studios because it reverses a question that tends to dominate in most architecture schools —what do I have to say about architecture? —

into what architecture can say through me? It is a fantastic path of discovery when you start going down the truth of that question and realize that the fault in our education is that we are always next to our work talking about it. We're explaining it to the professor and the studio crit; we are defending it to the jury at the end of the semester, etc. And such behavior schools us to believe that it is our intentions as architects that give meaning to the work. But in actual practice, when you hand your building over to inhabitation, your voice is forever silent. What you have to do is to empower the building to speak for itself. There is a wonderful phrase that Juhani writes in his book *"The Eyes of the Skin,"* that we lend our perceptions to the space, and the space turns to us its aura. And I think about that dialogue between the inhabitant and the aura. Isn't this what architecture demands of us? The word of advice I would give to students is to never explain your scheme by saying *'this is my concept'* because of X, Y, or Z. There is this wonderful story about Louis Kahn. He was talking to students, and he said, *"architecture is,"* and he paused, and the students thought he was searching for the next word, but he had completed his sentence. *"Architecture is."* And then he went on to explain that the spirit of architecture is internal and each individual work of architecture is some flawed attempt to reach that inner spirit and that we have to keep reaching for it.

MICHAEL J. CROSBIE: Alberto, do you want to comment on your experience as a Walton critic?

ALBERTO CAMPO BAEZA: Some people think that this critical strategy of mine (i.e., to use history) has to do with not wanting to attack contemporary architects. When my friend Bjarke Ingels smiles upon hearing a comment by me about his architecture, I am very nervous. That is why I don't like to use any adjective for this or that architectural work. I think that it is much better to learn from history, to learn from what proportion is, what scale is, what light is. Besides, nobody can offend light. Some critics or writers say, *"Mr. Campo Baeza is the harborer of light."* And I say, *"Oh no, light is the mother of all architecture. It is not mine. It is not my material. Light is the basis for architecture."* A friend of mine said something about music that resonates with my understanding of architecture and light. He said that music is air. When the air passes through an instrument, the instrument vibrates and delivers music, and in that act, it appears even more magnificent than the music. Similarly, when light goes through our spaces, we get how architecture *'sounds.'* Do you remember ancient Greek engineer Eupalinos? He said that there are buildings that are mute, buildings that speak, and this is our attempt, buildings that sing. There is a history of buildings that sing. They are the buildings that we study: the Pantheon, the Villa Savoye, and the Farnsworth house. It is possible to make buildings that sing. You guys can do it. You can do it. We can do it. It is possible. We teachers must transmit optimism in our classes. And in order to be optimistic, we cannot be professors pointing fingers, you know, like grandfathers. We must help, continue to learn, and be confident. It is possible. We can do it.

SUSAN JONES: I will just tell a quick story of architecture history professor Eduard Sekler who was my independent thesis advisor before I actually came to my senses, and it does have to do with the Walton program. I sometimes feel very humbled to be here but also almost hypocritical. Why do I say that? Because I started as a graduate student that I wanted to do a thesis on sacred space. I was so sure in all of my Harvard-GSD confidence that I knew what I was doing. So I went to professor Seckler, and I told him that I wanted to do a whole investigation of sacred spaces in the 20th century and that I didn't like any of them. *"I don't really like any,"* I said to Eduard Sekler, *"and I am going to do a compendium on all of them, research them, and show how sacred architecture really lost something since the 1950s."* This is my 24-year-old self talking to Seckler. So I finally write this whole compendium, a full 28 pages with beautiful images, many of them representing sacred buildings missing something that I am trying to explain in my writing to Seckler. And he is just how Juhani is: he is very gentle with me and very smiley, very patient with this poor young graduate student right here talking to him. When I finally finish, I don't get any words from him. He is just smiling, very friendly, very smiley, just looking at me. He says something gentle like, *"Well, if you went to visit some of these spaces, maybe you wouldn't have this feeling. Maybe there is something more,"* and so in my 24-year-old wisdom, I gave up this project, and thank goodness I gave it up. And I did some thesis with Alvaro Siza on a bridge in Vienna, and it was a fantastic experience, and I learned much more. But I realized at that moment that I would not have been capable of expressing the sacred: I am a 24-year-old beginner on this, I cannot be putting myself in front of my peers and my colleagues and talk about the sacred. And here I am now some 30 years later, and I am talking about the sacred, and I still feel like I cannot talk about *"it."* I can't. I am not sure, maybe Juhani, and Alberto, Mike, Eliana, Prem, and Julio could talk about it. But I still feel that we are still unable to express or to talk about it with any substance. And I think it is very brave of the Walton program to try and bring this sense of spiritual architecture into this school and to this young audience. I am also incredibly grateful for this conversation that we can have here today about emotion and spirituality in architecture. The care that we all brought to these words is very, very comforting, and very humbling. And it makes me feel very warm and connected to all of you here, so thank you very much.

MICHAEL J. CROSBIE: I would like to invite a couple of questions from the audience now. Okay students, there must be something burning that you want to know.

… The audience remains silent for a short time …

PALLASMAA TO CAMPO BAEZA: They must be very shy.

CAMPO BAEZA: Yes, they are very shy.

ERIC HOFFMAN (CUA Alumni): The panel talked a lot about discovering your passion and spirituality. I am a former Walton program student that went through the experience twice (Fall 2012 and 2013). I am now onto that path of being an emerging professional, an emerging architect, trying to continue this education, this discovery of spirituality in architecture beyond just college life. Are there any paths or ideas or initiatives you all took beyond college life to continue to build that education and that passion beyond?

ELIANA BÓRMIDA: Travel and study. Study and travel, and try to imagine from drawings, from plans, from sections what the place you are going to visit is going to be like. What you are going to feel when you visit it and then go and experience it for real. That is the best way to connect design work and feelings. Because design depends on representing reality, so you must learn through personal experiences how you can relate drawings, figures, and geometry with tangible things, with space and architecture or nature. You must try to connect those worlds, the world of sensations and reality —your perception — and the world of drawings and models that is called design. It is a fundamental process that you must engage in. So travel, travel, go out, and experience.

MICHAEL J. CROSBIE: The most crucial thing in answering your question is not to think that you are not a student anymore. You are a student for the rest of your life.

SUSAN JONES: We all are.

JUHANI PALLASMAA: I would like to add one more thing: read! Never stop reading.

ALBERTO CAMPO BAEZA: Never stop!

JUHANI PALLASMAA: When I was a student, I clas-sified my books into two categories: "architecture books" and "other books." And after a while, I realized the category of "other books" said much more about architecture than the so-called professional books because the other books were poetry and novels and what have you. They all spoke about life, which is the ground upon which architecture is based, whereas the professional books rarely talk about life. They speak about the same universal themes over and over again. I always advised my students never go to bed without having at least 3 or 4 good books next to your head on the night table. For me, books are magical objects. You don't even have to read them. When you have them near you, they will educate you.

ALBERTO CAMPO BAEZA: I second Juhani's wise words. I remember an old friend of mine, an-other architect who has more books of poetry than books of architecture in his library. And re-turning to Eric's question, my response is to work, work, work, work. Work is the common denominator among all of us here, from Michael to Eliana to Prem to Julio. This is a group of peo-ple that are working and working and working.

SUSAN JONES: Do the hard stuff which is the work. Do the stuff that doesn't feel good.

ALBERTO CAMPO BAEZA: And enjoy it! Enjoy, en-joy, enjoy, enjoy!

PREM CHANDAVARKAR: I would like to share a story that was life-changing for me. It was told in a lecture I heard about twenty years ago, given by a gentleman named Suresh Krishna, who ran a company that made radiator caps for au-tomobiles. This was a time when the Indian economy had just changed from a protected and isolated economy to a globally integrated one. And he somehow managed to land this large contract from General Motors to supply radi-ator caps. General Motors, in those days, was the biggest car company in the world. And their quality standard stated that in a million radiator caps, you couldn't have more than 120 defects, which means more than 99.99% right. That is a high standard. And he said that they didn't really know what they were doing, but they agreed to it. He said in the first year, they hit something like 60 or 70 defects. In the second year, they brought it down to 20, and in the third year, they hit 0. So he asked, "How did we do it?" To explain, he said he had to tell us a story. The story is about this young prince who was about to become a king, and he had to be trained to be fit to be a king. He was sent for this training to a mystic who lived on the edge of a forest. The mystic said to the prince, "I am not going to tell you anything. You must go live in the forest for three months and after that come and tell me what you heard." So the prince goes in, and after his return at the end of the three months, he was asked what he heard. And he narrated very dramatic things. He said, "I heard a thunderstorm; I heard a tiger killing a deer; I heard an elephant crashing through the forest." He was told by the mystic that he had not appropriately listened and must go back for three more months and listen more carefully. After this second stint of three months, the prince described sounds that were much more subtle. He spoke about water flowing in a brook, the rustle of wind through leaves, and things like that. Again, he was told, "No, you haven't listened properly. Go back for three more months and listen some more." This time the prince came out after one month, very excited, exclaiming, "I heard it! I heard it!" The mystic asked, "What did you hear?" The prince replied, "I heard sunlight hitting the ground; I heard a flower blooming; I heard dew forming on the grass." The mystic told him, "You can go home now. You are fit to be a king." So Suresh Krishna said, "We listened to the radiator caps that way. And that is how we did it." I have been trying in my own flawed way to listen to architecture that way. You've got to listen carefully.

MICHAEL J. CROSBIE: I want to thank our round table for sharing their perceptions, histories, and hopes. We can continue this discussion with questions outside this lecture hall during the reception and over the next few days. Thank you all for being here tonight.

APPENDIX

THE VOLUNTARY ARCHITECTURAL SIMPLICITY MANIFESTO
JULIO BERMUDEZ

THE CALL

Postmodern apathy, cynicism, and relativism notwithstanding, we are experiencing a fragmented and chaotic reality acted out in massively irresponsible behaviors across the Earth. Our world is shrinking under the relentless assault of our polluting and wasteful habits. Habits that come out of accepting life in the fast lane under the mantra of more, bigger, faster, better, and cheaper. Habits that keep on failing to provide what they promise and instead deliver only more unmet needs, grief, and stress. Despite the promises heralded by the advancing information age, continuous scientific breakthroughs, the prowess of technological evolution, and the myth of infinite growth and rationality, we always find ourselves returning, increasingly more frustrated, to the same ancient existential dramas born out of just being alive and trying to attain some peace, security, and contentment. Little, if any, have we advanced in these simple matters. Escaping this fact into the carefully crafted distractions geared to our most superficial desires and exercised through unchecked consumerism never quite works either. Worse still, we are beginning to see what some of these habits have brought us: global warming, unspoken poverty co-existing with opulent greed, violence, AIDS, terrorism, war, ecological devastation, and economic instability at a planetary scale. Although it is hard to admit it, we ourselves have been all too often shy accomplices of this state of affairs. Confused, distracted, and overwhelmed by the neurotic complexity of it all, we feel little more than irrelevant peons, floating astray in the rough seas of 21st Century civilization.

Architecture, the art of establishing the material order of a cultural order, cannot avoid but to reflect and respond to its surrounding reality. Not surprisingly, the current reality is requiring architectural responses defying all traditions. Contemporary architects increasingly find themselves with the task of redefining architecture's purpose, technology, functionality, and aesthetics based on the needs and visions of our seemingly ungraspable culture.

Professing architecture is no light matter in these circumstances. True professing demands that we hold a position, stand for something, make a vow in the name of a deep-seated passion for architecture, our fellow beings, and Earth. Professing also requires being able to technically and competently respond to architectural challenges. Professing is where belief and knowledge come together in the here and now of present reality. Hence, uncritically adopting off-the-shelf Postmodern, Modern, Classicist, Deconstructivist, and any other pre-digested style appears superficial and irresponsible.

So, how are we to profess architecture facing *this* reality? Can we truly make a committed and caring act in which we use our architectural skills for the sake of improving whatever is trusted to us as architects? Can we make a difference?

THE RESPONSE

We take on this question professionally. And, following the two meanings behind professing, it moves simultaneously in two parallel paths of commitment and embodiment.

The philosophical path offers a ***voluntary and critical direction*** that resists the forces of today's zeitgeist. The disciplinary path leads towards ***architectural clarity, sustainability, and essentialism*** as concrete ways to embody this resistance. The two-path road points towards a renewed aesthetics and ethics of 'less is more.' It encourages a turn towards the minimal, the fundamentally uncomplicated, the direct, and conscious as a potent antidote to our culture of excess, schizophrenia, and unconsciousness. We are talking about an architecture of presence. We will use Duane Elgin's book ***"Voluntary Simplicity"*** as a source of clarity and inspiration along this road.[1]

Starting the journey demands that, first and foremost, we do it ***voluntarily***. We must freely choose it from within and not feel that it is imposed on us from without. Second, this choice has to come out of some personal realization (conscious or unconscious) of its necessity. In other words, we cannot select it as a result of nostalgia or reactionary ideology. Rather it should ***grow out of*** our direct experience of the situation itself. "Growing-out-of" something means to have been in the midst of it and come out of it by first-hand learning and effort. It signifies that we embrace (and not to throw away) what has been overcome. In having been intimate with it at one time, we have understood it well enough to attempt to transcend it without narrow-minded resentment. In other words, it is not a position arrived at by intellectual reasoning or negative emotions. Instead, it is a decision founded in a concrete and personal experience of growth.

Thus, choosing simplicity grows out of our direct experience of living under unnecessary complexity. Seeking focus grows out of being tired of living in distraction. Pursuing essentialism grows out of realizing that superficiality offers little. And so on, the desire for clarity grows out of confusion, conservation out of wastefulness, austerity out of excess, integrity out of fragmentation, self-restraint out of empty consumerism and spending, poetry out of crude materialism, presence and slowness out of the fleetingness of a fast life, committed participation out of passive following, the minimum out of overcrowded and cluttered conditions, and order out of chaos.

We will call the resulting architecture, ***Voluntary Architectural Simplicity (VAS)***. The **VAS** Studio is wherein **VAS** is practiced by making use of basic or essential architectural principles, rules, ideas, experiences. VAS engages the hypothesis of simplicity as a critical, insight seeking, disciplinary, and conscious inquiry to confront the professional challenges of today.

There is an unspoken high power that is pushing us into **VAS** : ***spirituality***. We "sense" that today's huge problems will never be sincerely addressed (and thus solved) unless we acknowledge the ultimate meaning, wholeness, or trans-personal nature of reality and all beings. While this vision does not require a divinity, it doesn't shy away from the metaphysical either. In this sense, perhaps, our most urgent job as architects is to profess the sacredness of all space on Earth so that land development may be done with care and wisdom. The preservation, respect, and celebration of space can only come when we honor its sacred dimension. By bringing a spiritual sensibility to its fold, **VAS** may be able to positively affect a world in desperate need of truth, goodness, and beauty. **VAS** gives us the intellectual, emotional, and active space to discuss, explore, practice, and advance an architecture that fosters spiritual development by the sheer power of design quality.

Two disclaimers to end this manifesto. First, **VAS** is consciously naïve in seeking to resist the overwhelming forces of our time. It just makes non-sense to do so. Second, **VAS** is not self-righteous. Although it claims to do what is right, it does not see this path as the only or best path to address today's challenges. It only points at one possible way of professing architecture. It just professes, and in so doing offers, humbly, Voluntary Architectural Simplicity.

CHOOSING BEING: how to respond to today's unhealthy state of affairs
JULIO BERMUDEZ

SITUATION

There are three fundamental directions or foci in which our lives may advance: doing, having, or being.

We live in a world that expects from us continuous productive or consumption activity. Be it at work, in the market, or at school, we are being asked to do more and more. Doing, it seems, is the ticket to success. After all, the saying goes, you haven't seen anybody getting places by sitting on their butt. We love to boast about how much we have accomplished and, better still, how much there remains to do! Who can deny that we are competing with each other (and with ourselves) as to who is the one most overwhelmed with work? So, doing, getting-things-done is the mantra running our daily lives. We accordingly pack our days from dawn to dusk with activities aimed at achieving maximum benefit. And, naturally, we transfer this lifestyle to our kids whose schedules are so busy with extra-curricular activities (designed to put them ahead in adult life) that they have no time to … play! Our 'try-to-keep-busy' stoic attitude also cuts into our leisure time (i.e., we come back from vacation more tired than we left), the gym (Oh, boy! Do you know how much I lifted today!? … and that's nothing to what I still have to do in the coming weeks according to my new

work-out routine), and even spiritual practices (i.e., guess who is getting more enlightened, righteous, or closer to God?).

Of course, the striving for doing is only one side of the coin. The other side is the simultaneous expectation for uncritical consumption. Buying, getting, using up, having are not just legitimate ways in which to spend our free time, but a socially accepted (and surely needed) mechanism of psychological compensation. And more, much more. In fact, it has taken on patriotic value: the best contribution a concerned citizen could do right after 9-11 (as requested by the President himself) was … to go shopping! The message is loud and clear. If we are not busy doing, then be busy consuming, but be busy. Don't stop! Just keep on going.

Indeed, living in America today means to be 24/7 busy. So accustomed have we grown to this situation that even when we are not busy, we feel in need to fake that we are. Who hasn't found oneself pretending to be working when somebody is watching? It is as if the more it is demanded from us, the more we do, the more we buy or have, the busier we are, the higher is our self worth and placement in society, and, supposedly, the better we feel.

The socially accepted way to escape this onslaught is media. We are allowed to (often expected to) leave the busy and consumption cycles and plunge into digital entertainment and connections. Who hasn't been relieved to receive a phone call in the middle of some uncomfortable waiting or quiet time? Who hasn't quickly turned to our smartphone seeking some unnecessary information (so we can remain occupied)? TV, the internet, flicks, radio, Twitter, videogames — you name it — are ways for us to leave behind the little reality left in our lives lest we break the spell and return to some ugly, unacceptable, frightening world. Media consumption, the adult pacifier/drug par excellence, keeps us 'entertained' (i.e., from Latin: being in between, i.e., in limbo) and, in doing so, maintain us in a fabricated trance: comfortably numb, asleep.

Those people, practices, activities, discourses, or beliefs critical to or not fitting in this picture are quickly spotted and discredited. In our extreme neo-puritan ethics, hanging-out, idling, not doing are seen as parasitic, aberrant if not plain subversive acts. Not having a cell phone or TV/internet at home are looked down upon: what kind of weirdo are you? Not joining the shopping way of life risks socialist or anti-American condemnation. In short, social labels and judgments are readily available to explain any and all of these non-sense attitudes: ignorance, psychological disturbance, immaturity, naïve idealism, religious fundamentalism, leftist anarchism … We just need to keep the system going, and for this, we are reassured over and over again, we must have the production, consumption, and media machinery running undisturbed (now globally). Never mind the results of these actions.

Doing and having have won the day.

RESPONSE

Faced with this state of affairs, seeing it for what it is, we could decide to take an alternative path so that we can begin to heal and awake from this collective hallucination. Moving in the right direction is not that hard to figure out once we realize the situation. It just demands that we engage opportunities that focus on 'being' rather than 'doing' or 'having.'

And this starts by diminishing the enslaving cycles of unchecked production and consumption (material or virtual) and creating the mental-emotional-physical space-time wherein we can step back and become aware of our circumstances. We must find excuses and sanctuaries for guiltless idling: events, places, and times to find, enjoy, and expand being. To put it differently, by resisting the pressures to be busy, consume, and/or plunge into the mediasphere, we become able to notice our being alive. By deciding to provide ourselves with a necessary retreat from real-world disease, we promote healing, both at the individual and collective levels. By fostering and celebrating not-doing, not-having, stopping, and letting be, we begin to liberate ourselves from the bondage of socio-cultural programming. We will know if we succeed when we find ourselves in the here and now of our lives feeling whole, awakened, alive, and yes, joyful!

Developing being means to engage the subjective (personal, individual self), intersubjective (social, collective self), and objective (environmental, no-self) dimensions of human experience (i.e., first-, second- and third-person perspectives). It means to direct ourselves to observe, study, exercise, express, and taste being's mind, body, and connectivity with others and nature. This effort may need separation and connection at different times, often accepting opportunities to deal with ourselves in solitude, while other times seeking chances to come together in community and with nature.

Although it should be evident from these short considerations, growing being is professing the appreciation and support of all life — for being is life. Hence, affirming being, re-establishing a balance between 'having,' 'doing' and 'being' is a spiritual proposition, whether one is religious or not. This is because it demands us to "re-ligare" (i.e., the Latin root of religion), which means nothing else than to re-connect with the broadest and deepest realms of all — something

which has never been severed to start with —
only forgotten. Not surprisingly, several faith
traditions in the East and West do encourage
us to practice being over having and/or doing.
An excellent example, especially in the context
of this discussion, is the following statement by
Pope John Paul II:

> *"Ours is a time of continual movement
> which often leads to restlessness, with the
> risk of 'doing for the sake of doing'. We
> must resist this temptation by trying 'to be'
> before trying 'to do'."*[2]

Our *way to respond to today's unhealthy state of
affairs* is thus to **choose being** by affirming, developing, and celebrating its *unfolding* alone and in
community.

ON THE ARCHITECTURAL DESIGN PARTI
JULIO BERMUDEZ

Preliminary Note: This short essay presents meditations on the nature and function of the "parti" in architectural design. I wrote it back in 2006 after having to respond to students' frequent requests for an explanation of what-a-parti-is throughout my many years of teaching design studios. In this essay, I try to shed light on the matter without killing the magic and even esoteric quality of what the 'parti' stands for.[3]

What is an _Architectural Design Parti_? Better yet, what is the _architectural design parti_ of _your proposal_? If you can't answer this question, then you can't really go anywhere. Well, you can go many ways, but you are truly lost. Going home, finding your whereabouts, your direction – that's what it means to become aware of your _parti_.

So, what is a _parti_? Simply put, it's the most basic organizational principle that expresses your architectural design. It is the scheme, main concept, or idea that explains better than anything else the character and appearance of your design. It's the position your design takes in front of the world of infinite architectural possibilities. Very much like what a political party does amid the many political ideologies, it could embrace or address the state of affairs of a country, people, crisis, economy… After all, _parti_ comes from the French word similar to the Spanish word, _"partido."_ In Spanish, arriving at a _parti_ requires

"toma de partido," literally to "take a position." So selecting a _parti_ demands your declaration of affiliation, the commitment to a significant idea of architecture that resolves a given set of architectural challenges.

So the _parti_ is not neutral. It demands professing… professing a belief.

The _parti_ is the most comprehensive yet most profound description possible of your act of making. In a way, it comes foremost and first, before any language is applied. Hence you can have the same parti being used by Peter Zumthor, Jean Nouvel, Zaha Hadid, or Michael Graves. Of course, certain types of languages or positioning may preclude the selection of certain _partis_, very much like certain cultures may not accept or choose certain kinds of political or economic ideologies.

So, what is it? You see, if you answer this question, then you resolve all the questions, hence its importance and its difficulty. For a _parti_ permeates every single aspect of architecture: its formal manifestation, its tectonics and details, its engagement of program and site, its experience… Despite seeming to be 'intellectual,' the _parti_ is far from being intellectual – the _parti_ is the true nature of the design, its soul if you wish. It manifests its very essence and therefore, cannot be just intellectual. Naturally, it takes a sharp and agile mind to clarify the spirit of a work of architecture. But such an undertaking is more an act of observation than of thinking. Intellectualization often obscures or confuses what is in front of you. In a way, the essence, nature, or primary condition of the architectural being cannot be 'figured out' but instead needs to be 'seen' or 'felt.'

Of course, you start your effort by seeking a *parti* and once found, you steer the design process toward creating a building that materializes such character. Let's say you pick a 'juxtaposition' *parti*. This choice may be random, pre-assigned, chosen for good reasons (analysis, site, precedent, etc.). However, once you select this or that *parti*, then you are definitely moving toward this and not that direction. You now have an operative system for critiquing, developing, realizing your architecture.

In short, the *parti* is the overall and comprehensive schema, idea, or concept giving order, meaning, and rationale to a building. It provides a horizontal thrust that connects program, site, experience, form, space, and tectonics in such a way that, if very well done, it also points to a vertical dimension: philosophy and spirituality. The *parti* may start from a particular architectural concept interpreting a specific aspect of architecture (context, precedent, composition, materiality, program, etc.). However, in order to become a *parti*, it needs to become wholistic and cross-dimensional, bringing all aspects of a design within its domain.

ARCHITECTS ON THE ARCHITECTURAL DESIGN PARTI

"The most important matter in designing a building is to establish a design philosophy. Each building needs and should have its own appropriate principle that directs the design… Little by little the philosophy of the building starts to take shape in my mind and suddenly I have the feeling that it is ready…" Ricardo Legorreta[4]

"… making architecture is about making choices, which once made, exclude other choices. The choices one makes establishes a kind of testament…"
John Pawson[5]

"Without an IDEA, Architecture would be pointless, only empty form… An idea is capable of: serving (function), responding to a place (context), resolving itself geometrically (composition), materializing itself physically (construction)… Architecture is always a built IDEA. The history of Architecture is the History of built IDEAS. Forms change, they crumble, but the IDEAS remain, they are eternal."
Alberto Campo Baeza[6]

*"**Order is***
***Design** is form-making in order*
Form emerges out of a system of construction
Growth is a construction
*In **order** is creative force*
*In **design** is the means —where   with what   when with how much*
The nature of space reflects what it wants to be
………………………
Thru the nature —why
*Thru the **order**—what*
*Thru **design** — how"*
Louis Kahn[7]

TESTIMONIALS

It is essential to have the voice of the people that went through the Walton experience in this book. The students are the reason why the Walton Program and Studio exist. I sent an email to all the alumni for whom I had an electronic address. I asked them to comment on their experience. Respondents could remain anonymous if so chose. Below are their statements.

The testimonials are organized by the year the experiences happened, starting with the oldest Walton Studio and finishing with the most recent one. Within each studio, the accounts are alphabetically ordered by the alumni's last name. When possible, I included their student status at the time of having the experience. In several cases, individuals took two Walton Studios, and that's the reason why two years are sometimes marked.

2010 Walton Studio

I took part in the second Walton Studio with Craig W. Hartman and was greatly influenced during my thesis by the following year's Walton Critic Juhani Pallasmaa. Looking back now, the exposure that the Walton Studio gave me is even more important than perhaps I knew then. It has influenced me as a person in the way I see the world, and in practice, as it helps me narrow down my interests and beliefs. As a designer

working in the field, it is not always easy to stick to those beliefs, but this studio, along with the Spirit of Place program led by Travis Price, still guide my way and define my ethos. Being exposed to architects who successfully practice architecture in this way has been essential in determining my career path. It is one thing to think of a beautiful and meaningful idea but entirely another to make it materialize. The Walton Studio proves that it is possible. I remember feeling understood and excited that others wanted to rise to the challenge of creating spaces that pushed these boundaries.

In the years since, I have checked back and learned about new architects or have been excited to see that high profile professionals were aware of the Walton Program going on at CUA. Personally, even now, as a mother of two young children, it shapes how I would like them to be able to view the world. It is important as their teacher to be able to share the emotional and transcendent ways in which reality discloses itself. I hope that the Walton Studio program continues so that future students, CUA School of Architecture and Planning, and thereby the field of Architecture continues to advance for the benefit of society.

Chloe Rice *(graduate student)*

Reflecting on my time spent at Catholic University studying sacred architecture with Julio Bermudez, specifically in the Walton Studio, it feels odd to compartmentalize the kind of architecture we were analyzing, discussing, and creating from any other kind. To me, there is no distinction between spiritual architecture and non-spiritual architecture. Architecture is spiritual! This is the lens thru which I perceive the world — that the act of claiming and capturing space is itself a sacred and ancient human ritual. This belief feels so essential to my understanding of what architecture is, can, and should be that I struggle to recognize the origin.

Now a decade later, the element of the Walton Studio that remains most memorable and transformative was the advice and wisdom of Craig W. Hartman. I believe there is too often a disconnect between the study and practice of architecture, especially regarding less "practical" pursuits — the emotional, spiritual, ineffable quality of architecture. Mr. Hartman represented for me proof that the ideas we were passionately defending in the studio were not merely abstract concepts but real and powerful principles to be manifested in steel, glass, and stone.

There was never an issue of belief in the sacredness of architectural space, no doubt in the Why. What was unclear, and often remains murky as a young practicing architect, is the How. While navigating the complex practice of architecture, much of my energy is spent understanding less-than-sacred aspects of the profession; payroll, R-values, errors & omissions insurance, the best time to call the Baltimore City permit office (after lunch), etc. What guides my career are the lessons learned in the Walton Studio and instincts birthed and developed not simply intellectually, through intense study and debate, but emotionally through a journey of experiencing and perceiving the spiritual power of architecture.

Evan Wivell *(graduate student)*

2010 & 2011 Walton Studio

It was my great privilege to have my work at CUA critiqued by three Walton Critics: Craig W. Hartman, Juhani Pallasmaa, and Alberto Campo Baeza. And while the wisdom of these three architectural giants was invaluable, the most profound lesson came from Professor Julio Bermudez himself. Julio once opened a studio lesson by reminding us all that it was the fall equinox. And commenting on a great cultural disappointment: we live in a time and place in which most people have no lived understanding of the equinoxes and solstices. No real, lived understanding of the cycles of nature. No understanding of the cyclical nature of the place we all call home; the earth. Essentially, no understanding of place. An education in the Walton Studio at CUA is an education in the spirituality of place; of placemaking. It's been ten years since I started my education in the spirituality of placemaking. Now, as a mother of four, my focus is on the spirituality of home and on placemaking within the sacred space of the domestic church. The primary lesson I carry to this day from the Walton Studios is architecture, particularly sacred architecture, and the importance of place are not compartmentalized from "real life" or vice versa. They are a part of the very essence of each other. I was once told an architectural education is a classical education: that of educating the whole person. The Walton Studio is a great bastion of education for the whole person, aiming to imbue students of architecture with a great sense of the importance of spirituality in the making of a place.

Ashley Prince Rodriguez *(graduate student)*

2011 Walton Studio

To be able to sit beside Juhani Pallasmaa daily and discuss experiential architecture through the means of a school project is a priceless memory to have of my schooling years.

Today, working with a client to create/renovate their own space requires a deep dive into that person's life to truly design for and around them. The space guides them through their day to day, working for and with them on an experiential level.

It was discussions of "phenomenology" through the Walton Studio that made me understand the critical connection between person and architecture on a sensible human scale.

It is imperative for professional education to bring in diverse critics of many backgrounds to provide students opportunities to think and approach architecture through different lenses. The Walton Critic, no doubts, offers such skills. Outside of the Walton Studio itself, it is very valuable to have the Walton Critic as a tool of learning through guest teaching and jurying. I had the experience of having Alberto Campo Baeza sit and critique my final thesis presentation, which is an event I will never forget.

Andrew Baldwin (graduate student)

The Walton Studio was an incredible learning experience that undoubtedly altered my outlook and approach to design. Words will only begin to describe the experience, and they will likely fall short in conveying the impact. It fundamentally changed my perspective and thought process — to say it was "just" a studio would be a gross understatement and severely underrepresent the impact to me personally and professionally. There were long nights, many struggles, and challenges, but these were all welcomed.

The Walton Studio exposed me to a completely different way of approaching design. Until that point, design had been more formally driven and touched little upon actual experiences. I vividly remember reading Juhani Pallasmaa's *"The Eyes of the Skin"* and hanging on each and every word. It forced me to think about the architecture and the connection with the individual beyond the spatial "box." It really forced me to think about how we inform spaces and vice versa, how they, in turn, inform us. (Just as a side remark — this marked up, over-highlighted and underlined book still remains in my possession.).

The Walton Program is a huge draw for students, and it is consistently my first recommendation for any attending or incoming student. I sincerely hope it remains as-is.

Scott Gillespie (graduate student)

2011 & 2012 Walton Studio

A few years ago, I embarked on a spiritual pilgrimage of sorts and traveled more than 2,600 miles to attend graduate school at The Catholic University of America. The Walton Critic program, the Cultural Studies and Sacred Space graduate concentration, and the high caliber of faculty at CUA first attracted me to the school because it is unique and unlike anything that exists in the world. I hoped to gain an education that would enable me to become a successful architect of religious buildings, but I left with vastly more. Participating in the Walton Studios with the visiting critics impacted my understanding of the interconnectivity between architecture, culture, spirituality, ecology, and human experience. From a practical standpoint, my studio experiences taught me how to think with my hands, draw in my mind, and cultivate my imagination.

On a spiritual level, however, I was taught how to surrender my ego and be a humble architect open to new horizons, perspectives, challenges, and modes of discovery. I came to an existential awareness of my surroundings, which awakened within me the ethical necessity to defend the authenticity of human experience through architectural design. Likewise, revealing the sacred transcendental realm through architecture became a new priority for me. I came to understand that in order to transform chaos into cosmos, one must design with beauty and truth. But designing with beauty and truth required me to slow down and discern the fingerprint of the Creator's hands in the order, patterns, geometry, proportions, and principles found in nature. My design studio mentors also taught me that ethics and aesthetics are ultimately intertwined with a love for humanity. Designing buildings to protect the public's health, safety, and welfare is only the beginning; one must transcend those expectations with a desire to build a lasting and beautiful world which uplifts and inspires the human spirit.

I am truly grateful for the Walton Critic Program in Sacred Space and Cultural Studies; for it has positively shaped my work as an architect, my research as an emerging scholar, and my pedagogy as an educator. I hope that CUA continues to teach and profess spirituality in architectural education.

Brandon Ro *(graduate student)*

2012 Walton Studio

Taking the Walton Studio with Alberto Campo Baeza had a profound impact on my architectural studies at CUA. In a short time, the studio lessons with Alberto forever shaped my thoughts on space, light, and balance. As a self-described son of Mies van der Rohe, Alberto taught us about the beauty of balance and the logic of symmetry and form. The simplicity of modern clean lines, articulated with simple materials and complemented by the ever-changing sun as it casts light and shadows throughout the day, months, and seasons. The Walton Studio with Campo Baeza demonstrates the beautiful design power of "less with more" to elevate a person's experience of space with all their senses. To this day, I have frequently asked myself if what I have designed is logical and balanced.

If I were given the opportunity, I would retake the Walton Studio. It was an extraordinary opportunity to learn from a renowned architect how to think and develop a personal design

library and philosophy with which to build your own foundation of architectural thought. I hope that future generations of young architects will continue to have the opportunity to be exposed and learn from professionals that have mastered their craft.

Toni Lem *(graduate student)*

From a young age, I have been a determined and goal-oriented person. I set my mind into a goal and use that vision to carry me through the whole process. Back in 2012, the force and determination that pushed me forward for so many years were gone after I graduated with a bachelor's degree in architecture from The Catholic University of America. Ironically mixed with the pride I felt with such achievement, I was also left feeling empty, wondering if a higher education or even architecture was necessary for my modest way of living. I thought if the goal was to live a good life, then why to be part of such a draining and complicated effort in earning an education and later working in architecture when this will eventually consume my life. After many considerations and enticed by the chance of meeting a world-class architect, I thankfully decided to continue my education at CUA and participate in the Walton Program with Julio Bermudez and architect Alberto Campo Baeza.

The fall semester of 2012 was the first time I ever heard an architect and a professor didactically speak about their personal beliefs and philosophies so strongly, rendering architecture as an unavoidable mode of professing. I then understood that life does not come second to architecture, nor architecture is something we practice as a means to gain anything, but it is a consequence of who we are. Architecture is not the voice, but the conversation itself. It was Alberto's words that finally articulated the rambling thoughts in my mind, advocating for an architecture that is essential and without clutter. Those words still resonate with me as a professional.

Robin Munoz *(graduate student)*

2012 & 2013 Walton Studio

My educational and spiritual experience in the Walton Program is a significant turning point in my architectural and spiritual journey. I had come from an Islamic background with a focus on Sufism in search of spirituality. I had the privilege to learn, study, and ultimately experience spiritual architecture from different faiths around the globe. The openness of the Walton Program helped me critically question my faith and eventually grow through natural, cultural, and religious layers to spiritual essence. I had the chance to learn how spirituality can be manifested into space from two world-class architects (Alberto Campo Baeza and Claudio Silvestrin) who have successfully done so. The Walton Studios widened my perspective and showed me possibilities to advance spiritually and manifest this spirituality into habitable space.

The approach of this program is uniquely experiential. It provides the space for students to grow in both inward and outward directions spiritually. Readings and assignments help students contemplate the deep layers of their physical, psychological, and spiritual self, yet provide guidance and environment to explore the broader layers of our collective consciousness.

The Walton Program was a life-changing experience that gave me the courage to apply its deepest teachings to my professional and spiritual life.

Amirali Ebadi (graduate student)

I have had the honor of participating in the Walton Studio both as a student (twice) and as a teacher. They both have been unforgettable experiences by their intensity and the novelty they exposed me to.

I came from Spain after having finished my architectural studies in Madrid, to get a Master's degree in the U.S. The concentration in Sacred Space at CUA is what attracted me the most. I had never heard about a graduate program like it before. I thought that it was a unique opportunity to bring my faith and my work together. The very first semester I took the Walton Studio, I had the great surprise of finding as Walton Critic Alberto Campo Baeza, a professor/architect I admire, and whom I had had as a professor also earlier in Madrid.

As a graduate student, what impacted me the most was the human quality of the Walton Critics, which, at that time, I saw manifested in their dedication to the students and the passion they put when they talked about architecture. Later on, as one of the faculty in the 2016 Walton Studio, I saw the coherence between what the critics professed and their architecture.

One big difference of the Walton Studio and other studios is assignments that invite students into deep thinking. I will always remember the first site visit we did for our project in 2012, a monastery for 12 monks by the Potomac River in Washington DC. Julio had us stay there for a long time, just feeling the place in order to get the inspiration for our projects. The Walton Studio leaves an impact because it requires students to contemplate beyond what we see with our eyes and to express the invisible with our designs. Thus, faith and work, the sacred and the profane are not seen as separated aspects of our life, but on the contrary, parts of the same whole that enhance one other.

What I appreciate most about the Walton Studio is the non-conventional types of projects it uses as well as the close interaction between the Walton Critic and the students. The time he or she is in the studio creates a different atmosphere in the whole school. During these times, the students work hard, architecturally seeking the good and the beautiful, and this process occasions what seems to be a transformation of their being. I wish the residency of the guest critic could be longer!

Ana Maria Roman (graduate student)

2013 Walton Studio

The Walton Studio and the Sacred Space concentration not only gave me a deeper understanding of the world around me but also opened my eyes to the impact of spirituality in design. The studio with Claudio Silvestrin brought to light the experiential poetics of minimalist architecture and the lasting impression that a space can leave on the visitor. It changed my way of viewing architecture as a whole. I realized that design is not just a visual encounter but an emotional and spiritual experience as well.

Erica Donnelly (*graduate student*)

Contemporary architecture is routinely asked to address a whole host of societal, environmental, and physical challenges. Rarely is the effect of architecture upon the human spirit questioned or explored. The Walton Studio, with its focus on the spiritual and cultural potential of the built environment, provided a unique opportunity to plumb the depths of meaning and its translation into physical form. Speaking personally, the Walton Studio was my first architecture studio as a graduate student at CUA. In many ways it became a threshold for a new way of thinking — and feeling — about architecture in an academic context that deeply impacted the rest of my time at the university. While the scope of the program is unique on its own, it is strengthened by well-known voices from a global background who bring their own perspectives to the pursuits of the Walton Studio. In my studio's time with Claudio Silvestrin, we strived together to distill meaningful simplicity from challenging historical and social contexts. Looking back at a distance of several years, the introspection and thoughtfulness engendered by the Walton Studio remain close to my heart as I engage with the world in my role of architect each day.

Matthew Schmalzel (*graduate student*)

During my time in the Walton Studio, I came to understand a great amount about intuition in design and getting in touch with personal and spiritual decision making, specifically in architecture. This opened up design opportunities that I did not believe were possible for me. It also heightened my interest in creating physical connections with higher powers outside of and within myself. As an architect, I find that I trust my heart more than I would if I were not exposed to this type of design studio.

The most memorable part of the Walton Studio experience came from challenging my mind and instincts. The complexity around thinking outside of our typical notions and toward inward reflection is something that I will be forever grateful for. It impacted every design studio that I took following it and ultimately gave me confidence in my decision making for my Master's Thesis and beyond. I carry this experience with me in my design work today.

One major part of the success of this studio is Julio's guidance, influence, and trust in his students. Without his leadership, none of this would be possible nor as profound as this program has been over the years. For him, I am always grateful.

Kristen Weller (*graduate student*)

Figure 20-1. Walton Program alumni reunion (2018). From left to right. Gabrielle Oakes, Julio Bermudez, Kristen Weller, Anh-Tu Nguyen, and Matthew Schmalzel. Photograph by Julio Bermudez.

2013 & 2014 Walton Studio

I see the Walton Studios as more than just classes. Compared to other coursework at that time, they felt like something much more profound. They not only seek to uncover and convey a meaningful understanding of the phenomenological potential of design but are also an opportunity for observation and introspection. There is an emphasis on architecture's connection to the greater world around us that can be very difficult to find, in both academia and in the "real" world. Likewise, the journey towards understanding that connection, primarily through the design process, is rightfully treated with equal importance. I am very thankful to have had the chance to participate in two of these studios, for what I learned in them I have carried with me even to this day.

John Allen (graduate student)

The Walton Studios helped shape my point of view on design in a way that I do not believe could have been easily realized on my own. We were guided by our critics to think about the projects and design challenges that they gave us in ways that I can confidently say have directly influenced the manner in which I approach my work daily. The topics of the studios were not always necessarily unique from other studio focuses; the subjects were not chosen because they could be defined as spiritual spaces — that would have totally missed the point. The goal, or at least my goal, became to be able to view any space as experiential. The user's interaction with the built environment was what we were really creating, with architecture as the medium. We were shown how to see the impact that the built environment can have on individuals, and this has allowed me to view architecture and space in a way that I have come to consider invaluable.

Megan Gregory (graduate student)

2014 Walton Studio

Six years after the fact, I often find myself thinking about my time in the 2014 Walton Studio with Julio Bermudez and Eliana Bórmida. It was the first semester of my Master of Architecture program, and although I had received a B.S. in Architecture from CUA in 2008 and had been working in the industry, I didn't have a passion for the profession.

I consider my Walton Studio a turning point in both my education as well as my career so far. Eliana and Julio introduced me to the concept of Voluntary Architectural Simplicity — or "VAS" — as a philosophical design concept. It teaches that the architect has the opportunity and responsibility to respond to overwhelming cultural forces by creating spiritually uplifting and enriching environments; in a world prone to excess and instability, consciously designed spiritual spaces can enrich and heal.

The VAS philosophy shaped how I understand the built world, as well as my personal role as an architect. Designing for meaningful sensory experience through the VAS lens became a foundational professional approach of mine. Now, my passion for design is rooted in the goal to effect positive change where I can, and I have that first semester in 2014 to thank.

Victoria Wallace (graduate student)

2014 & 2015 Walton Studio

Relative to other students at the school of architecture, I was older when I took the Walton Studios. I was a 60-year-old practicing professional with over 30 years of design and construction experience when I decided to complete a Master's degree in Architecture. Yet, the entire Sacred Space and Cultural Studies graduate concentration under the direction of Professor Julio Bermudez proved to be an eye-opening experience and one that will remain with me and guide me through life. Although I consider myself a spiritual person with a sense of appreciation for design and the built environment, I found myself in new uncharted waters. With the help of the studio process and the Walton Critics, I was able to develop new paths and open new doors that I was not aware of before. The experience was one similar to a searching journey of mind and heart to a place of enchantment such as Jerusalem, Mecca, or Tibet. The studio became a hermitage, and sessions became an experience to look forward to.

I would recommend the program to any design students or professional who wishes to expand their way of thinking and open their mind to new challenges that go beyond day to day manmade constraints of the design process. A unique feature of the Walton Program is the fact that its visitors come from across the globe, ready and willing to share their thoughts and feelings; this experience is one that is impossible to duplicate. Often studio sessions would move on to dinners or walks in nature, and the journey continued. I hope that I could attend the program again to further my personal and spiritual growth as well as furthering my education in architecture. The selection of Professor Bermudez to manage the program, in my opinion, is key to its success. Julio breaks down the barriers of preconceptions and logic to get the student to experience new thoughts and patterns.

Sina Moayedi (*graduate student*)

2015 Walton Studio

Going through the Walton Critic Program, architecture made me take a deeper dive than I thought I could. I thought I already knew something about the spirituality of architecture, and how it affects/can affect people. This studio challenged me to design a space in the cosmopolitan city of Washington, where people could rest, refresh, and reconnect with themselves and their natural environment, not an easy task.

The final jury was the most memorable part. It was because the design process had been difficult for me, getting out of my shell/comfort zone, especially at the beginning. Seeing that I was capable of creating a new space for people to reconnect on a spiritual level made me realize that the life path I charted for myself, architecture, is not so much a profession as it is a vocation, a calling.

For students, getting to work closely with not just an architect, but a world-renowned one at that, when they might not yet have worked professionally, is quite an honor and an opportunity not to miss. It gives them a chance to learn from someone great, and to talk about/explain their own ideas and possibly convince the architect of the merits of their designs. That helps build confidence, clarity of thought, and makes them find out what they are capable of coming up with and refining it.

Along with my Thesis, the Walton Studio was the personal highlight of my architecture education, and I think my best project as a student. Honestly, it felt like I successfully made it out of architecture "boot-camp". It was a great feeling of accomplishment finishing the rigorous studio. Plus, the added benefit and real joy of working with Joan Soranno and Susan Jones, along with Michael J. Crosbie that year, made it that much more impactful.

Matthew Hoffman (*graduate student*)

2016 Walton Studio

The Walton Studio gives students a once in a lifetime experience to interact with architects that can truly broaden their mind and design process. There is "deep thinking." The main project challenged students to ponder deeply about the implications of their architectural moves. The studio focused on the ideas behind the project and not just the project itself.

Anonymous

The Walton Studio and the Sacred Space and Cultural Studies concentration at The Catholic University of America did not only impact me as a designer but influenced me as a person and has probably touched every aspect of my life in some way. The program helped shape my daily perspective on life and had me asking questions I otherwise never would have. How do you make a building speak? What does it want to say? Who does it want to be? How does this space make me feel? It became less about inventing forms and more about creating spaces that do the most essential things in life — how to form a relationship with a person.

I will never forget when I was in the Walton Studio, before going to the site of our new studio project, Prem Chandavarkar told us to walk the site asking ourselves some of the following questions: What do you hear? How do you feel? What do you smell? Listen to the site breathe. I was instructed to experience a place with all my senses, and I will never forget how valuable those questions were. I was to look at the site not as a place of potential or as data that needed to be collected, but step one was to experience it exactly as it was — for who it was.

The Walton program impacts almost all who encounter it, and the more someone is willing to be vulnerable to uncertainty, risk, and emotional exposure, the more they will attain. The Walton Studio goes far beyond just terrestrial thoughts and opens a whole new angelic dimension.

Amanda Ocello *(graduate student)*

We never actually experience the spaces we make as students, but we never forget the emotion we aim to evoke. At the core of an entire Walton Studio project is one space, one moment, where a spiritual metaphor is realized spatially. To produce a design that clearly articulates a sense of the sacred requires dedication to communicating a specific spiritual message. As a student, dedicating my time to a product of passion allowed me to evolve internally. This type of internal growth will spark a fire within your spirit that will lead to a life-long appreciation for the sacred.

Madeline Wentzell *(graduate student)*

2016 & 2017 Walton Studio

The Walton Studio was my first design course at Catholic and my first experience with Julio as a professor. I remember that I struggled a bit at the very beginning because I had been working very rigidly in an architectural firm for the previous three years. The poetic and emotional warm-up exercises were not what I was expecting at all. I remember there was one assignment where my partner, Madeline Wentzell, and I were called out for creating something too predictable. I was very grateful that we were in partnerships and that mine helped guide me to loosen up and experiment.

The partnership especially helped with understanding Prem Chandavarkar's approach, which emphasized that design was a discourse between metaphor and scale. It was a process of stepping back and checking that every idea aligned with the concept but worked in detail as well. In a building for finding vocation, which can manifest in so many ways, Madeline was a great sounding board for working through all the wild ideas. The methodology rather than ego facilitated the collaborative process, and it became us vs. the project and what it wanted to be.

The following year with Rick Joy was individual; rather than having a partner to work with, we had to consider the profile of a client and how their family approached the world. Designing a family home went much further into detail and asked us to establish all their eccentricities and habits in a step-by-step sequence: how did they arrive home? What is the transition between the car/garage and the front door? Where do they put their keys after they enter? Etc. It forced us to empathize with a particular lens of spirituality and how they meditated or drew inspiration from the various moments of the home design.

I think the Walton experience was extremely beneficial for graduate school because it continuously asked of us to consider our approach in design and vocation. That Prem's studio was literally begging us to figure out how one finds vocation while we were figuring out our own paths in architecture was a challenge that, in the end, strengthened my resolve to continue pursuing this career. I realized I was going through the same motions that I was asking of the users of my project. Similarly, the family project made me realize how design can be an infrastructure that enables the users' lives to enrichen the space. So rather than throwing everything at a project and seeing what sticks, I learned to work toward understanding what the project wants to be and how it manifests itself through the details. Integrating spirituality and sensory perception into a design is something that will stay with me for a long time. Previous instructors have emphasized technical competency or contextual relevance, and those are essential facets of the profession, but also widely taught in architectural education. The Walton Studio provides a refreshing change of pace and methodology to the design curriculum that is not offered anywhere else.

Anh-Tu Nguyen (*graduate student*)

I had the privilege of being a part of two Walton Studios during my time at CUA. The first was with Prem Chandavarkar in 2016, and the second with Rick Joy in 2017. I consider both of these studios formative experiences of my architectural education. Prem challenged me to question my sometimes over-analytical mind and redefine to myself what it meant to design. In his studio, we were asked to prioritize the state of mind of our building's users. One day he told us that "architecture is not a problem-solving activity." This sentiment is something I repeat to myself to this day when I find myself looking for the "solution" rather than the sublime.

In some ways, Prem's studio broke me down as a designer. A year later, in Rick Joy's studio, I began to build myself up. Rick gave me room to explore one beautiful idea deeply, and I learned that was enough. In his studio, I felt what it truly means to have a breakthrough. Early in the semester, I felt like the challenge before me was insurmountable. I had been asked just to let go. To me, that was like being asked to change my personality fundamentally. One day I reached inside, pulled out what was in my heart and mind, and put it on paper. From that moment, the rest of the semester felt almost effortless. All I had to do was whatever supported that piece of my heart. At the end of the studio, I felt a confidence in myself I never had before. Today, when I grow frustrated with design, I take a deep breath and look to my heart, knowing that I will find what I'm looking for with trust and time.

Emily Oldham (*graduate student*)

2017 Walton Studio

The Walton Studio exceeded my expectations in every way. I looked forward to class, I loved the project assignments, and I admired the professor. I believe I grew in my ability as a designer, learned a great deal about good architecture, and produced work that was a great addition to my portfolio.

Anonymous

Having the Walton Critic's new perspective coming in and adjusting the curriculum every year keeps the class exciting and fresh. Working closely with a renowned architect was an honor, and I am very thankful to have had that opportunity.

Anonymous

The Walton Studio really benefits from the outside critic in challenging the norm of architectural design studios. I think having a notable professional architect come and share their process with us was the best part of the course. In general, I feel the Sacred Space and Cultural Studies graduate concentration is particularly attuned to asking the student to be compassionate and inclusive in their design work by considering the experiences of the end-users of architecture.

Anonymous (graduate student)

What if instead of starting a project with a budget and program, you started with a symphony and a finger painting? The Walton Studio illustrates how beauty and chaos can awaken a project. How you can elevate a simple program to become an environment of enlightenment. The Walton Studio is an invaluable experience. Whether you are the pupil, professor, or decorated designer, this course will remind you how your profession can become your devotion.

As a student, I was most impacted by the philosophical and theoretical exercises we were tasked with. They inspired me to reflect on my life, my impact on the environment and how I could bet-

ter serve my community. The best part – is that I was not alone on my journey. There is a group of you, students and teachers, that are all asking the same questions of themselves. It is a community I still cherish today as my "Sacred Brothers and Sisters."

As a professional, it is easy to be persuaded by budgets and other restrictions. But after participating in the Walton Studio, I believe our responsibilities extend beyond a list of deliverables. I believe it is our duty and our gift as designers to bring truth, spirit and story into our work.

Madeline Amhurst (graduate student)

2017 & 2018 Walton Studio

I wish every architecture student and design professional could have the fortune of studying under Julio and the guest critics of the Walton Studio. Not only did the studios bring our class face-to-face with architectural giants, living legends who appeared by my studio desk as if in a dream, but personally and perhaps more importantly, the course crystallized my understanding of architectural practice as a vocational endeavor — as a means by which truth, goodness, and beauty can be presented to the world.

Figure 20-2. Amirali Ebadi, Brandon Ro, and Kara Borton with Walton Critic Alberto Campo Baeza. Photograph by Julio Bermudez

Profound, moving, and utterly beautiful, the subject matter of the Walton Studio sometimes evaded description. We often tried to capture the indescribable, the delicate translation of emotion into concrete, or light into a story, how time can work as an element of design, where a grieving woman might go to cry. These things are difficult to convey in words and challenging to design. But in practice, in an architecture that commands attention not just from the eyes, but from the soul, this understanding of spiritual space made visible needs no such description. It is simply felt. The Walton Studio, for this reason, is an unparalleled dive into the very heart of architecture.

I remember my two semesters in the Walton Studio with immense gratitude. Julio Bermudez is a brilliant professor, and through his truly tireless and compassionate leadership, I believe the Walton Studio has become an academic program of incomparable rigor and depth. Its uncompromising commitment to excellence in design and its humble, empathetic approach towards the human spirit was formative and enlightening. My time in the Walton Studio was undoubtedly one of the greatest gifts of my architectural education, one I will treasure for many years to come.

Caroline Winn (graduate student)

2018 Walton Studio

Until that point, I had taken a passive and unemotional approach to architectural design, unaware of the human aspect of it. Generally, I am not a very emotional person, and I hide a lot of my feelings. But in the Walton Studio, my biggest takeaway was that the best expression of architecture is truthful to oneself and honest to others. It taught me that people in architecture are individuals with stories, needs, and feelings in a deep life-long journey for a sense of fulfillment, not something I would've given second thought without taking the studio. The Walton Studio teaches you to care on a much deeper level and to get in touch with your inner emotional headspace about what makes you feel the way you do and how differently it translates to others' feelings. This type of thought has added a certain richness to my life that I can't quite explain even though it shows more obviously through my work. I take into consideration the experience of others and how they feel or think when designing and what it means to them.

I remember a pinup where, in the weeks leading up to it, I was head-locked and convinced about things that were mostly occurring in my head. It seemed like I was trying to hide, architecturally, something, or was scared. Without encouragement, I don't think the final product would have ever come to fruition, but somehow, with a swift kick from my instructor, he drew it out of me, and I made the decision to break free of the safety of my bubble. It felt very liberating to be able to fully express these vulnerable feelings and positions symbolically, without judgment or restraint.

The Walton Studio gives students a rare chance to meet and work with some of the world's most prominent architectural figures for some invaluable experience. The things it teaches, like compassion and understanding, are excellent life skills to have throughout one's life and career. The studio is a fascinating study not only on the topics of the course but a more in-depth look into oneself. I think every student of architecture deserves an experience like this. The Walton Studio is not something one quickly forgets and will most likely stick with me for the rest of my life.

Gino-Angelo Brentana (senior undergraduate student)

The Walton Studio was truly one of the best studios I ever took at CUA. It focuses on human thinking, existentialism, and spirituality. While some of its projects may not be feasible, the studio allows students to explore and discuss ideas that transcend problem-solving studio projects.

At the beginning of the Walton Studio, I was

told we were to design a funerary complex. As a functionally driven individual, I began tackling the program and phases of the project. As I analyzed precedents and presented programmatic solutions, I realized that the ideas about functionality were not going to be enough to be the drivers of the design. I was forced to look deeper into the process of death, dying, and grieving. As a twenty-one-year-old, I had never pondered so much about death. In my mind, death was a topic for future me. I am not a deeply religious person, so I choose to believe in death as a part of every-day life. To some, this may appear depressing, not to have something to look forward to after death. Therefore, for me, this meant that I must cherish my time on earth because it may be all I have. As this realization came to me, I had an inspiration to incorporate this idea into my project.

For me, the most memorable moment was when Alberto Campo Baeza destroyed the plan of my project during midterms. This moment was also the most valuable lesson because I had solely designed an intricate ceremonial hall for my complex and subsequently laid out the remaining functions in a pragmatic manner. After this critique, I carefully and intentionally laid my plans primarily according to the emotion and intentions of the users while still abiding to function. This lesson has had a tremendous impact on how I have proceeded to lay out my plans in every project since and will work on in the future.

This learning experience instilled in me an understanding of how architecture can affect users on an emotional and spiritual level. The Walton Studio made me look at architecture from a completely different perspective. It made me face my fears and take part in conversations about life and death that I perhaps would not have had for another decade.

Frederico Witzke *(senior undergraduate student)*

2019 Walton Studio

The 2019 Walton Studio was an incredibly rewarding experience due to the unique approach to designing architecture. The first portion of the studio focused on exploration by creating art though rip-and-tear models and photograph. This was a different procedure for developing a parti concept. I initially doubted the method since it was so foreign from prior studios. The process proved to be fruitful and enlightening, as the studies developed into the most thought-provoking project I have designed. Professor Julio Bermudez mentored an approach that balanced keeping the unorthodox, evocative designs developed in the explorative portion of the studio and developing an architectural design that was structurally feasible. The result was twelve architectural designs that pushed the boundaries of modern architecture and celebrated the human experience of being.

Morgan Allen *(graduate student)*

The Walton Studio has changed my life. It has challenged me in a way that I did not know I needed. The work is so important and so different than the norm... really a powerful program, and this studio is something I will never forget.

Anonymous *(senior undergraduate student)*

Personally, The Walton Studio opened so many doors that I did not know existed. Collaborating with world-class professionals who believe and succeed in creating phenomenological spaces was so impactful. The Walton Studio has changed my understanding of what architecture can and should be. Of course, architecture should be functional and beautiful, but also can be highly experiential and furthermore, sacred. These objectives are what we strived for in the Walton Studio, and these qualities are what I look for when I enter a new space. Working with the masters has bolstered my hopes for the profession, as well as increased my drive to hold myself and my work to a higher standard and meaning.

Andrew Beiner *(senior undergraduate student)*

The Walton Studio experience truly was a spiritual time in my life. I had the honor of having worked by Daniel Libeskind, who taught us to look at architecture in a very different way. In the intense workshop that he directed, we were constantly reminded that no matter our outcome by the end of the week, and there were many very different ones done by my studio peers, that we all came from the same initial points of inspiration. This, in itself, seems like an elementary lesson, but it made me very aware of my own thought processes and how I perceived the world before, during, and after the workshop. Now when looking at anything in this world, I am aware of the steps through which I analyze. This is, in fact, a very architecturally inspired process, beginning with foundations, then moving on to spaces, and finishing with visual/conceptual attributes. I now allow myself to break down the world into things and find inspiration in everything, all because of my Walton experience.

Something very memorable to me was hearing Daniel Libeskind, one of my favorite architects, say some very simple yet encouraging words to me. After a presentation on analyzing different forms of art, he said, *"Now see, you have approached this in a very structured, but different way than your classmates, and that is something very special."*

This seems like a normal, motivational thing for any professor to say, but it made me happy and proud of my own thought process. It was a simple but validating thing to hear from someone whom your revere, and it makes you aware that your voice can be impactful and important. After this experience, I have become more confident in my ideas and my mind as a creative tool. The Walton Studio is a once in a lifetime experience.

Isabella Laccetti *(senior undergraduate student)*

The Walton Studio allowed me to explore my purpose as a design-oriented person. Through close collaboration with my peers and the incredible faculty, I was able to unlock/REdiscover a piece of my soul that provided a sense of purpose and fulfillment. I was able to explore the design process and the process of creating new abilities. Spirituality and phenomenology, form and function, sacred and profane facets of spaces and architecture were explored and investigated in ways I had previously not attempted. The human experience of architecture is something so timeless, yet so new. Each time we encounter a space, there is a certain uniqueness to our journey. I think one of the things I appreciated so much in the Walton Studio was the exploration of ritual as a course of action predicting experience. My semester in The Walton Studio is one I will forever cherish as it impacted me not only as a designer but as a person of faith.

Abigail Sekely *(senior undergraduate student)*

Figure 20-3. Walton Program alumni reunion (2016). From left to right. Kristen Weller, Devon Brophy, Emily O'Loughlin, Erica Donnelly, Megan Gregory, Donald Brandon Moore, Scott Gillespie, Julio Bermudez, a guest, Andrew Metzler, and 2016 Walton Critic Prem Chandavarkar. Photograph by Julio Bermudez.

CONTRIBUTORS

Eliana Bórmida is principal of Bórmida & Yanzón Arquitectos, an international, award winning office operating from Mendoza, Argentina. Their portfolio contains remarkable projects related to nature, wine, lodging, agro-industrial architecture and more. Balancing contemporary demands and consciousness with the values of local tradition, their buildings are beautiful, simple, tectonic, and sophisticated. It is an experiential architecture that defines a spatial narrative full of sensations and emotion that kindly invites our actions and always grounds us to the local nature, culture, and history. Bórmida & Yanzón's work has been covered in the international press and published extensively. Bórmida was a professor of architecture history and urbanism at the Universidad de Mendoza for 30 years where she founded and directed the Institute of Architectural and Urban Culture. She was awarded the Stella dell'Ordine della Solidarietā Italiana bestowed by the Presidency of Italy in 2007, named "Outstanding Woman" by the Mendoza Federation of Business Leaders in 2012, and Illustrious Citizen of the City of Mendoza in 2014.

Alberto Campo Baeza is a Spanish architect internationally known for his luminous, simple yet nuanced, and always provocative architecture, the result of a long, continuous and disciplined investigation of the miracle of light and space. By professing an axiology of 'more with less,' Campo Baeza is able to focus on the essence of architectural ideas, experience, and program. His work has received extensive, worldwide recognition. In 2014, he was elected Full Member to the Royal Academy of Fine Arts of San Fernando of Spain. In 2015, he was awarded the BigMat in Berlin, the International Prize of Spanish Architecture, and the 1st Prize Ex Aequo to build the new Louvre. Most recently, he received the Gold Medal for Spanish Architecture (2019) and the National Prize for Architecture in Spain (2020). His built work, drawings, and writings have been published in 5 languages. He teaches at ETSA-UPM, in Madrid, since 1976 and has lectured at many American and other foreign universities.

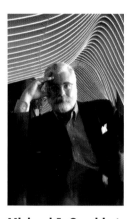

Prem Chandavarkar is the managing partner of CnT Architects, a 60-person award-winning and widely published architectural practice based in Bangalore, India. CnT's seeks to construct a collaborative practice where design excellence is pursued in an organizational form that does not center on a few specific personalities. CnT's work is known for mediating design spectacularity and human habitation by "an aesthetics of absorption," that is, by making architectures that absorb and accrue meaning rather than flaunt it. Chandavarkar is a former Executive Director of Srishti School of Art Design & Technology in Bangalore, and has been a guest lecturer at architecture colleges in India, the United States, New Zealand, and Switzerland. Besides design practice at CnT, he writes and lectures on a wide variety of subjects covering architecture, urbanism, art, spirituality, cultural studies, politics, and education.

Michael J. Crosbie has made significant contributions in the fields of architectural journalism, research, teaching, and practice. He has served as an editor at Architecture, The AIA Journal, Progressive Architecture, ArchitectureWeek.com, and since 2001 as editor-in-chief of Faith & Form, a quarterly journal on interfaith religious art and architecture. He is the author of more than 20 books on architecture and has edited and contributed to approximately 20 others. Dr. Crosbie is Professor of Architecture at the University of Hartford and has lectured and served as a visiting critic at many architecture schools in North America and abroad. He has been one of the leaders of the Architecture, Culture, and Spirituality Forum (ACSF) since 2013. Professor Crosbie is a recipient of the Edward S. Frey Memorial Award in recognition of his contributions made to religion, art, and architecture, bestowed by the Interfaith Forum on Religion, Art, and Architecture.

Craig W. Hartman, FAIA, is SOM's Senior Consulting Design Partner, serving over 30 years as the firm's partner for its West Coast practice. His US and international work ranges from entire urban districts to singular works of architecture and interior space. His projects have been widely published and examples of the work are held as part of SFMOMA's permanent collection. Hartman's architecture is characterized for environmental sustainability, humanism, and its nuanced consideration of the relationships between material, structure, form and natural light. Among his well-known buildings are the U.S. Embassy in Beijing, the United States Courthouse in Los Angeles, the Library of Virginia in Richmond, San Francisco's International Airport Terminal at SFO, and the Cathedral of Christ the Light in Oakland. At the Cathedral Dedication, Hartman received the Vatican's Knighthood (Sylvestrine Order). Hartman's work has been recognized with over 240 awards for design and innovation, including 10 National AIA Honor Awards for Architecture, Interior, and Urban Design. Hartman has taught, lectured, and juried work at multiple architecture programs in the

Susan Jones is founder and principal of atelierjones, an architecture, urban and ecodesign firm. Started in 2003, the office brings design, research, and community engagement to generate projects of reclamation: of forgotten urban sites and buildings, or of waste/scrap materials to create renewable and beautiful architecture. The firm designs new ways of living and working in the city: from homes to urban housing, spiritual spaces, the rehabilitation of commercial structures, and the preservation of historic structures. atelierjones' work has received numerous international, national, and local design awards. Her book, *"Mass Timber | Design and Research"* was published in 2018 by ORO Editions. Susan Jones has been a visiting design professor and critic at numerous universities and is Affiliate Associate Professor of Architecture at the University of Washington. A native of the Pacific Northwest, she became a Fellow of the AIA in 2010, and has been working for architects since she was sixteen.

Rick Joy is founder and principal of Studio Rick Joy, a 32-person architecture and planning firm established in 1993 in Tucson, Arizona. SRJ is internationally recognized for its contemporary, lifestyle centered, contextually responsive, and beautiful approach to architecture. SRJ has participated in multiple exhibitions and has been featured in over 150 publications worldwide. Joy has lectured extensively throughout the United States and around the globe. He is considered a contributor to the global discourse on modern architecture. Joy has received many national recognitions including the 2002 American Academy of Arts and Letters Award in Architecture, the prestigious National Design Award from the Smithsonian Institute/Cooper-Hewitt Museum in 2004, multiple Record House Awards (1997, 2001, 2005, 2009, 2010), and the 2013 Jeff Harnar Award for Contemporary Architecture. Rick Joy periodically serves as a visiting professor at the Harvard Graduate School of Design, Rice University, University of Arizona, and M.I.T.

Polish-American architect, **Daniel Libeskind** is an international figure in architecture and urban design. Informed by a deep commitment to music, philosophy, and literature, Mr. Libeskind aims to create architecture that is resonant, original, and sustainable. Libeskind established his architectural studio in Berlin, Germany, in 1989 after winning the competition to build the Jewish Museum in Berlin. In February 2003, Studio Libeskind moved its headquarters from Berlin to New York City to oversee the master planning for the World Trade Center redevelopment, which is being realized in Lower Manhattan today. Daniel Libeskind's practice is involved in designing and realizing a diverse array of urban, cultural and commercial projects around the globe. The Studio has completed buildings that range from museums and concert halls to convention centers, university buildings, hotels, shopping centers and residential towers. As Principal Design Architect for Studio Libeskind, Mr. Libeskind speaks widely on the art of architecture in universities and professional summits. His architecture and ideas have been the subject of many articles and exhibitions, influencing

Finnish architect **Juhani Pallasmaa** is one of the most lucid architectural theoreticians and educators in the world today. His many books, writings, exhibitions, and buildings are internationally renowned. For example, his *"The Eyes of the Skin"* has become a classic book of architectural theory all over the world and his exhibitions of Finnish architecture have been displayed in more than 30 countries. Former professor and dean of architecture at the Helsinki University of Technology and former Director of the Museum of Finnish Architecture, Pallasmaa travels around the world to lecture and lead workshops that prompt architects, scientists, philosophers, and others to consider the most important topics of today. For many years, he served as a jury member of the Pritzker Prize, the most prestigious architectural award in the world.

Antoine Predock received the 2006 American Institute of Architects (AIA) Gold Medal — the highest honor conferred by the AIA on an architect whose significant body of work has had a lasting influence on the theory and practice of architecture. He is the principal of Antoine Predock Architect PC, based in Albuquerque, N.M. Predock's U.S. projects include the La Luz community in Albuquerque, the Nelson Fine Arts Center at Arizona State University, the Tang Teaching Museum and Art Gallery at Skidmore College, and the San Diego Padres' Petco Park, whose design reinvents the concept of a ballpark as a garden rather than solely a sports complex. His international work includes the National Palace Museum Southern Branch in Southern Taiwan and the Canadian Museum for Human Rights in Winnipeg, Manitoba, Canada. He has lectured all over the world and taught at many American universities, including the University of New Mexico, University of Oklahoma, SCI-Arc, CalPoly Pomona, Clemson University, Harvard University, and Arizona State University.

Architect **Claudio Silvestrin** is based in London and Milan and the author of an internationally recognized oeuvre that covers not only architecture but also a wide range of design scales and interests. His works are distinguished by being austere but not extreme, contemporary yet timeless, calming but not ascetic, strong but not intimidating, elegant but not ostentatious, simple but not soulless. His aim is to raise human awareness of an evolution which is not merely technological and material, but which fundamentally encompasses emotion and spirit, man and nature, and has beauty as its compass. He pursues this conviction with a thought process based on depth, integrity, clarity of mind, inventiveness, and concern for details. Claudio Silvestrin's thoughts on today's challenges as well as his work have been featured in four books, many professional magazines and journals, exhibitions, and many media outlets.

Thomas Walton's 25-year career in teaching at The Catholic University of America's School of Architecture and Planning focused on design and buildings as expressions of social and cultural values. These essential themes emerge in his research and writing on such topics as the great 1920s skyscraper race in New York City, the history of the planning and development of Washington, DC, and his volume on corporate architecture in the late Twentieth century. Following these commitments, in 2003 he joined the U.S. General Services Administration in its Design Excellence Program, an initiative that has reinvigorated the importance of federal building as a symbol of our open government and democratic values. He envisioned and funded the Walton Distinguished Critic in Design and Catholic Stewardship at CUA in 2008 which he continuously engaged with and supported until his unexpected passing in May 2020. Walton had received his M.Arch (1976) and Ph.D. (1980) from The Catholic University of America, lectured at organizations such as the American Institute of Architects and the Smithsonian Institution, and served as a consultant to the National Endowment for the Arts.

EDITOR

Professor **Julio Bermudez** has directed the Sacred Space and Cultural Studies graduate program at the Catholic University of America School of Architecture and Planning since 2010. Dr. Bermudez's interests are focused on the relationship between architecture, culture, and spirituality through the lens of phenomenology and neuroscience. He has widely lectured, led symposia, and published in these areas, including *"Transcending Architecture. Contemporary Views on Sacred Space"* (CUA Press 2015) and *"Architecture, Culture and Spirituality"* (Routledge 2015). His current research uses neuroscience to study contemplative and sacred spaces. Bermudez has received several national and international recognitions, including the 1998 AIA Education Honors Award, the 2005 Arturo Montagu Creative Career Prize (bestowed by Latin American SiGraDi), the 2010 Sasada Award for significant record in scholarship and service (conferred by CAADRIA, Asia), and the 2021 ACSA Distinguished Professor Award. He is the president of the Architecture, Culture, and Spirituality Forum, a 650-member international organization that he co-founded in 2007 (http://www.acsforum.org/).

ENDNOTES, BIBLIOGRAPHY, INDEX

ENDNOTES

SPIRITUALITY IN THE DESIGN STUDIO. INTRODUCING THE WALTON PROGRAM

1. Edmund O'Sullivan, "Emancipatory Hope," in *Holistic Learning and Spirituality in Education*, eds. By John P. Miller, Selia Karsten, Diana Denton, Deborah Orr, and Isabella Colalillo Kates (Albany, NY: SUNY Press, 2005), 69-78, citation in p.70.

2. The biases against addressing spirituality in the architectural academy and profession are discussed by Michael Crosbie, "The Sacred Becomes Profane," in *Architecture, Culture, and Spirituality*, eds. Thomas Barrie, Julio Bermudez, and Phillip Tabb (New York: Routledge, 2015), 59-69; Michael Benedikt, *God, Creativity and Evolution. The Argument from Design(ers)* (Austin, TX: The Center for American Architecture and Design, 2008); Julio Bermudez, "The Extraordinary in Architecture," *2A* 12 (2009): 46-49; Karla Britton, *Constructing the Ineffable* (New Haven, CT: Yale School of Architecture, 2011); and Renata Hejduk and Jim Williamson, "Introduction: The Apocryphal Project of Modern and Contemporary Architecture," in *The Religious Imagination in Modern and Contemporary Architecture. A Reader*, eds. R. Hejduk and J. Williamson (New York: Routledge, 2011),1-9.

3. *"Higher education has given ample proof of its viability over the centuries and of its ability to change and to induce change and progress in society. Owing to the scope and pace of change, society has become increasingly knowledge-based so that higher learning and research now act as essential components of cultural, socio-economic and environmentally sustainable development of individuals, communities and nations. Higher education itself is confronted therefore with formidable challenges and must proceed to the most radical change and renewal it has ever been required to undertake, so that our society, which is currently undergoing a profound crisis of values, can transcend mere economic considerations and **incorporate deeper dimensions of morality and spirituality.**"* (emphasis added). UIA Architectural Education Commission, *UIA and Architectural Education. Reflections and Recommendations* (Paris, France: International Union of Architects — UIA, 2002), 77. URL http://citeseerx.ist.psu.edu/viewdoc/download?doi=10.1.1.549.4828&rep=rep1&type=pdf (accessed July 9, 2020). The UIA document is actually quoting a paragraph from the preamble of UNESCO, *Higher Education in the Twenty-first Century: Vision and Action, v. 1: Final Report* (Paris, France: UNESCO, 1999), 20. URL: https://unesdoc.unesco.org/ark:/48223/pf0000116345 (accessed July 9, 2020).

4. "Göbekli Tepe" in UNESCO World Heritage. https://whc.unesco.org/en/list/1572/ . See also Andrew Curry, "Gobekli Tepe: The World's First Temple?" *Smithsonian Magazine* (Nov 2008). URL: https://www.smithsonianmag.com/history/gobekli-tepe-the-worlds-first-temple-83613665/ (accessed July 13, 2020). Charles C. Mann, "The Birth of Religion," *National Geographic* 219, no.6 (June 2011): 34-59.

SPIRITUALITY IN ARCHITECTURAL EDUCATION. MEDITATIONS

1. Parker J. Palmer and Arthur Zajonc with Megan Scribner, *The Heart of Higher Education. A call to Renewal* (San Francisco, CA: Jossey Bass, 2010), 49.

2. See chapter 17 "Learned Ignorance" in Edward Harrison, *Masks of the Universe* (New York: McMillan, 1985), 273-278. Harrison's piece is based on *"De Docta Ignorantia"* by philosopher/theologian Nicholas of Cusa (1440). From a "learned ignorance" perspective, *"the more we know, the more aware we become of what we do not know"* (Harrison, p.273). Learning thus becomes a process of coming to know and humbly accept our ignorance.

3. Searches of articles relevant to architectural or

design education using keywords such as "spirituality," "spirituality and education," obtained only one relevant result, and "spirituality and architectural education" obtained only one relevant result in the journal *Space and Culture* and another in *Design Issues*: Andrejs Kulnieks, Dan Roronhiakewen and Kelly Young, "Tramping the Mobius: A Curriculum of Oral and Literary Tradition as a Primer for Rural Education," *Space and Culture* 21, no.1 (Nov. 8, 2017): 60-71. Alain Findeli, "Rethinking Design Education for the 21st Century: Theoretical, Methodological, and Ethical Discussion," *Design Issues* 17, no.1 (Winter 2001): 5-17. Disappointing results were also obtained from the *International Journal of Islamic Studies*: only two out of over 80 articles in its 8 volumes were related to architectural education, namely: Anat Geva, "Revisiting a Graduate Design Studio on Sacred Architecture: A Mosque Design in Yazd, Iran," *International Journal of Islamic Architecture* 4, no.1 (2015): 161-187; and Ashraf Salama, "Reflections on Architectural Education of the Muslim World within a global World," *International Journal of Islamic Architecture* 9, no1(2019): 33-41.

4. Examples of articles reporting on educational experiences addressing spirituality are hard to find. Searches using keywords are useful but often miss papers that deal with spiritual issues but employing a different, more "secular" language such as "ethics", "social justice," and so on. Although I will not claim to have gone through the whole record of ACSA conference proceedings (i.e., I read the abstract of every paper that the searches highlighted but only went into their full text if the abstract directly or indirectly referred to spirituality or a spiritual-like theme), the systematic searches along with a random sampling of proceedings (which I also did) does provide a relatively fair perspective about the published record. In this regard, there are conference proceedings found to contain no articles covering spirituality in architectural education at all. In other cases, one or two are found. For example, Ping Xu, "Design with Meanings: Feng-shui and Cosmology in Architecture," in *85th ACSA Annual Meeting Proceedings*, ed. Lawrence W. Speck (Washington DC: ACSA, 1997), 255-260; and Gregory S. Pallermo, "Ethical Premises in Student Proposals: Well-Being, Virtue and Change," in *87th ACSA Annual Meeting Proceedings*, eds. Geraldine Forbes and Marvin Malecha (Washington, DC: ACSA, 1999),183-188. Sometimes, a proceeding contains several papers but this is rare and usually happens when the conference topic invited such reflections. For example, "*The Ethical Imperative*" topic of the 106 ACSA Annual meeting in 2018, edited by Amir Ameri and Rebecca O'Neal Dagg (Washington DC: ACSA, 2018). Here we find four articles: Keith Diaz Moore, "A Place-Based Ethic of Care: The Beginnings of the Utah School," pp. 231-235. Alexis Gregory, "Empathizing with Clients: Teaching Students How to Design for 'The Other'," pp. 236-243. Lauren Matchison,

"Creating an Academic Community of Inquiry: Educating Architects to Embrace a People-Centered View," pp. 244-249. However, even here the level of interest or coverage of spirituality in architectural education is low when compared to the total number of published articles: out of about 100 average published papers per annual meeting (the range goes from 80 to about 120), about 4 papers were found. In most other proceedings the number was 1 or 2 papers at best.

5. The range of 25-35 papers is due to the difficulty in determining what constitutes "spirituality" when the actual word is not used and-or the article focus is only indirectly addressing it. In terms of the variability of found papers per NCBDS conference proceeding, three examples will make my point: [1] Three articles were discovered in the *Proceedings of NCBDS 33: Begin W/Why: Ethics and Values in Beginning Design* eds. Erin Carraher et al (Salt Lake City, UT: University of Utah, 2017): Elisa Kim, "Beginning with 'Environmentality'," 263-266; Stephen Temple, "Necessity for Learning Abstraction in Representational Thinking," 420-42; and Roger Vitello, "Introducing Empathy into the Classroom: Becoming my Brother's Keeper," 466-473. [2] Only one article came up in the *Proceedings of NCBDS 34: Time*, eds. Kristyn Benedyk et al. (Cincinnati, OH: University of Cincinnati, 2018): Jacob A. Gines, "Practicing Conscious Architectural Experience." And [3] Two papers were retrieved from the *Proceedings of NCBDS 30: Materiality. Essence + Substance*, eds. Leslie Johnson et al (Chicago, IL: Illinois Institute of Technology, 2014): Amber Ellett, "Measures of Place: The Eidetic Image in Design," 44-48; and Chad Schwartz, "Spiritual Tectonics: Exploring Dualities in the Design Studio," 529-535. URLs: http://ncbds.la-ab.com/33_Proceedings.pdf ; https://journals.uc.edu/index.php/ncbds/issue/view/62 and https://www.beginningdesign.org/2014-Mies-s-I-I-T respectively. The full archive of proceedings is available at https://beginningdesign.org (accessed June 15, 2020).

6. Julio Bermudez, "Turning the Light Inward: Applying the 'Know Thyself' Injunction in Architectural School." Paper presented at the *11th Architecture, Culture, and Spirituality Forum Symposium*, Taliesin West, AZ, May 16-19, 2019. http://www.acsforum.org/symposium2019/works/Bermudez.pdf > (accessed July 15, 2020). A major motive for creating ACSF was the lack of attention to spirituality in architecture and its allied disciplines (landscape architecture, interior architecture, urban planning, etc.). While there is reason for optimism for the changes happened over the past 13 years, the situation has not advanced as much as one would have expected. See Tom Barrie, Julio Bermudez, Anat Geva, and Randall Teal, "Architecture, Culture and Spirituality. Creating a forum for scholarship and discussion of spirituality and meaning in the built environment (April 13, 2007)," *The ACSForum. org*, http://www.acsforum.org/acsforumnew/wp-content/

uploads/2017/11/ACS_founding_whitepaper_2007.pdf (accessed July 15, 2020). In full disclosure, I was one of the four co-founders of ACSF in 2007. (accessed July 12, 2020). There is a variety of resources that cover the teaching and learning of Islamic art and architecture like, for example 31 course syllabi. However, there is little actual scholarly discussion or analysis of spirituality or faith in architectural education. For more refer to https://archnet.org/collections/808 (access July 12, 2020).

8. Here are two examples of the very few findings from open internet searches (which demanded much more than going through the abstracts and word search parameters): Marga Jann, "Revamping Architectural Education: Ethics, Social Service, and Innovation," *International Journal of Arts and Sciences* 3, no.8 (2010): 45-89. Michael Karassowitsch, "Architecture is not Technology: The Space of Differentiation in Architectural Education," *Open House International* 40, no.3 (x 2015): 17-23.

9. Refer to endnote #2 of Chapter 1.

10. Louis Kahn, *Louis Kahn: Conversations with Students* (Architecture at Rice) (Houston, TX: Rice University School of Architecture, 1998).

11. About John Hejduk see for example: J. Kevin Story, *The Complexities of John Hejduk's Work* (New York, Routledge, 2020). Beliefnet, " John Hejduk: A Remembrance" article retrieve from URL: https://www.beliefnet.com/entertainment/2000/08/john-hejduk-a-remembrance.

12. Crosbie, "The Sacred Becomes Profane," articulates why this is the case in architecture.

13. Recent polls have found, for example, that, 80% of Americans believe in God and 74% in heaven. For specific details, refer to the 2018 Pew Research Center survey on belief in God: https://www.pewforum.org/2018/04/25/when-americans-say-they-believe-in-god-what-do-they-mean/ and the 2015 Pew Research Center survey on belief in heaven: https://www.pewresearch.org/fact-tank/2015/11/10/most-americans-believe-in-heaven-and-hell/ (accessed June 11, 2020).

14. Higher Education Research Institute, UCLA, *"Attending to Students' Inner Lives: A Call to Higher Education,"* white paper, April 4-6, 2011, p.3. URL https://spirituality.ucla.edu/docs/white%20paper/white%20paper%20final.pdf (accessed July 18, 2020). *"Fully four in five students tell us that they 'have an interest in spirituality and that they 'believe in the sacredness of life,' and nearly two-third say that 'my spirituality is a source of joy.' Students also hold strong religious beliefs. More than three-fourths believe in God, and more than two in three say that their religious/spiritual beliefs 'provide me with strength, support, and guidance.' Finally, three-fourths of the students report feelings of a 'sense of connection with God/Higher Power that transcends my personal self'."* Alexander W. Astin, Helen S. Astin, and Jennifer A. Lindholm. *Cultivating the Spirit. How college can enhance students' inner lives* (San Francisco, CA: Jossey-Bass, 2011),

citation in 3 but also see pages 6 and 39. These statistics are backed by others such as Braskamp et al, *Putting Students First*; Conrad Cherry, Betty DeBerg, and Amanda Porterfield, *Religion on Campus* (Chapel Hill, NC: The U of North Carolina Press, 2001); and Robert J. Nash, *Religious Pluralism in the Academy: Opening the Dialogue* (Lang, Peter Publishing, 2001).

15. Regarding faith in the world, a 2012 WIN-Gallup International poll on religiosity and atheism found that 59% of the world's population is religious, 23% are not religious (but do not call themselves "atheist", suggesting an openness to non-organized spiritual belief or practice) and only 13% report to be atheist. In this 2012 survey, U.S. population was found to be 60% religious, 30% non-religious (but open to spiritual beliefs), 5% atheist, and 5% not responding. See: https://sidmennt.is/wp-content/uploads/Gallup-International-um-trú-og-trúleysi-2012.pdf , (accessed June 11, 2020).

16. William Bloom, *The Power of the New Spirituality* (Wheaton, IL: Quest Books, 2011). Lucy Bregman, "Guest Editorial: Defining Spirituality: Multiple Uses and Murky Meanings of an Incredibly Popular Term," in *The Journal of Pastoral Care & Counseling* 58, no.3 (Fall 2004): 157-167. Jane Dyson, Mark Cobb, and Dawn Forman, "The Meaning of Spirituality: A Literature Review," *Journal of Advanced Nursing* 26 (1997): 1183-1188. Martin Fowler, John D. Martin, and John L. Hochheimer, *Spirituality: Theory, Praxis and Pedagogy* (Leiden, Netherlands: Brill, 2020). Doug Oman, "Defining Religion and Spirituality," in *Handbook of the Psychology of Religion and Spirituality*, eds. Raymond F. Paloutzian and Crystal L. Park (New York: The Guilford Press, 2013), 23-47. Walter Principe, "Toward Defining Spirituality," *Studies in Religion* 12, no.2 (Spring 1983): 127-41. Philip Sheldrake. *Spirituality. A Brief History* (New York: Wiley-Blackwell, 2013). Ruth A. Tanyi, "Towards clarification of the meaning of spirituality," *Journal of Advanced Nursing*, 39, no.5 (2002): 500-509.

17. Parker J. Palmer. *The Courage to Teach* (San Francisco, CA, Jossey-Bass, 2007), 5.

18. Astin et al., *Cultivating the Spirit*, 137.

19. bell hooks, *All About Love: New Visions* (New York: HarperCollins Publishers, 2000), 77.

20. I like the following quote because it connects some dots: *"The Big Picture comes as a result of depth encounters with the sacred."* O'Sullivan, *"Emancipatory Hope,"* 69. "Sacred" should be here understood in its widest meaning, that is, as things of ultimate significance in life.

21. Pew Research Center, "'Nones' on the Rise," (Oct 9, 2012). URL: https://www.pewforum.org/2012/10/09/nones-on-the-rise/. See also Pew Research Center, "In U.S., Decline of Christianity, Continues at Rapid Pace,"(oct 17, 2019). URL: https://www.pewforum.org/2019/10/17/in-u-s-decline-of-christianity-continues-at-rapid-pace/ (both accessed July 12, 2020).

22. William James. *The Varieties of Religious Experience* (New York: Simon & Schuster, Inc. 2004), 41. book dealing with architecture and design from this second-person perspective is: Michael Benedikt, *Architecture Beyond Experience* (San Francisco: AR+D publishing, 2020).

24. Astin et al., *Cultivating the Spirit*, 127-8

25. Palmer & Zajonc, *The Heart of Higher Education*, 108.

26. See for instance, Sean Esbjorn-Hargens, Jonathan Reams and Olen Gunnlaugson, *Integral Education. New Directions for Higher Learning* (Albany, NY: SUNY Press, 2010). Anthony T. Kronman, *Education's End. Why Our Colleges and Universities Have Given Up on the Meaning of Life* (New Haven, CT: Yale University Press, 2006). Harry R. Lewis, *Excellence without Soul: Does Liberal Education Have a Future?* (New York: Public Affairs, 2007); John P. Miller. *Education and the Soul. Toward a New Curriculum* (Albany, NY: Sunny Press, 2000). John P. Miller, Selia Karsten, Diana Denton, Deborah Orr, and Isabella Colalillo Kates, *Holistic Learning and Spirituality in Education* (Albany, NY: SUNY Press, 2005). Palmer and Zajonc, The Heart of Higher Education.

27. Palmer and Zajonc, *The Heart of Higher Education*, 10.

28. Astin et al., *Cultivating the Spirit*, 1.

29. Robert Kegan, *The Evolving Self: Problems and Process in Human Development* (Cambridge, MA: Harvard University Press, 1982). William G. Perry, Jr., Forms of Intellectual and Ethical Development in the College Years (San Francisco, CA: Jossey-Bass Inc., 1999). Ken Wilber, Integral Spirituality (Boston, MA: Shambala, 2006).

30. Miller et al, *Holistic Learning and Spirituality in Education*. Regarding the pressure and situation of colleges and universities vis-à-vis society, see the following article (and referred books): Jonathan Zimmerman, "What Is College Worth," *The New York Review of Books* (July 2, 2020). URL: https://www.nybooks.com/articles/2020/07/02/what-is-college-worth/ (accessed June 21, 2020).

31. Astin et al, *Cultivating the Spirit*, 140.

32. Lewis, *Excellence without Soul*, xiv.

33. Ronald Barnett, *A Will too Learn: Being a Student in an Age of Uncertainty* (New York: Open University Press, 2007). James Thompson, *Narratives of Architectural Education. From Student to Architect* (New York, Routledge, 2019). See Chapter 3 in particular.

34. Ronald Barnett and Søren S.E. Bengtsen, *Knowledge and the University. Re-claiming Life* (New York: Routledge, 2019)

35. Astin et al., *Cultivating the Spirit*. See also, Higher Education Research Institute, "Attending to Students' Inner Lives: A Call to Higher Education."

36. Astin et al, *Cultivating the Spirit*, 157.

37. These fragmentations are a combination of the diagnosis of several authors about our contemporary situation. Most notably, Palmer and Zajonc, *The Heart of Higher Education*; and John P. Miller. The Holistic Curriculum (Toronto, University of Toronto Press, 2007).

38. John P. Miller makes the same point: *"… precisely because these dangers exist, they demand public scrutiny, so religion and spirituality must be understood as critical parts of the human 'mess' that higher education should help students engage. Excluding religion and spirituality from serious study in secular settings is a stunning form of irrationality in itself. Religion and spirituality are among the major drivers of contemporary life (as one can readily see in any daily newspaper) and of any historical epoch one can name."* Miller, *The Holistic Curriculum*, 47.

39. Jost Schieren, "The Spiritual Dimension of Waldorf Education," *Waldorf Resources*. Accessed July 12, 2020, https://www.waldorf-resources.org/articles/display/archive/2014/08/27/article/the-spiritual-dimension-of-waldorf-education/ Reflecting on Waldorf Education, a good example of a spirituality-integrated model of education, Schieren points out that even though spirituality greatly challenges today's prevailing rational-scientific paradigm, its rejection has much more to do with "socio-historical habit of thought." Society generally perceives spirituality as unacceptable or dangerous due to these four traits: *"Exclusiveness: Spiritual knowledge is initiate knowledge, and as such is the property of a select few … Devotion [personal subjugation, fanatism] … Dogmatism: Spiritual doctrines often take the form of statements of ultimate wisdom … Sectarianism: The charge of sectarianism encompasses all the previous points."*

40. Warren A. Nord, *Religion and American Education: Rethinking a National Dilemma* (Chapel Hill: University of North Carolina Press, 1995), 6-7.

41. Ibid., 378-79.

42. Jorge N. Ferrer, Marina T. Romero, and Ramon V. Albareda, "Integral Transformative Education. A Participatory Proposal," in *Integral Education*, eds. Esbjorn-Hargens et al., 79-103, citation in p.97.

43. Astin et al., *Cultivating the Spirit*, 138. For more details, readers should refer to Chapter 8 and particularly the summary in pages 135-36.

44. See Chapter 9 in Astin et al, *Cultivating the Spirit*, 137-57.

45. Aditya Adarkar and David Lee Keiser, "The Buddha in the Classroom: Toward a Critical Spiritual Pedagogy," *Journal of Transformative Education* 5, no.3 (2007): 246-61. Shauna L. Shapiro, Kirk Warren Brown, and John Astin. "Toward the Integration of Meditation into Higher Education: A Review of Research Evidence." *Teachers College Record* 113, no.3 (2011): 493-528. Michael D. Waggoner, "Spirituality and Contemporary Higher Education," *Journal of College and Character* 17, no.3 (2016): 147-56. Arthur Zajonc, "Contemplative Pedagogy: A Quiet Revo-

lution in Higher Education," *New Directions for Teaching and Learning* 134 (2013): 83-94.

46. The first amendemnt to the United States Constitution states *"Congress shall make no law respecting an establishment of religion, or prohibiting the free exercise therof..."* I should acknowledge that legislation requiring the separation of religion and government may only apply to a few countries other than the U.S. In those other nations, perhaps, this issue may not be so divisive or problematic.

47. Elizabeth J. Tisdell, *Exploring Spirituality and Culture in Adult and Higher Education.* This is one particularly good reference because it (1) addresses the difference between religion and spirituality vis-à-vis culture and (2) considers the separation of church and state mandate in light of our ealier discussions.

48. Miller, *Education and the Soul*, 140

49. In Zorach v. Clauson (1952), the Supreme Court supported accommodating religion in secular education in recognition that U.S. *"institutions presuppose a Supreme Being"* and that such acknowledgment of God by no means signifies the institutionalization of a state church, something the Constitution forbids. Some of the Supreme Court's arguments are worth quoting: *"We are a religious people whose institutions presuppose a Supreme Being. We guarantee the freedom to worship as one chooses. We make room room for as wide a variety of beliefs and creeds as the spiritual needs of man deem necessary… Government may not finance religious groups nor undertake religious instruction nor blend secular and sectarian education nor use secular institutions to force one or some religion on any person. But we find no constitutional requirement which makes it necessary for government to be hostile to religion and to throw its weight against efforts to widen the effective scope of religious influence."* See more on this see: Supreme Court, "Zorach et al. v. Clauson et al." in *Legal Information Institute, Cornell Law School*, https://www.law.cornell.edu/supremecourt/text/343/306 (accessed August 6, 2020)

50. Astin et al, *Cultivating the Spirit*, 7.

51. Jon F. Wergin, "Foreword," in *Putting Students First*, eds. Braskamp et al., 11-12.

52. Gregory A Kalscheur, "Revitalizing the Catholic Intellectual Tradition," in *C21 Resources: Exploring the Catholic Intellectual Tradition* edited by Robert P. Imbelli (Boston, MA: The church in the 21st Century Center at Boston College, Spring 2013), 11.

53. I personally know about 40 architecture faculty in North America that regularly (i.e., about once every 2-3 years) teach a course or studio with spirituality in mind. While not a significant number when looking at the big picture (ACSA claims that the approximate total number of architecture faculty is 5,000 faculty), it does mean that the topic, very limitedly, is being addressed.

54. The two exceptions of spirituality-seeking architectural course(s) being official parts of an architectural

curriculum (that I know of) are the Walton Studio (and a couple of classes in the Sacred Space and Cultural Studies graduate concentration) at CUA (that this book covers) and the foundation course "Sacred Places" (ARCH1007) taught by Associate Professor Tammy Gaber at Laurentian University School of Architecture in Ontario, Canada. For more on the latter see Tammy Gaber, "Continuity of the Sacred in Architectural Pedagogy." Paper presented at the *11th Architecture, Culture, and Spirituality Forum Symposium*, Taliesin West, AZ, May 16-19, 2019. http://www.acsforum.org/symposium2019/works/Gaber.pdf (accessed July 15, 2020)

55. Thompson, *Narratives of Architectural Education,* 54.

56. It is possible to deal with any issue (spirituality included) keeping a "safe" intellectual, analytical distance. For example, we can design a moderately successful courthouse by giving appropriate response to the required program after reviewing architectural precedents, studying the judicial process, meeting the clients, etc. but without involving ourselves (i.e., emotionally, ideologically, physically, spiritually) with the actual project and the very notion and experience of justice, the good, etc.. In other words, we could approach the task technically, dispassionately, in third-person.

57. In Astin et al., *Cultivating the Spirit*, 6-7 and 139-41, the authors provide an eloquent explanation of why university faculty avoid associating what they do with anything "spiritual." Their reason extend beyond the three major concerns earlier stated (indoctrination or irrationality, irrelevance to the educational task, and church-state separation mandate) to include (a) considering the topic private and therefore not appropriate to inquire about it, (2) lack of expertise, and (3) the potential negative academic and political fallout of doing it. Astin et al. also point out that the discomfort faculty feel with the word "spirituality" considerably diminished when they are able to replace it for a phrase like "search for meaning and purpose."

58. Thomas Barrie and Julio Bermudez, "Spirituality and Architecture", in *The Routledge International Handbook of Spirituality and Society and the Professions*, eds. Laszlo Zsolnai and Bernadette Flanagan (UK: Routledge, 2019), 345-55.

59. The professional practice of architecture demands important ethical considerations in line with spirituality.

60. Although these categories may seem forced (reality is a whole), they provide useful viewpoints, which, if well synchronized, may allow good insights into how architecture and spirituality interact and affect each other. See Wilber, *Integral Spirituality*.

61. See the warm-up project Susan Jones used in her 2018 Walton Studio. Another example is the workshop that Antoine Predock led in his 2009 Walton Studio. Other pointers include the already cited Amber Ellett,

"Measures of Place: The Eidetic Image in Design," 44-48; and Chad Schwartz, "Spiritual Tectonics: Exploring Dualities in the Design Studio," in *Proceedings of NCBDS* University professor Anat Geva's Advanced History of Building Technology (ARCH 649) offered at her Department of Architecture.

62. Palmer and Zajonc, *The Heart of Higher Education*, 3.

63. Many see the ultimate goal of education is emancipatory: to liberate the learner's mind so that the true human potential may be unleashed, pursued, and realized. Paulo Freire, *Pedagogy of the oppressed* (New York, NY: Bloomsbury, 1970). John Dewey, *Democracy and Education* (New York: The Free Press, 1966).

64. Romantic English poet John Keats called "negative capability" the skill enabling to work under ambiguity and contradictions without having to resort to fact and reason for resolution (or become upset). For more see Stephen Hebron, "John Keats and 'negative capability,'" 15 May 2014, *The British Library*, in URL: https://www.bl.uk/romantics-and-victorians/articles/john-keats-and-negative-capability (accessed July 19, 2020).

65. Palmer and Zajonc, *The Heart of Higher Education*, 94-95. See also Arthur Zajonc, "Cognitive-Affective connections in teaching and learning: The relationship between love and knowledge," *Journal of Cognitive Affective Learning* 3, no.1 (2006).

66. Alberto Perez-Gomez, *Built Upon Love* (Cambridge, MA: The MIT Press, 2006).

67. Pope John Paul II, *Letter of His Holiness Pope John Paul II to Artists* (1999). The Vatican. Following is another beautiful and related citation from the same document that is worth transcribing: *"Every genuine art form in its own way is a path to the inmost reality of man and of the world. It is therefore a wholly valid approach to the realm of faith, which gives human experience its ultimate meaning."* URL: http://www.vatican.va/content/john-paul-ii/en/letters/1999/documents/hf_jp-ii_let_23041999_artists.html

68. Morris Berman, *The Reenchantment of the World* (Ithaca, NY: Cornell University Press, 1981).

69. The following citation makes this point clear: *"We believe that faculty who are in touch with their own spirituality and who sees the importance of spirituality in their own lives are likely to exhibit certain behaviors, both in and outside the classroom, that support the development of caring in their students . Such faculty members are also more likely to engage in conversations with students about values, and about the meaning and purpose of life, all of which can affect students' spiritual growth and development."* Astin et al., *Cultivating the Spirit*, 75.

70. Palmer, *The Courage to Teach*. This excellent book focuses on the internal dimension of the educator, something of central concern in a spirituality informed architectural education.

71. I presented a version of such vision in written and lecture format. Julio Bermudez, "Arguments for a Spiritual Urbanism." *IN_BO (Ricerche e progetti per il territorio, la città e l'architettura)* 9 (2016): 104-115. Julio Bermudez, "Seeking a Spiritual City," (Richard H. Driehaus Foundation Lecture on Architecture) at the *Chicago Humanities Festival,* Chicago (Nov.4, 2017). Lecture available online in YouTube at: https://youtu.be/jri7rFw_E9Y (accessed July 27, 2020)

72. A good discussion on the origin and evolution of this adage is offered in the website "quoteinvestigator. com" (URL: https://quoteinvestigator.com/2014/09/07/forgotten/#note-9696-15 (accessed July 2, 2020). Versions by Albert Einstein, B.F. Skinner. James Bryant Conant and others are put forward.

73. Michael Polanyi, *Personal Knowledge. Towards a Post-Critical Philosophy* (New York: Harper & Row, 1964).

74. See: Martin J. Packer and Jessie Goicoechea, "Sociocultural and Constructivist Theories of Learning: Ontology, Not Just Epistemology," *Educational Psychologist* 35, no.4 (2000): 227-21. Stanton Wortham and Kara Jackson, "Educational Constructionisms," in *Handbook of Constructionist Research*, eds. James. A. Holstein and Jaber. F. Gubrium (New York: The Guilford Press, 2008), 107-28. *30: Materiality. Essence + Substance*, eds. Leslie Johnson et al (Chicago, IL: Illinois Institute of Technology, 2014), 529-35. An excellent (but unpublished) teaching example is Texas A&M

THE WALTON STUDIO

1. bell hooks, *Teaching to Transgress. Education as the Practice of Freedom* (New York: Routledge, 1994), 207.

2. This is a well-known and often used quote. This or similar versions have been attributed to Socrates, Plutarch, and others. A good discussion about the origin and authorship of this quote is available at "quoteinvestigator.com": https://quoteinvestigator.com/2013/03/28/mind-fire/ (accessed July 13, 2020)

3. Julio Bermudez, "Introduction," in *Transcending Architecture*, ed. Julio Bermudez (Washington, DC: CUA Press, 2015), 8-9.

4. The 1-2-3-person perspective cycling is implied in "Integral Education" and in the seminal work of Ken Wilber. Refer to Esbjorn-Hargens, Jonathan Reams and Olen Gunnlaugson, "The Emergence and Characteristics of Integral Education," in Integral Education, eds. Esbjorn-Hargens et al, 1-16; and Wilber, *Integral Spirituality*.

5. Pope Francis. *Visit To The Pontifical Catholic University Of Chile. Address of the Holy Father* (January 17, 2018), The Vatican. http://www.vatican.va/content/francesco/en/speeches/2018/january/documents/papa-francesco_20180117_cile-santiago-pontuniversita.html

6. Shunryu Suzuki, *Zen Mind, Beginner's Mind* (New York: Weatherhill, 1973).

7. Julio Bermudez, "Zen and/in Beginning Design Education," in *Developing Creative Thinking in Beginning Design*, ed. Stephen Temple (New York: Routledge, 2018), 90-106.

8. The teaching materials utilized in 10 Walton Studios (i.e., syllabi, assignments, references, etc.) are accessible in the teaching tab of my homepage: http://juliobermudez.com/teaching.htm . Examples of students' work from some of the studios is available here: http://www.sacred-space.net/studentwork.htm. The record of three exhibits of work from Walton Studios is available in my page in Academia.edu: https://cua.academia.edu/JulioBermudez/Exhibits,-Videos,-and-Performances (all sites accessed July 21, 2020).

9. Lewis Mumford, *Faith for Living* (New York: Harcourt, Brace & Company, 1940), 216.

2019 - 2009 WALTON STUDIOS

1. Daniel Libeskind. *The Edge of Order* (New York, Crown Publishing Group, 2018).

2. Karen Armstrong, *Twelve Steps to a Compassionate Life* (New York: Alfred A. Knopf, 2010), p.97

3. Jeanne Halgren Kilde, "A Method of Thinking About Power Dynamics in Christian Space," in *Sacred Power, Sacred Space: An Introduction to Christian Architecture and Worship*, ed. Jeanne Halgren Kilde (New York: Oxford University Press, 2008). Keith Anderson, *The Digital Cathedral* (New York: Morehouse Publishing, 2015).

4. The aphorisms may be read in Franco Bertoni, *Claudio Silvestrin* —translated by Lucinda Byatt (Basel, Switzerland: Birkhäuser 1999).

5. Le Corbusier, "The Core as the Meeting Place of the Arts", in T*he Heart of the City: towards the human-ization of human life*, eds. J. L. Sert, E. N. Rogers, and J. Tyrwhitt: (London: Lund Humphries & Co. Ltd., 1952), 41-52.

6. Alberto Campo Baeza, *The Built Idea* (Philadelphia, PA: Oscar Riera Ojeda Publishers, 2011). Alberto Campo Baeza, *Principia Architectonica* (Madrid, Spain: Mairea Libros, 2012).

7. Ortega y Gasset, "Anejo: En torno al Coloquio de Darmstadt, 1951," in *Obras Completas* (Madrid: Revista de Occidente-Alianza, 1962-83, vol.9, 625-644).

8. Alejandro de la Sota, *Alejandro de la Sota: Arquitecto* (Madrid: Ediciones Pronaos, 1990).

9. E.H. Gombrich, *The Preference for the Primitive: Episodes in the History of Western Taste and Art* (New York: Phaidon Press, 2006), 27. The quote of Cicero may be also found in the original: Cicero, *De Oratore*, book 3, 96.

10. Juhani Pallasmaa, *The Eyes of the Skin* (New York: Wiley, 2005). Juhani Pallasmaa, Encounters (Helsinki, Finland: Rakennustieto Publishing, 2008). Juhani Pallasmaa, *The Architecture of Image: Existential Space in Cinema* (Finland: Rakennustieto Publishing, 2008). Juhani Pallasmaa, *The Thinking Hand* (New York: Wiley, 2009). Juhani Pallasmaa, The Embodied Image (New York: Wiley, 2011).

11. Andrey Tarkovsky, *Sculpting in Time: Reflections on the Cinema* (London: The Bodley Head, 1986), 110.

12. Jean-Paul Sartre, "What is Literature," *Jean-Paul Sartre: Basic Writings*, ed. Stephen Priest (London: Routledge, 2001), 272.

13. Rainer Maria Rilke, "Letter to Jacob Baron Uexkull, " Paris, dated August 19 , 1909.

14. Martin Heidegger, "What Calls for Thinking?", *Martin Heidegger: Basic Writings*, ed. David Farrell Krell, (New York: Harper & Row Publishers), 356-7.

15. Iain McGilchrist, *The Master and His Emissary: The Divided Brain and the Making of the Western World*, New Haven, CT: Yale University Press, 2009),142.

16. Gernot Böhme, *Critique of Aesthetic Capitalism* (Milan: Mimesis, 2017).

17. Maurice Merleau-Ponty, as quoted in McGilchrist, *The Master and His Emissary*, 409.

APPENDIX

1. Duane Elgin. *Voluntary Simplicity* (New York: William Morrow Co. 1993).

2. John Paul II, Pope. *Novo Millennio* Ineunte (January 6, 2001), The Vatican. Accessed May 31, 2020. http://www.vatican.va/content/john-paul-ii/en/apost_letters/2001/documents/hf_jp-ii_apl_20010106_novo-millennio-ineunte.html

3. The text of this essay has remained basically the same since 2006 because it has been helpful with my students and readers. In fact, if I go by internet "hits," this is the most popular piece I have ever written with nearly 24,000 views so far, counting both its English and Spanish versions (as of early August 2020).

4. Ricardo Legorreta in "Aspects of Minimal Architecture." *Architectural Design Profile* 110 (London: Academy Editions, 1994), 16.

5. John Pawson, in "Aspects of Minimal Architecture." *Architectural Design Profile* 110 (London: Academy Editions, 1994), 42.

6. Alberto Campo Baeza, in "Aspects of Minimal Architecture." *Architectural Design Profile* 110 (London: Academy Editions, 1994), 22.

7. Louis Kahn, "Order and Form," *Perspecta* 3 (1955): 46-63.

BIBLIOGRAPHY

Adarkar, Aditya, and David Lee Keiser. "The Buddha in the Classroom: Towards a Critical Spiritual Pedagogy." Journal of *Transformative* Education 5, no. 3 (2007): 246-61.

Albareda, Ramon V., Marina T. Romero, and Jorge N. Ferrer. "Integral Transformative Education. A Participatory Proposal." In *Integral Education*, edited by S. Esbjorn-Hargens, J. Reams, and O. Gunnlaugson, 79-103. Albany, NY: SUNY Press, 2010.

Anderson, Keith. The Digital Cathedral. New York: Morehouse Publishing, 2015.

Armstrong, Karen. *Twelve Steps to a Compassionate Life*. New York: Alfred A. Knopf, 2010.

Astin, Alexander W., Helen S. Astin, and Jennifer A. Lindholm. Cultivating the Spirit: *How College can enhance students' inner lives*. San Francisco, CA: Jossey-Bass, 2011.

Astin, John, Kirk Warren Brown, and Shauna L. Shapiro. "Toward the Integration of Meditation into Higher Education: A review of Research Evidence." T*eachers College Record* 113, no. 3 (2011): 493-528.

Barnett, Ronald. *A Will to Learn: Being a Student in an Age of Uncertainty*. New York: Open University Press, 2007.

Barnett, Ronald, and Soren S. E. Bengsten. *Knowledge and the University: Re-claiming Life*. New York: Routledge, 2019.

Barrie, Thomas, and Julio Bermudez. "Spirituality and Architecture." In *The Routledge International Handbook of Spirituality and Society and the Professions*, edited by L. Zsolnai and F. Flanagan, 345-55. New York: Routledge, 2019.

Barrie, Tom, Julio Bermudez, Anat Geva, and Randall Teal. (2007). "Architecture, Culture, and Spirituality : Creating a forum for scholarship and discussion of spirituality and meaning in the built environment." White Paper, April.

Accessed October 2, 2021. http://www.acsforum.org/acsforumnew/wp-content/uploads/2017/11/ACS_founding_whitepaper_2007.pdf.

Benedikt, Michael. *Architecture Beyond Experience*. San Francisco: AR+D publishing, 2020.

——.*God, Creativity, and Evolution: The Argument from Design(ers)*. Austin, Texas: The Center for Architecture and Design, 2008.

Berman, Morris. *The Reenchantment of the World*. Ithaca, NY: Cornell University Press, 1981.

Bermudez, Julio. "Introduction." In *Transcending Architecture*, edited by Julio Bermudez, 8-9. Washington, D.C.: CUA Press, 2015.

——. "Zen and/in Beginning Design Education." In *Developing Creative Thinking in Beginning Design*, edited by Stephen Temple, 90-106. New York: Routledge, 2018.

——. "Turning the Light Inward: Applying the 'Know Thyself' Injunction in Architectural School." Paper presented at the 2019 Architecture, Culture, and Spirituality Symposium (ACSF 11). Accessed October 2, 2021. http://www.acsforum.org/symposium2019/works/Bermudez.pdf

Bertoni, Franco. *Claudio Silvestrin*. Translated by Lucinda Byatt. Basel: Birkhauser, 1999.

Bloom, William. *The Power of the New Spirituality*. Wheaton, IL: Quest Books, 2011.

Bohme, Gernot. *Critique of Aesthetic Capitalism*. Milan, Italy: Mimesis, 2017.

Bregman, Lucy. "Guest Editorial: Defining Spirituality: Multiple Uses and Murky Meanings of an Incredibly Popular Term." *The Journal of Pastoral Care & Counseling* 58, no. 3 (2004): 157-167.

Britton, Karla. Constructing the Ineffable. New Haven, CT: Yale School of Architecture, 2011.

Buber, Marin. *I and Thou*. New York: Touchstone, 1970.

Campo Baeza, Alberto. *Principa Architectonica*. Madrid: Mirea Libros, 2012.

———. *The Built Idea*. Philadelphia: Oscar Riera Ojeda Publishers, 2011.

———. "Aspects of Minimal Architecture." *In Architectural Design Profile* 110, edited by M. Toy and I. Spens, 22. London: Academy Editions, 1994.

Cicero, Marcus Tullius. *De Oratore. Book III*, edited by David Mankin. Cambridge: Cambridge University Press, 2011.

Crosbie, Michael. "The Sacred Becomes Profane." *In Architecture, Culture, and Spirituality*, edited by T. Barrie, J. Bermudez, and P. Tabb, 59-69. New York: Routledge, 2015.

Curry, Andrew. "Gobekli Tepe: The World's First Temple?" *The Smithsonian Magazine*, November 2008. Accessed October 2, 2021. https://www.smithsonianmag.com/history/gobekli-tepe-the-worlds-first-temple-83613665/.

Dewey, John. *Democracy and Education*. New York: The Free Press, 1966.

Diaz Moore, Keith. "A Place-Based Ethic of Care: The Beginnings of the Utah School." In the *106th ACSA Annual Meeting Proceedings*, edited by A. Ameri and R. O'Neal Dagg, 231-235. Washington, DC: ACSA, 2018.

Dyson, Jane, Mark Cobb, and Dawn Forman. "The Meaning of Spirituality: A Literature Review." *Journal of Advanced Nursing* 26 (1997): 1183-1188.

Elgin, Duane. *Voluntary Simplicity*. New York: William Morrow Co., 1993.

Esbjorn-Hargens, Sean, Jonathan Reams, and Olen Gunnlaugson. *Integral Education: New Directions for Higher Learning*. Albany, NY: SUNY Press, 2010.

Findeli, Alain. "Rethinking Design Education for the 21st Century: Theoretical, Methodological, and Ethical Discussion." *Design Issues* 17, no. 1 (2001): 5-17.

Fowler, Martin, John L. Hochheimer, and John D. Martin. Spirituality: *Theory, Praxis and Pedagogy*. Leiden, Netherlands: Brill, 2020.

Freire, Paulo. *Pedagogy of the Oppressed*. New York: Bloomsbury, 1970.

Gaber, Tammy. "Continuity of the Sacred in Architectural Pedagogy." Paper presented at the 2019 Architecture, Culture, and Spirituality Symposium (ACSF 11). Accessed October 2, 2021. http://www.acsforum.org/symposium2019/works/Gaber.pdf.

Geva, Anat. "Revisiting a Graduate Design Studio on Sacred Architecture: A Mosque Design in Yazd, Iran." *International Journal of Islamic Architecture* 4, no. 1 (2015): 161-187.

Gombrich, E.H. *The Preference for the Primitive: Episodes in the History of Western Taste and Art*. New York: Phaidon Press, 2006.

Gregory, Alexis. "Empathizing with Clients: Teaching Students How to Design for 'The Other'." In the *106th ACSA Annual Meeting Proceedings*, edited by A. Ameri and R. O'Neal Dagg, 236-243. Washington, DC: ACSA, 2018.

Esbjorn-Hargens, Sean, Jonathan Reams, and Olen Gunnlaugson. "The Emergence and Characteristics of Integral Education." In *Integral Education*, edited by S. Esbjorn-Hargens, J. Reams and O. Gunnlaugson, 1-16. Albany, NY: SUNY Press, 2010.

Harrison, Edward. *Masks of the Universe*. New York: McMillan, 1985.

Hebron, Stephen. "John Keats and 'negative capability'." *The British Library* (May 15, 2014). Accessed October 2, 2021. https://www.bl.uk/romantics-and-victorians/articles/john-keats-and-negative-capability.

Heidegger, Martin. "What Calls for Thinking." *In Martin Heidegger: Basic Writings*, edited by D. Farrell, 356-357. New York: Harper & Row Publishers, 1978.

Hejduk, Renata, and Jim Williamson. "Introduction: The Apocryphal Project of Modern and Contemporary Architecture." In *The Religious Imagination in Modern and Contemporary Architecture*, edited by R. Hejduk and J. Williamson, 1-9. New York, New York: Routledge, 2001.

hooks, bell. *All About Love: New Visions*. New York: HarperCollins Publishers, 2000.

———. *Teaching to Transgress: Education as the Practice of Freedom*. New York: Routledge, 1994.

James, William. *The Varieties of Religious Experience*. New York: Simon & Schuster, Inc., 2004.

Jann, Marga. "Revamping Architectural Education: Ethics, Social Service, and Innovation." *International Journal of Arts and Sciences* 3, no. 8 (2010): 45-89.

Kahn, Louis. *Louis Kahn: Conversations with Students (Architecture at Rice)*. Houston, TX: Rice University of Architecture, 1998.

Kahn, Louis. *"Order and Form."* Perspecta 3 (1955): 46-63.

Kalscheur, Gregory A. "Revitalizing the Catholic Intellectual Tradition." In *C21 Resources: Exploring the Catholic Intellectual Tradition*, edited by R. P. Imbelli, 11. Boston: The Church in the 21st Century Center at Boston College, 2013.

Karlowitsch, Michael. "Architecture is not Technology: The Space of Differentiation in Architectural Education."

Open House International 40, no. 3 (2015): 17-23.

Kegan, Robert. *The Evolving Self: Problems and Process in Human Development.* Cambridge: Harvard University Press, 1982.

Kilde, Jeanne Halgren. "A Method of Thinking About Power Dynamics in Christian Space." In *Sacred Power, Sacred Space: An Introduction to Christian Architecture and Worship*, edited by J. Halgren Kilde. New York: Oxford University Press, 2008.

Kim, Elisa. "Beginning with 'Environmentality'." In *NCBDS 33 Proceedings: Begin W/Why: Ethics and Values in Beginning Design*, edited by E. Carraher, 263-266. Salt Lake City: NCBDS, 2017.

Kronman, Anthony T. *Education's End: Why Our Colleges and Universities Have Given Up on the Meaning of Life.* New Haven: Yale University Press, 2006.

Kulnieks, Andreis, Dan Roronhiakewen, and Kelly Young. "Tramping the Mobius: A Curriculum of Oral and Literary Tradition as a Primer for Rural Education." *Space and Culture* 21, no. 1 (2017): 60-71.

Le Corbusier. "The Core as the Meeting Place of the Arts." In *The Heart of the City: Towards the Humanisation of Urban Life*, edited by J. L. Sert, E. N. Rogers and J. Tyrwhitt, 41-52. London: Lund Humphries & Co. Ltd, 1952.

Legorreta, Ricardo. "Aspects of Minimal Architecture." In *Architectural Design Profile 110*, edited by M. Toy and I. Spens, 16. London: Academy Editions, 1994.

Lewis, Harry R. *Excellence without Soul: Does Liberal Education Have a Future?* New York: Public Affairs, 2007.

Libeskind, Daniel. *The Edge of Order.* New York: Crown Publishing Group, 2018.

Mann, Charles C. "The Birth of Religion." *National Geographic*, June 2011. Accessed October 2, 2021. https://www.nationalgeographic.com/magazine/article/gobeki-tepe

Matchison, Lauren. "Creating an Academic Community of Inquiry: Educating Architects to Embrace a People-Centered View." In the *106th ACSA Annual Meeting Proceedings*, edited by A. Ameri and R. O'Neal Dagg, 244-249. Washington, DC: ACSA, 2018.

McGilchrist, Iain. *The Master and His Emissary: The Divided Brain and the Making of the Western World.* New Haven: Yale University Press, 2009.

Miller, John P. *Education and the Soul. Toward a New Curriculum.* Albany, NY: SUNY Press, 2000.

——. *The Holistic Curriculum.* Toronto: University of Toronto Press, 2007.

Miller, John P., Selia Karsten, Diana Denton, Deborah Orr, and Isabella Colalillo Kates, eds. *Holistic Learning and Spirituality in Education.* Albany: SUNY Press, 2005.

Mumford, Lewis. *Faith for Living.* New York: Harcourt, Brace & Company, 1940.

Nash, Robert J. *Religious Pluralism in the Academy: Opening the Dialogue.* New York: Peter Lang Publishing, 2001.

Nord, Warren A. *Religion and American Education: Rethinking a National Dilemma.* Chapel Hill, NC: University of North Carolina Press, 1995.

Oman, Doug. "Defining Religion and Spirituality." In *Handbook of the Psychology of Religion and Spirituality*, edited by R. F. Paloutzian and C. L. Park, 23-47. New York: The Guilford Press, 2013.

Ortega y Gasset, Jose. *Anejo: En torno al Coloquio de Darmstadt*, 1951. Vol. 9, Obras Completas. Madrid: Revista de Occidente-Alianza, 1962-1983.

O'Sullivan, Edmund. "Emancipatory Hope." In *Holistic Learning and Spirituality in Education*, edited by J. P. Miller, S. Karsten, D. Denton, D. Orr, and I. Colalillo Kates, 69-78. Albany, NY: SUNY Press, 2005.

Packer, Martin J., and Jessie Goicoechea. "Sociocultural and Constructivist Theories of Learning: Ontology, Not Just Epistemology." *Educational Psychologist* 35, vol. 4 (2000): 227-21.

Pallasmaa, Juhani. *The Embodied Image.* New York: Wiley, 2011.

——. *The Thinking Hand.* New York: Wiley, 2009.

——. *The Architecture of Image.* CITY?, Finland: Rakennustieto Publishing, 2008.

——. *The Eyes of the Skin.* New York: Wiley, 2008.

Palermo, Gregory S. "Ethical Premises in Student Proposals: Well-Being, Virtue and Change." In the *87th ACSA Annual Meeting Proceedings*, edited by G. Forbes and M. Malecha, 183-188. Washington: ACSA, 1999.

Palmer, Parker J. *The Courage to Teach.* San Francisco, CA: Jossey-Bass, 2007.

Palmer, Parker J., Arthur Zajonc, and Megan Scribner. *The heart of higher education: A call to renewal.* San Francisco, CA: Jossey-Bass, 2010.

Pawson, John. "Aspects of Minimal Architecture." In *Architectural Design Profile 110*, edited by M. Toy and I. Spens, 42. London: Academy Editions, 1994.

Perez-Gomez, Alberto. *Built Upon Love.* Cambridge, MA: The MIT Press, 2016.

Perry, William G., Jr. *Forms of Intellectual and Ethical Development in the College Years.* San Francisco: Jossey-Bass Inc., 1999.

Pew Research Center. *"In U.S., Decline of Christianity Continues at Rapid Pace"* (October 2019) Accessed October 2, 2021. https://www.pewforum.org/2019/10/17/in-u-s-decline-of-christianity-continues-at-rapid-pace/

———. "When Americans Say They Believe in God, What Do They Mean?" (April 25, 2018). Accessed October 2, 2021. https://www.pewforum.org/2018/04/25/when-americans-say-they-believe-in-god-what-do-they-mean/ .

———. "Most Americans Believe in Heaven and Hell" (November 10, 2015). Accessed October 2, 2021. https://www.pewresearch.org/fact-tank/2015/11/10/most-americans-believe-in-heaven-and-hell/

Polanyi, Michael. *Personal Knowledge*: Towards a Post-Critical Philosophy. New York: Harper & Row, 1964.

Pope Francis. "Visit to the Pontifical Catholic University of Chile." *The Vatican* (January 17, 2018). Accessed October 2, 2021. http://www.vatican.va/content/francesco/en/speeches/2018/january/documents/papa-francesco_20180117_cile-santiago-pontuniversita.html.

Pope John Paul II. "Letter of His Holiness Pope John Paul II to Artists." *The Vatican* (1999). Accessed October 2, 2021. http://www.vatican.va/content/john-paul-ii/en/letters/1999/documents/hf_jp-ii_let_23041999_artists.html .

———. "Novo Millennio Ineunte." *The Vatican* (January 2001). Accessed October 2, 2021. http://www.vatican.va/content/john-paul-ii/en/apost_letters/2001/documents/hf_jp-ii_apl_20010106_novo-millennio-ineunte.html .

Porterfield, Amanda, Betty Deberg, and Conrad Cherry. *Religion on Campus*. Chapel Hill, NC: The U of North Carolina Press, 2001.

Principe, Walter. "Toward Defining Spirituality." *Studies in Religion* 12, no. 2 (1983): 127-141.

Rilke, Rainer Maria. *Letter to Jakob Baron Uexkull*. Translated by Jane Bannard Greene and M.D.Herter Norton. New York: W.W.Norton Company, Inc., 1945

Salama, Ashraf. "Reflections on Architectural Education of the Muslim World within a global World." *International Journal of Islamic Architecture* 9, no. 1 (2019): 33-41.

Sartre, Jean-Paul. "What is Literature." In *Jean-Paul Sartre: Basic Writings*, edited by Stephen Priest, 272. London: Routledge, 2001.

Schieren, Jost. "The Spiritual Dimension of Waldorf Education" (August 27, 2014). Accessed October 2, 2021. https://www.waldorf-resources.org/single-view/the-spiritual-dimension-of-waldorf-education .

Schwartz, Chad. "Spiritual Tectonics: Exploring Dualities in the Design Studio." In *NCBDS 30 Proceedings: Materiality. Essence + Substance*, edited by Leslie Johnson, 529-35. Chicago: Illinois Institute of Technology, 2014.

Sheldrake, Philip. *Spirituality: A Brief History*. New York: Wiley-Blackwell, 2013.

Schinkel, Anders, "Wonder, Mystery, and Meaning." Philosophical Papers 48, n.2 (2019): 293-319.

Sota, Alejandro de la. *Alejandro de la Sota: Arquitecto*. Madrid: Ediciones Pronaos, 1990.

Story, J. Kevin. *The Complexities of John Hejduk's Work*. New York: Routledge, 2020.

Suzuki, Shunryu. *Zen Mind, Beginner's Mind*. New York: Weatherhill, 1973.

Tanyi, Ruth A. "Towards clarification of the meaning of spirituality." *Journal of Advanced Nursing* 39, no. 5 (2002): 500-509.

Tarkovsky, Andrey. *Sculpting in Time: Reflections on the Cinema*. London: The Bodley Head, 1986.

Temple, Stephen. "Necessity for Learning Abstraction in Representational Thinking." In *NCBDS 33 Proceedings: Begin W/Why: Ethics and Values in Beginning Design*, edited by E. Carraher, 420-42. Salt Lake City: NCBDS, 2017.

Thompson, James. *Narratives of Architectural Education: From Student to Architect*. New York: Routledge, 2019.

Tisdell, Elizabeth J. *Exploring Spirituality and Culture in Adult and Higher Education*. San Francisco, CA: Jossey-Bass, 2003.

Trautvetter, Lois Callan, Kelly Ward, and Larry A. Braskamp. Putting Students First: *How Colleges Develop Students Purposefully*. San Francisco, CA: Jossey-Bass, 2006.

UCLA. "Attending to Students' Inner Lives: A Call to Higher Education." *Higher Education Research Institute*, (April 2011). Accessed October 2, 2021. https://spirituality.ucla.edu/docs/white%20paper/white%20paper%20final.pdf .

UIA Architectural Education Commission. *UIA and Architectural Education. Reflections and Recommendations. Paris: International Union of Architects*, 2002. Accessed October 2, 2021. http://citeseerx.ist.psu.edu/viewdoc/download?doi=10.1.1.549.4828&rep=rep1&type=pdf.

UNESCO World Heritage. "Gobekli Tepe." Accessed October 2, 2021. https://whc.unesco.org/en/list/1572/ .

UNESCO. "Higher Education in the Twenty-first Century: Vision and Action, v. 1: Final Report." Report of *World Conference on Higher Education, 1998*. Paris: UNESCO, 1999.. Accessed October 2, 2021. https://unesdoc.unesco.org/ark:/48223/pf0000116345.

Vitello, Roger. "Introducing Empathy into the Classroom: Becoming my Brother's Keeper." In *NCBDS 33 Proceedings: Begin W/Why: Ethics and Values in Beginning Design*, edited by E. Carraher, 466-473. Salt Lake City: NCBDS, 2017.

Waggoner, Michael D. "Spirituality and Contemporary Higher Education." J*ournal of College and Character* 17, no. 3 (2016): 147-156.

Wilber, Ken. *Integral Spirituality*. Boston: Shambala, 2006.

Wortham, Stanton, and Kara Jackson. "Educational Constructionisms." In *Handbook of Constructionist Research*, edited by J. A. Holstein and J. F. Gubrium, 107-128. New York: The Guilford Press, 2008.

Xu, Ping, and Lawrence W. Speck. "Design with Meanings: Feng-shui and Cosmology in Architecture." In the *85th ACSA Annual Meeting Proceedings*, edited by L. W. Speck, 255-260. Washington, DC: ACSA, 1997.

WIN-Gallup International. *Global Index of Religiosity and Atheism* (2012). Accessed October 2, 2021. https://www.webpages.uidaho.edu/~stevel/251/Global_INDEX_of_Religiosity_and_Atheism_PR__6.pdf

Zajonc, Arthur. "Cognitive-Affective connections in teaching and learning: The relationship between love and knowledge." *Journal of Cognitive Affective Learning* 3, no. 1 (2006): 1-9.

——. *Contemplative Pedagogy: A Quiet Revolution in Higher Education. New Directions for Teaching and Learning*, no. 134 (2013): 83-94.

Zimmerman, Jonathan. "What is College Worth?" *The New York Review of Books* (July 2020). Accessed October 2, 2021. https://www.nybooks.com/articles/2020/07/02/what-is-college-worth .

INDEX

academic, leadership, 20
academic, performance, 20
academics, architectural, xiii, 13, 24
academy, architectural, 23, 30, 32, 250n2
academy, the, 5, 8, 22, 35, 58, 193
ACSA (Association of Collegiate Schools
of Architecture), 13, 248, 251m4, 254n53
ACSF, acsforum (Architecture, Culture,
and Spirituality Forum), xiii, 13, 23, 243,
248, 251n6, 254n54
aesthetic, 8, 24, 25, 98, 175, 177, 192,
256n16
aestheticized, 166, 177
aesthetics, 37, 98, 175, 216, 217, 229,
243
age, industrial, 55
age, information, 56, 216
age, our, 8, 176
age, secular. *See* secular
AIA, American Institute of Architects, xii,
42, 246, 247
amazing, 9, 57, 58, 162
ambiguity, ambiguous, 17, 28, 255n64
American, 115, 4, 7, 14, 19, 23, 62, 115,
136, 138, 140, 142, 152, 161, 205,
220, 242, 252n13, 253n40
analysis or analyses, 8, 9, 13, 22, 56, 131,
223, 252n7
analysis, precedents, 40, 182
analysis, site, 62, 114
analytical, 16, 20, 235, 254n56
anxiety, 4, 32, 71
apathy, 216
apprenticeship model, 31
architectural academics, xiii
architectural academy, 23, 30, 32, 250n2
architectural aesthetics, 98
architectural career, 30
architectural challenge, 186, 216, 222
architectural clarity, 76, 88, 217
architectural community, 3

architectural curriculum, 12, 27, 30,
254n54,
architectural design, 8, 12, 38, 62, 122,
150, 166, 175, 222, 228, 236, 237,
238
architectural discipline, 3, 13, 24, 113
architectural discourse, 37
architectural education, 2, 3, 4, 5, 6, 7,
8, 12, 13, 14, 23, 24, 25, 26, 27, 28,
29, 31, 32, 35, 39, 42, 43, 58, 97,
132, 159, 160, 175, 200, 202, 205,
227, 229, 233, 235, 237, 251n3,
251n4, 252n7, 252n8, 255n70
architectural educators, 3
architectural experience, 130, 175, 177,
251n5
architectural history, xvi, 150
architectural idea or ideas, 46, 76, 136,
150, 156, 242
architectural imagination, 29
architectural inquiry, 28, 30, 38, 41, 120
architectural issues, 26, 73
architectural language, 68, 166
architectural object, 25, 26, 131
architectural pedagogy, 38, 73, 193,
254n56
architectural practice, 32, 175, 203, 236,
243
architectural practitioner, xiii, 3, 13, 14
architectural precedent, 41, 104, 114,
254n56
architectural professing, 2, 25, 27, 32, 39,
43, 216, 218
architectural quality or qualities, 62, 131,
192
architectural scholars, 3, 13
architectural schooling, 16, 25, 27
architectural simplicity, 76, 88. *See also*
Voluntary Architectural Simplicity
architectural space, 72, 131, 227
architectural task, 76, 204

architectural teaching, 13, 14
architectural training, 26
architectural transcendence, 35, 36, 37
architectural vision, 32
architectural work, 4
architecture schools, 3, 24, 99, 131, 211,
251n6
architecture students, 2, 26, 85
architecture, experiential, 129, 130, 131,
228, 242
architecture, religious. *See* religious architecture
architecture, sacred, 7, 8, 110, 212, 227,
251n3
architecture, spiritual. *See* spiritual
architecture
ARCHNET, 13, 251n7
art of architecture, 46, 166
art of teaching, 7, 8, 150
assessment, xiii, 28, 38, 42, 100, 101, 200
Astin, Alexander W., 14, 16, 17, 252n14,
252n18, 253n24-31-35-36-43-44-
45, 254n50-57, 255n69
atheism, 252n15
atheists, 15, 19, 113, 205, 252n15
atmosphere, 8, 55, 57, 68, 131, 177, 188,
230
attention, xiii, 3, 4, 8, 16, 20, 22, 30, 38,
43, 59, 120, 182, 192, 211, 237
attention, lack of, 4, 13, 251
attention, particular, 27, 115, 196
aura, 8, 196, 211
authentic, 4, 6, 8, 131, 166, 176, 208
authenticity, 8, 9, 13, 14, 21, 22, 31, 37,
41, 43, 120, 130, 177, 182, 228
authority, 97
autonomous, 99, 177
autonomy, 97
awareness, 9, 14, 15, 16, 19, 24, 25, 39,
56, 73, 120, 122, 132, 191, 228,
247

awe, 14, 98, 166, 192, 206

Bach, Johann Sebastian, 161, 163
Baroque, xv
beautiful, the, 37, 230
beauty, 7, 8, 14, 15, 22, 29, 36, 72, 85,
    146, 150, 162, 163, 175, 177, 182,
    192, 203, 204, 207, 208, 217, 229,
    236, 247
beginner's mind, 30, 39, 255n5
being, human, 4, 46, 202, 211
being, whole, 14, 15
beings, human, 4, 6, 7, 17, 56, 85, 110,
    114, 116, 193, 202, 209
belief, xvi, 3, 15, 19, 73, 85, 104, 110,
    114, 207, 216, 222, 227, 252n13,
    252n15
belief(s), spiritual, 104, 114, 252n14,
    252n15
beliefs, 7, 15, 16, 19, 37, 47, 55, 85,
    113, 114, 154, 220, 226, 229,
    252n15, 254n49
beliefs, personal, 175, 229,
beliefs, religious, 21, 170, 252n14
Berman, Morris, 29, 255n68
bias/biases, 21, 28, 22, 37, 250n2
Bible, 115, 204
big picture, 18, 42, 43, 252n20, 254n53
body, 6, 16, 18, 38, 39, 46, 68, 122, 125,
    131, 132, 193, 196, 207, 220
Boyer report, 3
breath, 56, 163, 235
Brunelleschi, Filippo, 176
Buddhism, 39
Buddhism, Zen. See Zen
Buddhist tradition, 40

capricious, 26, 162
care, 19, 25, 29, 31, 32, 43, 105, 192,
    212, 217, 237, 251n4, 252n16
cathedral, 73, 114, 116, 145, 190, 193,
    256n3
Cathedral of Christ the Light (Oakland,
    CA), 8, 190, 192, 193, 194, 244
Cathedral, Cologne (Germany), 203, 210
Cathedral, St. James (Seattle), 69
Catholic, 41, 204, 234,
Catholic University of America, xii, xv,
    22, 73, 85, 97, 114, 159, 200, 227,
    228, 229, 234, 247
chapel, 40, 66, 68, 69, 117, 123, 145,
    150, 151, 155, 182, 183, 194, 196,
    203
Chapel of Ronchamp, France (by architect
    Le Corbusier), 8, 192
Chapel, Bruder Klaus Field (by architect
    Peter Zumthor), 8, 192, 193
chapel, burial, 40, 166, 167, 171, 177
Chapel, Rothko, 160,

Chapel, Thorncrown (by architect E.Fay
    Jones), 8, 192, 193
Chowdhury, Morad, 101
Christ, Jesus, 145, 146
Christian faith or tradition, 40, 104, 113,
Christian space, 256n3
Christian teaching, 182
Christianity, 22, 107, 252n21
church (as building), xvi, 26, 73, 74, 112,
    145,
church (as institution in general), 203,
    227, 254
church and state (separation), 3, 18, 20,
    21, 254n47, 254n57
Church of Christ The Worker (by archi-
    tect Eladio Dieste), 8, 192
Church, Catholic, xv, 193
Cicero, 163, 256n9
civilization, 8, 20, 46, 166, 191, 216
Clarence Walton
Fund for Catholic Architecture, xv, xvi
clarity, 8, 22, 25, 37, 73, 136, 150, 154,
    217, 233
clarity, architectural. See architectural
Classic, classical, 161, 162, 227, 246
Classicist, 216
climate change, 24, 62
cognicentric, 8, 16, 17, 23, 32
cognition, 16, 18
cognition, meta, 27
cognoscere, 16, 17, 32, 38,
collaboration, 16, 28, 113, 176, 239
collaborative, xv, 36, 38, 39, 234, 243
Cologne Cathedral. See Cathedral
commitment, xi, xii, xiii, 3, 4, 5, 9, 14,
    22, 25, 28, 29, 30, 57, 166, 177,
    182, 217, 222, 237, 245, 247
common sense, 19, 25, 39
commonality, 18, 37, 139
communal, 28, 62, 85, 106, 122, 142
community, xii, xiii, 3, 15, 19, 20, 24, 26,
    28, 36, 50, 62, 72, 92,98, 104, 106,
    110, 115, 116, 201, 220, 221, 236,
    244, 246, 251n4
compassion, 6, 14, 16, 21, 30, 38, 43,
    101, 166, 237
compassionate, 8, 14, 15, 21, 29, 85, 236,
    237, 256n2
competence or competency, 25, 100, 101,
    202, 235
competition, xiii, 129, 245
complexity, 4, 31, 161, 191, 216, 217,
    231
connectedness, 14, 21, 27
connection(s), 14, 18, 22, 29, 32, 47, 68,
    72, 73, 85, 92, 100, 105, 107, 114,
    122, 126, 161, 191, 205, 210, 220,
    228, 231, 232, 252n13, 255n65
connectivity, 191, 220
conscious, 7, 37, 207, 211, 217, 251n5

consciousness, 14, 15, 50, 57, 94, 98,
    177, 210, 242
construction, 24, 26, 37, 58, 131, 145,
    146, 162, 176, 192, 204, 223, 233
consumerism, 177, 204, 216, 217
consumption, 5, 32, 40, 182, 219, 220
contemplation, 92, 110, 202
contemplative, 5, 27, 28, 39, 41, 52, 120,
    136, 253n45
contemplative practice, 20, 150
contemplative space, 192, 248
contradiction, 28, 94, 255n64
conventional, 19, 88, 101, 114, 130, 230
conventions, 36, 55, 58, 98
conviction(s), 9, 22, 145, 247
Coronavirus or COVID-19 (pandemic),
    xi, 85
cosmic, 166, 182
creativity, 28, 29, 39, 56, 97, 98, 104,
    136, 205, 206, 250n2
Creator, 145, 229
criticism, 3, 16, 20, 22, 24, 36, 30, 37,
    42, 136
critique, 4, 20, 22, 24, 76, 130, 166, 228,
    238, 256n16
cultural criticism, 23, 37, 42, 46
culture, 2, 7, 9, 13, 15, 16, 27, 35, 37,
    38, 76, 98, 120, 131, 177, 182, 191,
    200, 204, 206, 207, 208, 216, 217,
    228, 242, 245, 248, 251n3
Cummings, E.E., 4
curiosity, 4, 21
curriculum, 2, 3, 5, 15, 23, 24, 25, 26,
    27, 29, 30, 58, 100, 101, 196, 206,
    236, 251n3, 253n26, 253n37,
    253n38, 254n54
curriculum and pedagogy, 16, 24
curriculum, architectural, 12, 27, 30, 99,
    100
curriculum, pedagogy-centered, 101
cyberspace, 55
cynical, 55, 162
cynicism, 19, 216

darkness, 71, 130, 146, 193, 209, 210
death, 6, 24, 37, 41, 62, 66, 68, 71, 166,
    170, 172, 177, 238
deconstructivist, 216
democracy, 97, 255n63
democratic, 19, 140, 247
demographic, 104, 114
demoralized, 43
design, xii, xvi, 2, 3, 6, 7, 9, 13, 24, 25,
    36, 37, 38, 39, 40, 42, 46, 55, 62,
    68, 76, 88, 98, 104, 105, 113, 116,
    120, 130, 131, 136, 142, 145, 146,
    154, 160, 167, 177, 178, 183, 198,
    201, 202, 204, 206, 207, 213, 222,
    223, 228, 229, 230, 232, 233, 234,

236, 237, 238, 239, 243, 244, 245, 246, 247, 251n4, 251n5, 252n23, 254n56, 256n61

design assignment, 114

design charrette, 40, 46

design education, 26, 250n3, 255n7

design method/methodology, 7, 27, 29, 35, 36, 38, 40, 41, 62

design parti, 8, 9, 222, 223

design practice. *See* practice

design problem, 114, 115

design process, xii, 25, 28, 29, 38, 71, 116, 120, 124, 129, 131. 132, 136, 150, 182, 232, 233, 234, 239

design quality, 145, 217

design studio, 2, 8, 13, 24, 26, 29, 36, 46, 98, 99, 100, 116, 166, 229, 231, 251n3, 251n5, 254n61

design work, 63, 71, 77, 85, 89, 121, 159, 213, 230

design workshop, 39, 41

design, architectural. *See* architectural

design, the essence of. *See* essence

destiny, 2, 58

development (building, urban), 24, 97, 115, 120, 217, 245, 247, 250n3

development (human, cultural), 17, 20, 22, 24, 32, 43, 88, 114, 253n29, 255n69

development (program), xvi

development, spiritual. *See* spiritual

developmental psychology, 17

Dewey, John, 27, 255n63

dialogic/dialogical, 8, 16, 26, 28

dialogue, 20, 36, 46, 80, 177, 211, 252n14

Dieste, Eladio, 8, 192

dignity, human. *See* human

dimension, artifactual, 35, 38

dimension, communicative, 25, 35, 38

dimension, emotional, 31

dimension, essential, 15, 206

dimension, existential. *See* existential

dimension, intersubjective, 46, 220

dimension, objective, 46, 166, 220

dimension, ontological, 23

dimension, phenomenological. *See* phenomenological

dimension, political, 97

dimension, sacred. *See* sacred

dimension, semiotic. *See* semiotic

dimension, spiritual. *See* spiritual

dimension, subjective, 46, 166, 220

dimension, transcendent. *See* transcendent, 14, 46, 56, 76, 166

dimension, transformative. *See* transformative

discipline, xv, 18, 23, 25, 26, 38, 132, 175, 251n6

discipline, architectural. *See* architectural

discovery, 72, 78, 92, 101, 142, 208, 211, 213, 228

discovery, self. *See* self

disempowered, 43

divinity, 14, 36, 217

dogma, 37, 145, 182, 208

doubt, xiv, 4, 12, 17, 22, 23, 31, 132, 227, 228

drawing, 73, 196, 209, 213, 242

dwelling, 46, 58, 76, 166, 192

earth, 2, 7, 19, 32, 56, 62, 85, 92, 114, 122, 138, 146, 150, 182, 192, 193, 204, 216, 217, 227, 238

Eckhart, Meister, 208

ecological, 18, 32, 38, 98, 115, 177, 216

ecology, 98, 228

economic, 15, 18, 24, 114, 216, 222, 250

economy, 166, 213, 222

education, xi, xii, 2, 3, 4, 13, 14, 15, 17, 18, 19, 20, 21, 27, 30, 32, 33, 35, 43, 100, 101, 140, 176, 203, 205, 206, 207. 211, 213, 227, 228, 229, 230, 232, 233, 243, 250n1, 254n57, 255n63

education system, 205, 206

education, architectural. *See* architectural

education, business model. *See* model

education, design. *See* design

education, formal, 206, 207

education, higher, 3, 8, 12, 15, 16, 17, 18, 20, 22, 23, 24, 26, 31, 35, 38, 200, 229, 250n1, 250n3, 252n14, 253n26, 253n35, 253n38, 253n45, 254n47, 255n62, 255n65

education, integral, 22, 253n26, 253n42, 255n4

education, professional, 12, 97, 136, 228

education, secular. *See* secular

education, spiritual, 207

education, spirituality-minded, 28, 33, 43

education, transformative. *See* transformative

education, true, 16, 27, 38, 203

education, Waldorf. *See* Waldorf

educational practice, 18, 20

ego, 6, 7, 27, 38, 39, 145, 146, 161, 202, 228, 234

egocentric, non-, 21, 136

egocentrism or egocentric, 14, 26, 32, 169,

El Greco, 160

Elgin, Duane, 182, 217, 256n1

Eliot, T.S., 7, 161, 162, 163,

embodiment, 5, 7, 8, 18, 37, 41, 120, 150, 217

emotion, 28, 41, 62, 71, 72, 163, 177, 202, 208, 212, 234, 237, 238, 242,

emotional experience. *See* experience

empathic, 6, 15, 24, 28, 42, 176, 202,

empathy, 8, 14, 16, 21, 30, 38, 47, 120, 129, 166, 176, 251n5

empirical, 16, 23, 28, 205

empower(ment), 18, 27, 97, 211

enchanted, 98, 100, 101

encompassing, all, 14, 15, 18, 21, 62

Encyclical, Laudato Si, 114, 115

engagement, community, 104, 244

enlightenment, 46, 77, 97, 141, 211, 236

ephemeral, 129, 162

equanimity, 14, 21

esoteric, 2, 35, 145, 222

essence, 146, 175, 191, 192, 222, 223, 227

essence of architecture, 166, 242

essence of design, 55

essence of learning. *See* learning

essence, spiritual, 193, 230

essense of being human, 113

essentialism, 37, 217

eternal, 145, 146, 166, 223

ethereal, 145, 146, 184

ethics, 15, 22, 24, 37, 55, 175, 217, 220, 229, 251n4, 251n5, 252n8

ethnocentrism, 14

ethos, 12, 191, 226

everyday life, 58, 68, 88, 116, 120, 124

evolution, 145, 191, 216, 247, 250n2, 255n72

existence, xv, 21, 22, 43, 52, 98, 170, 175, 206

existential, 5, 22, 28, 37, 41, 62, 120, 150, 166, 170, 175, 176, 178, 216, 228

existential awareness, 120, 228

existential dimension, 177, 201

existential experience, 177

existential meaning, 8, 204

experience, 3-5, 8, 15, 16, 18-20, 22, 23, 25, 26, 29, 36-39, 42, 46, 56-58. 62, 66, 73, 76, 85, 99, 100, 101, 115, 120, 124, 129, 130, 1402, 166, 176, 177, 178, 186, 188, 196, 203, 207, 209, 210, 212, 217, 226, 228, 230, 235, 236, 237, 239, 242, 254n56

experience, architectural. *See* architectural

experience, architecture as, 129, 132

experience, design of, 120

experience, educational, 43, 251n4

experience, emotional, 20, 88, 204

experience, first, 99, 234

experience, human, 192, 201, 205, 220, 228, 238, 239, 255n67

experience, intellectual, 37, 120

experience, invaluable, 236, 237

experience, learning, 16, 38, 196, 228, 238

experience, life, 17, 204, 207

experience, lifetime, 234, 239

experience, own, 23, 71, 104, 114, 202

experience, personal, 113, 138, 175, 209, 213, 217

experience, religious, 210, 252n22

experience, spiritual, 203, 230, 231

experience, transcendent, 36

experience, unique, 58, 150

experience, Walton, 226, 235, 239

experiential, architecture. *See* architecture

experiment, experimentation, or experimental, 3, 9, 35, 39, 41, 46, 136, 166, 192, 234

expertise, 29, 36, 101, 254n57

extraordinary, 9, 29, 57, 162, 163, 204, 229, 250n2

Eyes of the Skin, The, 29, 211, 228, 246, 256n10

faith, xii, xvi, 7, 12, 13, 14, 15, 19, 20, 22, 23, 24, 31, 32, 37, 38, 66, 68, 76, 97, 100, 101, 104, 110, 145, 150, 201, 204, 208, 219, 230, 239, 252n7, 252n15, 255n67, 256n9

faith tradition, 97, 101, 104, 113, 221

faith-based higher education, 22, 23

faith-based schools of architecture, 3

faith-based university, 22, 205

Farnsworth house (by architect Mies van der Rohe), 212

fear, 12, 14, 18, 19, 22, 71, 72, 172, 238

firmitas, utilitas and venustas, 192, 204

flourishing, 6, 8, 39

fragmentation, 18, 21, 23, 38, 217, 253n37

fragmented, 15, 16, 17, 32, 108, 176, 216

framework, 14, 15, 16, 18, 166

Frampton, Kenneth, 58, 159

Francis, Pope, 38, 114, 115, 255n5

Frankfurt School of Philosophy, 20

freedom, 3, 35, 57, 97, 98, 100, 254n49, 255n1

freedom, practice of. *See* practice

Freire, Paulo, 27, 255n63

future, xvi, 3, 9, 21, 32, 36, 55, 58, 104, 113, 140, 191, 200, 204, 206, 226,229, 238, 253n26

future citizen, 21, 32

future of sacred space. *See* sacred space

future professionals, 21, 202

geometry, 146, 150, 154, 188, 193, 206, 207, 213, 229

Giedion, Sigfried, 58

Giza Pyramids (Egypt), 9

global warming, 24, 216

Gobekli Tepe (Turkey), 9, 58, 250n4

God, 14, 24, 29, 32, 46, 56, 66, 88, 106, 108, 110, 115, 145, 150, 152, 166, 192, 204, 219, 250n2, 252n13,

252n14, 254n49

Gombrich, E.H., 161, 163, 256n9

good life, the, 37, 41, 99, 229

good, the, 15, 16, 19, 22, 175, 230, 254n56

good, the true, and the beautiful, 37, 166

goodness, 7, 14, 22, 212, 217, 236

Gospel, 156

Gothic, xv

grace, 162

gratitude, xi, xii, xiii, 8, 98, 237

grief, 6, 62, 71, 73, 166, 172, 178, 216

growth, 18, 38, 42, 88, 216, 217, 223, 234

growth, spiritual. *See* spiritual

guru, 30, 101, 209

habit, 5, 23, 57, 58, 57, 120, 132, 206, 216, 235, 253n39,

habits, professional, 7, 146

Hamlet, 56

haptic, 132, 177, 196

harmonious, xv, 15, 38

harmony, 81, 98, 100, 146, 191

heal, 166, 220, 232

healing, 16, 46, 170, 220

health, 22, 24, 36, 106, 115, 170, 205

health, mental, 205

health, safety, and welfare, 36, 229

healthy, 121, 161

heaven, 56, 68, 152, 252n13

Heaven and Earth, 7, 56, 146

Hedjuk, John, 13, 252n11

Heidegger, Martin, 162, 176, 252n11, 256n14

higher education. *See* education

Hinduism, 208, 209

Hippocratic oath, 55

history of architecture, xvi, 56, 150, 212, 223, 242

history, cultural, 130, 207

holistic, 14, 25, 85, 250n1, 253n37, 253n38

holistic learning. *See* learning

Holy Bible. *See* Bible

Holy Spirit, 145, 146

homeless, 40, 106, 115, 136

homeless shelter, 40, 136

Homo sapiens, 191

hooks, bell, 14, 35, 43, 252n19, 255n1

human dignity, 36, 41, 166

humanism, 8, 193, 244

humanity, 2, 8, 13, 14, 16, 24, 25, 39, 82, 97, 110, 146, 191, 192, 202, 204, 208, 210, 229

humble, 7, 12, 14, 39, 72, 146, 202, 228, 237

humbleness, 29

humility, 98, 176, 202, 208

hunger, 145, 202

Husserl, Edmund, 56

idealism, 97, 220

identity, xv, 7, 113, 129, 130, 131, 175, 176

ideology, 97, 98, 204, 217

Ignatian spirituality, 38

immanent/immanence, 8, 25, 145

immaterial, 130, 145

immeasurable, 13

immigration, 40, 136, 138, 140, 142

improvisation, 5, 6, 7, 40, 41, 136

incarnated, 166

individualism, 6, 7, 16, 18

indoctrination, 18, 19, 22, 254n57

ineffability, 192

ineffable, 13, 33, 130, 166, 227, 250n2

inhabitation, 76, 211

inner call, 59

inner life, 16, 17, 18, 252n14

inner reality, 7, 175

inner self, 18, 92, 101, 145, 205

inner spirit, 211

inner voice, 6, 100, 101

inner world, 28, 43, 209

inquiry, 7, 20, 23, 23, 28, 40, 104, 150, 200, 201, 217, 251

inquiry, architectural, 28, 30, 38, 41, 120

inquiry, spiritual, 22, 41

inquisition, 19

insecurity, 4, 28, 62

inspiration, 4, 136, 192, 217, 230, 235, 238, 239

inspiring, xvi, 7, 28, 35, 42, 73

institutionalized, 15, 62

instrumental, 2, 3, 8, 16, 17, 32, 100

instrumentalism, 6

integrity, 15, 22, 217, 247

intellect, 38, 39

intellectual, 14, 16, 18, 20, 22, 39, 98, 100, 114, 131, 145, 150, 163, 191, 192, 205, 217, 222, 253n29, 254n52, 252n56

interdisciplinarity, 5, 20, 26

interdisciplinary, 15, 38, 46

interfaith, 20, 243

internet, 59, 220, 252n8, 256n3

interpersonal, 15, 16, 26

intersubjective, 15, 26, 46, 220

interval, 56

intimacy, 7, 28, 78, 101, 129, 130

intimate, 30, 32, 33, 188, 192, 202, 217

intuition, 7, 12, 28, 38, 39, 41, 76, 131, 136, 231

intuitive, 20,26, 28, 56, 62, 131

intuitive action, 39, 46, 196

irrational, 18

Islamic, 13, 19, 230, 251n3, 252n7

Jerusalem, 233
Jesus Christ, 145, 146
Jewish, 113, 245
John Paul II, Pope, 28, 29, 221, 255n67,
    256n2
Jones, E. Fay, 8, 192
journey, inner. *See* inner
journey, outer. *See* outer
joy, 36, 98, 209, 233, 252n14
judgment, 21, 237
justice, economic, 15
justice, racial, 19
justice, social, 4, 19, 24, 36, 41, 251n4

Kahn, Louis, 3, 13,176, 196, 211, 223,
    252n10, 256n7
know thyself, 27, 31, 38, 251n6
Krishna, Suresh, 213, 214

Laudato Si, Encyclical, 104, 114, 115
Le Corbusier, xv, 150, 162, 256n5
leadership academic, 20
leadership skills, 18
leadership training, 20
leadership, college, 17
learned ignorance, 12, 250n2
learning architecture, xii, 2, 8, 32
learning environment, 31
learning experience. *See* experience
learning model, 6
learning outcomes, 18, 20
learning process, 8, 27, 28, 29, 30, 38
learning, essence of, 7, 176
learning, holistic, 15, 38, 253n26, 253n30
learning, integral, 16
learning, service-, 15, 20, 24
learning, styles, 31
learning, teaching and. *See* teaching and
    learning
liminal, xv, 56
listen, 17, 88, 202, 203, 209, 214, 234
listening, 4, 38, 100, 120, 203
loss, 62, 73, 115, 166, 170, 177
love, xi, 6, 9, 14, 24, 25, 30, 88, 91, 98,
    99, 101, 110, 161, 172, 229,
    252n19, 255n65
love, epistemology of, 28
luminous, xv, 150, 242

materialism, 98, 136, 217
mathematics, 57, 58
Matisse, Henri, 160
meaning of life, 27, 28, 78, 253n26,
    255n69
meaning, existential, 8, 175, 177, 204
meaning, search for, 52, 204, 254n57
meaning, spiritual, xvi, 92,
meaning, transcendent, 5

meaning, ultimate, 36, 217, 255n67
measurable, 16, 55, 196
Mecca, 126, 233
meditation(s), 8, 9, 12, 13, 24, 25, 27, 28,
    31, 41, 57, 88, 120, 122, 124, 136,
    142, 184, 222, 253n45
melancholia, 116, 178
Melnikov, Konstantin, 7, 161, 163
Mendel, Menachen, 55
Merleau-Ponty, Maurice, 177, 204,
    256n17
Merton, Thomas, 27, 182
metaphor, 205, 234
metaphysical, 2, 29, 36, 166, 170, 217
methodology. *See* design *and also* teaching
    method(s)
Michelangelo, 176
Mies van der Rohe, 162, 229
Millennials, 104, 114
mimesis, 176, 256n16
mindfulness, 176, 256n16
minimal/minimalism, 37, 46, 123, 154,
    182, 217, 231, 256n4, 256n5,
    256n6
miracle, 57, 242
miraculous, 57, 58, 150
model, apprenticeship. *See* apprenticeship
model, business (of education), 17, 23
model, educational, 3
model, integral (of education), 17
model, integrated (of education), 252n39
modernity, 6, 97, 98, 99, 100, 101
monastery, 40, 150, 152, 154, 156, 159,
    230
moral(s), 22, 97, 250n3
mortality, 55, 169
mortals, 7, 146, 166
motivation, 17, 20, 24
multi-ethnic, 55
multi-religious, 55
multicultural, 55, 193
Mumford, Lewis, 43, 256n9
Muslim, 13, 41, 251n3
mystery, 14, 28, 29, 39, 52, 78, 186
myth, 20, 204, 216

naïve, 12, 19, 37, 220
naïve, consciously, 218
narrative, 5, 62, 76, 120, 205, 242
narrative, architectural, 13
narrow-minded or narrow-mindedness,
    20, 32, 57, 217
nature of architecture, 130, 150
nature, personal, 71
nature, trans-personal, 36, 217
nature, true, 203, 222
NCBDS (National Conference on the
    Beginning Design Student), 13,
    251n5, 254n61

Neruda, Pablo, 88
news, 48, 59, 253n38
news, fake-, 17
news, good, 23, 25
9-11 (September 11, 2001), 219
nones, 7, 15, 113, 252n21
nostalgia, 166, 217
nothing, 12, 29, 55, 57, 58, 176, 204,
    205
nothingness, 166
numinous, 36

O'Donohue, John, 206
objective dimension. *See* dimension
objective education, 19
objective reality, 12, 55
objective world, 16, 28
objectivity, 6, 20, 162
ontological, 16, 18, 23, 24, 169
ontological turn, 17, 24
openness, xii, 9, 21, 35, 43, 175, 230,
    252n15
optimism, 166, 212, 251n6
Ortega y Gasset, 161, 162, 256n7
outer, journey, 12
outer, lives, 18
outer, world, 16, 209
overwhelming, xv, 57, 184, 218, 232

Palmer, Parker J., 12, 14, 250n1, 252n2,
    253n25, 253n26, 253n27, 253n37,
    255n62, 255n65, 255n70
pandemic, 24, 85
Pantheon, 208, 212
paradigm, 15, 16, 17, 33, 39, 129, 130,
    253n39
paradise, 35
paradox, 28, 98
paradoxical, 36, 162
parti, 8, 9, 222, 223, 238
participation, 28, 39, 217
participatory, 24, 27, 253n42
passion, 6, 30, 37, 101, 175, 201, 203,
    213, 216, 230, 232, 234
pedagogic, 2, 3, 12, 13, 16, 26, 31, 35,
    39, 132, 136
pedagogical practice. *See* practice
pedagogies, 20, 29, 30, 38
pedagogy, vii, 3, 5, 6, 7, 8, 25, 27, 28, 29,
    39, 42, 46, 58, 62, 100, 191, 206,
    229, 251n16, 253n45, 254n63
pedagogy of vocation, 88
pedagogy, 1-2-3 cycling, 38
pedagogy, architectural. *See* architectural
pedagogy, curriculum and. *See* curriculum
    and pedagogy
pedagogy, first-person, 38
pedagogy, integral, 38
pedagogy, second-person, 38

pedagogy, Socratic, 30
perception, 19, 62, 68, 98, 130, 132, 213, 235
Perez-Gomez, Alberto, 28, 255n66
performance, academic, 20
performative, 31, 177
person, first-, 16, 18, 26, 28, 38
person, second-, 15, 16, 18, 26, 28, 38, 253n23
person, third-, 9, 15, 16, 18, 26, 28, 38, 220, 254n56
person, whole, 227
personal knowledge, 32, 73, 255n73
personal mastery, 101
perspective, 9, 14, 18, 19, 21, 26, 27, 28, 38, 42, 77, 207, 228, 230, 234, 236, 238, 250n2
perspective, multiple, 21
perspective, non-egocentric, 21
perspective, non-ethnocentric, 21
perspective, relational, 15
perspective, social, 15
perspective, taking, 15
perspective, transcendental, 15
phenomenological dimension, 26
phenomenology, 24, 37, 38, 41, 56, 211, 228, 239
philosophy, 36, 37, 56, 150, 161, 166, 182, 223, 229, 232, 253n23, 255n4
philosophy, design, 129, 223
Picasso, Pablo, 160
pilgrimage, 126, 182, 228
playing, 46, 163
poetics, 8, 120, 192, 193, 231
poetry, 57, 58, 159, 161, 163, 176, 213, 217
Polanyi, Michael, 32, 255n73
political, 13, 19, 24, 76, 97, 222, 254n57
politics, 55, 59, 177, 243
positivistic, 20
postmodern, 23, 216
power, 6, 12, 14, 46, 73, 76, 101, 113, 145, 196, 202, 207, 211, 227
practice,
practice of freedom, 35, 255n1
practice, architectural. See architectural
practice, contemplative. See contemplative
practice, cultural, 22
practice, design, 177, 243
practice, educational. See educational
practice, pedagogical, 3, 100
practice, professional, 2, 3, 28, 36, 56, 97, 98, 129, 254n59
practice, religious. See religious practice
practice, social, 22, 88
practice, spiritual. See spiritual
practice, teaching,
prayer, xvi, 115, 120, 125, 146
pre-modern, 98
preconceptions, 30, 85, 136, 233

prejudice, 15, 37
presence, divine, 109, 116, 145, 150
profane, 19, 154, 156, 230, 239, 250n2, 252n12
professing, 14, 25, 216, 217, 220, 222, 229, 242
professing, true, 32, 216
professional education. See education
professional habits. See habits
professional practice. See practice
purpose (of life), 14, 15, 16, 17, 21, 22, 29, 37, 50, 82, 94, 98, 99, 239, 254n57, 255n69

quest, architectural, 39, 55, 59
quest, spiritual. See spiritual
question(s), spiritual. See spiritual
questioning, 5, 43, 88, 113, 136, 208
questioning, architectural, 5
questioning, cultural, 5, 37
questioning, intellectual, 22
questioning, spiritual. See question(s)
questions, big, xii, 5, 14, 15, 16, 17, 20, 28, 29, 35, 37, 41, 43

rational education, 19
rationality, 20, 136, 172, 208, 216
reason, 19, 20, 98, 100, 132, 204, 250n64
reason, critical, 19
reason, instrumental, 100
rebirth, 124, 136
relation between architectural education and spirituality, 3, 13
relation between architecture and spirituality, xii, 5, 32
relationship with nature, 41, 120, 191, 203
relationship, personal, 16
relationship, student-teacher. See student and teacher
relativism, 20, 23, 216
religion, 12, 13, 14, 17, 19, 20, 21, 22, 66, 97, 104, 108, 113, 114, 115, 145, 201, 204, 208, 220, 243, 250n4, 252n14, 253n38, 253n40, 253n46, 254n47, 254n49
religion, definition, 15, 252n16
religion, organized, 104, 110, 113, 114
religious architecture, 24, 113, 201
religious beliefs. See beliefs
religious buildings, 3, 40, 114, 166, 228
religious colleges or universities, 22, 23
religious experience. See experience
religious institution, 19, 22
religious practice, 26, 37, 104, 113
resistance, 18, 21, 22, 24, 217
respect, 28, 31, 38, 217
rethinking, 5, 99, 182, 251n3, 253n40
reverence, 14, 19, 29, 39, 191

rigor, 20, 25, 72, 101, 150, 182, 205, 233, 237
Rilke, Rainer Maria, 175, 256n13
risk, 4, 20, 59, 71, 72, 73, 221, 234
risk-taking, 30, 88
ritual, 5, 120, 124, 145, 156, 182, 227, 239
Romanesque, xv
romantic, 130, 255n64
Rome, 208
Ronchamp, Chapel of (by architect Le Corbusier), 8, 192
Rothko, Mark, 160, 163

sacred and profane, 154, 155, 230, 239
sacred architecture. See architecture
sacred building(s), 145, 212
sacred dimension, 6, 25, 56, 217
sacred place(s), 114, 116, 145, 146, 150, 254n54
sacred space, xvi, 3, 7, 24, 40, 41, 42, 62, 98, 100, 104, 108, 110, 113, 114, 115, 116, 145, 182, 196, 200, 212, 227, 228, 230, 234, 250n2, 254n54, 256n3
sacred space and cultural studies, xii, 2, 41, 97, 200, 228, 229, 230, 231, 233, 234, 236, 248, 254n54
sacred space, future of, 104, 113, 114
sacred space, situational, 104, 114, 116
sacred space, substantive, 104, 114, 116
sacred task of architecture, 5, 56, 166
sacred, the, 5, 14, 19, 37, 41, 55, 56, 97, 98, 100, 101, 104, 114, 116, 156, 200, 212, 230, 234, 239
sacredness, 76, 99, 104, 116, 146, 154, 217, 227, 252n14
sanctuary, 105, 193, 220
sapere, 16, 17, 32, 33, 38
Sartre, Jean Paul, 175, 256n12
school(s) of architecture. See architecture
science, 16, 20, 27, 28, 57, 58, 68, 85, 162, 204
secular, xvi, 19, 40, 251n4
secular age, 9, 55
secular education, 17, 19, 205, 254n49
secular environment, xvi, 253n38
secular realm, 7
secular space, 40, 46
secular, colleges and universities, 3, 21, 22, 23
secularism, 19, 97
security, 80, 106, 216
self-knowledge, 12
self-absorption, 99, 100
self-actualization, 105
self-autonomous, 99
self-centered, 98
self-confidence, 209

self-destructive, 209, 210
self-discovery, 17, 27, 208
self-referential, 7, 146
self-sacrifice, 161, 162
self-esteem, 18, 20
self-understanding, 21, 207
self, collective, 220
self, deep, 17, 27, 37, 88
self, inner. *See* inner self
self, no-, 220
self, personal, 220, 252n14
self, sense of, 7, 94, 175, 176
self, spiritual, 146, 230
self, superficial, 27
self, true, 27, 31, 88, 135
selfless, xiii, 7, 169
semiotic, 25, 132
semiotic dimensions, 26
sensations and emotions, 62, 132, 242
sense of place, 52, 184
sense of self. *See* self
sense of the sacred, 7, 116, 234
sense of unity. *See* unity
senses, the, 28, 88, 91, 99, 122, 124, 130,
    163, 207, 212, 229, 234
sensibility, 3, 6, 15, 57
sensibility, spiritual. *See* spiritual
separation between church and state, 3,
    18, 20, 21, 254n46, 254n47,
    254n57
service-learning. *See* learning
shelter, 9, 105, 192
silence, 8, 13, 14, 99, 115, 130, 136, 163,
    163, 170, 188, 205
simplicity, 7, 41, 62, 76, 88, 136, 150,
    153, 161, 163, 188, 217, 229, 231
simplicity, voluntary. *See* voluntary, 182,
    217, 256n1
Siza, Alvaro, xv, 212
skeptical, 19, 43
slow down, 115, 229
slowness, 217
social justice. *See* justice
society, 14, 15, 18, 19, 21, 27, 37, 38, 39,
    43, 56, 58, 76, 97, 106, 110, 136,
    166, 204, 219, 226, 250n3, 253n29,
    253n39
Socratic, 29, 30
solipsism, 20
sorrow, xiv, 166, 177, 178
Sota, Alejandro de la, 7, 161, 162, 163,
    256n8
soul, xv, xvi, 6, 24, 27, 28, 55, 62, 85,
    101, 126, 222, 237, 239, 253n26
spiritual, 3, 5, 7, 9, 14, 15, 21, 30, 36,
    38, 42, 46, 55, 56, 59, 88, 106,
    108, 113, 120, 193,200, 201,
    202, 203, 205, 207, 211, 227,
    228,231,234,238, 239, 251n4,
    253n39, 253n45, 254n49, 254n57,

255n71
spiritual architecture, 201, 209, 212, 227,
    230, 230
spiritual awareness, 24, 39
spiritual being, 21, 52, 166, 202, 207
spiritual belief, 104, 114, 252n14,
    252n15
spiritual concern(s), 3, 19, 24, 35
spiritual considerations, 23, 26
spiritual development, 18, 20, 217
spiritual dimension, 2, 5, 8, 14, 25,
    27, 30, 31, 42, 43, 58, 201, 202,
    207, 253n39
spiritual engagement, 9, 23
spiritual experience. *See* experience
spiritual growth, xi, 2, 15, 28, 32, 233,
    255n69
spiritual home, 5, 7, 76, 115, 193
spiritual inquiry, 21, 22, 30, 37, 41
spiritual issues, 13, 22, 25, 30, 37, 40
spiritual journey, 35, 230
spiritual knowledge, 145, 253n39
spiritual life, 14, 43, 104, 114, 230
spiritual meaning, xvi, 92,
spiritual practice, 5, 14, 15, 23, 30, 41,
    55, 85, 88, 104, 113, 182, 203, 219
spiritual pursuit, 19, 24, 104, 208
spiritual quest, 23, 31, 39, 114
spiritual questioning, 26, 29, 37
spiritual questions, 16, 27, 39, 120, 113,
    207
spiritual self, 146, 230
spiritual space, 203, 232, 237
spiritual thinking, 21, 22, 23
spiritual tradition(s), 35, 39, 205, 208
spiritual values, 4, 55, 182, 208
spiritual world, 7, 38, 146
spiritual worldview, 27, 37
spiritual, sensibility, 9, 21, 23, 28, 31, 36,
    39, 120, 217
spirituality - definition, 14-15
spirituality - resistance, 18-22
spirituality in faith-based institutions,
    22-23
spirituality in higher education, 15-18
spirituality in schools of architecture,
    23-31
spontaneity, 4, 136
stewardship, 2, 247
Stonehenge, 9
style, 7, 177
style (in architecture), 162, 216
style, learning, 31
style, life-, 14, 219
subjective dimension. *See* dimension
subjectivity, 6, 38, 93, 100, 131, 209
suspicion, 97, 98, 113
sustainability, 24, 37, 104, 114, 217, 244

teacher and student, 29-31, 100, 101,
    176, 206
teaching and learning, 5, 8, 31, 43, 202,
    252n7, 253n45, 255n65
teaching experience, 5
teaching method(s), 18, 20, 23, 29, 30,
    35, 36
teaching, art of, 7, 8, 150
teaching, authentic, 8
teaching, compassionate, 8
technology, 9, 76, 129, 216, 252n8
tectonics, 26, 41, 62, 73, 222, 223, 251n5
temple, 9, 19, 58, 145, 146, 250n4
terrorism, 24, 216
thinking and behavior, 14, 18
thinking and doing, 39, 136
thinking, critical, 28
thinking, deep, 230, 234
thinking, design, 28
thinking, group, xiii
thinking, irrational, 28
thinking, lateral, 136
thinking, philosophical, 3
thinking, re-. *See* rethinking
thinking, religious, 22
thinking, spiritual. *See* spiritual
tradition, 22, 40
tradition, faith. *See* faith
tradition, spiritual. *See* spiritual
traditional, xvi, 3, 9, 12, 16, 17, 20, 24,
    31, 38, 39, 57, 97, 115, 156
transcendence, xv, 7, 22, 25, 35, 36, 56,
    76, 170, 182, 207, 210
transcendence, architectural. *See* architec-
    tural
transcendent, 5, 14, 15, 18, 32, 55, 78,
    104, 182, 202, 209, 226
transcendent and immanent, 8, 25, 145
transcendent experience, 36
transcendent meaning, 5
transcendent values, 5
transcendental, 2, 57, 130, 150
transcendental dimension, 14, 46, 56, 76,
    166
transcendental perspective, 15
transcendental realms, 14, 88, 228
transformative, 31, 100, 277
transformative dimension, 31
transformative education, 253n42,
    253n45
transformative power, 6, 73
transformative process, 23, 32
travel abroad, 20, 203, 213
true education. *See* education
true love, 98
true professing. *See* professing
true questioning, 5
true self. *See* self
true teaching, 176, 209
trust, 4, 16, 17, 31, 38, 206, 211, 217,

231, 235
trustworthiness, 15, 17, 28
truth, 14, 58, 100, 101, 175, 204, 236, 237
truth, post-, 17
type of pedagogy, 18, 29. *See also* teaching method(s)
type of students, 31
type, building, 35, 40, 62, 76, 81, 166

uncertainty, 28, 141, 234, 253n33
unconscious, 8, 120, 176, 177, 217
unconsciousness, 37, 217
understanding, limited, 56
understanding, phenomenological, 129
understanding, *see*king, 14, 22
understanding, self-, 21, 207
understanding, visceral, 76
understanding, way of, 19, 56
unhealthy, 219, 221
unity, sense of, 14, 150
unknown, 56, 68, 72, 170
Upanishads, the, 101
urban civilization, 8, 114
urban development, 24
utilitarian, 16, 17, 23, 32, 177
utilitas, firmitas, and venustas, 192, 204

values, 15, 16, 17, 21, 22, 31, 39, 46, 48, 100, 130, 131, 162, 176, 192, 193, 205, 206, 250n2, 251n5, 255n69
values of humanity, 14
values, Catholic, 22
values, modernity's, 6
values, patriotic, 219
values, spiritual. *See* spiritual
values, system, 20, 129
values, transcendent, 5
Vatican, 255n5, 255n67, 256n2
Vatican II (Second Ecumenical Council of the Vatican), 193
venustas, utilitas and firmitas, 192, 204
Villa Savoye (Poissy, France, by architect Le Corbusier), 212
violence, 114, 216
Vitruvius, 192, 204
vocation, 2, 5, 6, 21, 22, 28, 40, 41, 43, 59, 88, 90, 92, 94, 233, 234, 235
vocation, definition, 98-99
vocation, pedagogy of, 88
Voluntary Architectural Simplicity (VAS), 8, 37, 41, 182, 216, 217, 218, 232
voluntary simplicity, 182, 217, 256n1
vulnerability, 28, 72
vulnerable, 31, 202, 234, 237

Waldorf education, 19, 253n39
Walton, Clarence, xv, xvi

Walton, Thomas, xi, xiv-xvi, 197, 247
warm-up (assignment), 5, 39, 62, 88, 99, 178, 254n61
web of life, 15
wellbeing (or well-being), 18, 24, 32, 39, 40, 104, 115, 251n4
whole, 14, 55, 106, 176, 220, 230, 231, 234, 254n60
whole being, 14, 15
whole person, 227
wholeness, 22, 36, 217
Wilde, Oscar, 209
wisdom, xv, 19, 176, 188, 204, 217, 227, 253n39
wonder, 4, 5, 13, 21, 29, 51, 55, 57, 58, 115, 206
worldview, 3, 14, 15, 18, 19, 20, 21, 27, 28, 30, 37, 38, 76, 98
worship, 9, 85, 104, 110, 115, 194, 254n49, 256n3

xenophobia, 18, 24

Zen Buddhism, 23, 39, 109, 211, 255n6, 255n7
Zumthor, Peter, 8, 192, 193, 222